My Life and Medicine

My Life
❧❧ *and*
Medicine

an autobiographical
memoir by

Paul Dudley White, M.D.

with the assistance of Margaret Parton

Gambit INCORPORATED
Boston · 1971

Excerpts on pages 197–201 from *Hearts—Their Long Follow-Up,* by Paul Dudley White, M.D. Copyright © 1967 by W. B. Saunders Company.

Figure 1 (heart circulation) reprinted by permission of the publishers and The Commonwealth Fund, from Helen B. Taussig, *Congenital Malformations of the Heart.* Cambridge, Mass.: Harvard University Press, Copyright, 1947, 1960, 1961, by The Commonwealth Fund.

Figure 2 (electrocardiogram) from *Heart Disease,* by Paul Dudley White, M.D. Copyright © 1951 by The Macmillan Company.

FIRST PRINTING

Dedicated in tribute to all those who have helped me along
the way: family, friends, colleagues and patients all over
the world, and to the gods who have been so kind to me.

Preface

This book has been written for several reasons, foremost of which is my belief that it may serve both as a warning and a stimulus for young people contemplating entering the profession of medicine; a stimulus because I have found it the most absorbing and exciting life imaginable, and a warning because I have been so absorbed that it has been difficult to play an adequate role in the amenities of life with family and friends. Another reason is that many of my colleagues, patients, and other friends have urged me during the last decade or more to put on paper an account of my life and its adventures, intermingled with some advice pertaining thereto. This I have tried to do.

I also want to emphasize the difficulties of writing an autobiography. It is far easier, I am sure, to write a biography of someone else. One knows too much about oneself and is apt to overemphasize experiences which, while they have been or have seemed of much importance to oneself, make for dull reading to the general reader. I hesitated, in part for this reason, to make the book a chronological report based on my diaries and Memindices which I have kept since childhood, but finally I gave way to this plan because its advantages are greater than its disadvantages. I have added enough chapters of special interest to break somewhat the possible monotony of chronology. Finally, one fears a criticism of egotism, or at least of egoism, in the presentation of things one has done or promoted, but the ego is naturally involved, and an autobiography must by nature be egoistical.

From the days of the First World War when I personally encountered many of the tragedies and very little of the so-called glories of war, I have been interested in world peace. More recently I have been painfully distressed by the horrors of the Second World War and its aftermath of cold wars and active conflicts all over the world. For many years I have treasured the idea of the possibility that the physicians of all nations, with only the health and happiness of their patients to consider, might bring together not only their colleagues in a united crusade against disease but their multitudes of patients, to promote international friendship, and thereby world peace. In May, 1970, when world peace seemed as remote as ever and the efforts at securing it as crude and primitive as medicine was several centuries ago, I coined a new word both in Greek and in English: "Irenology" in English and (εἰρηνόλογος) in Greek, meaning "The Science of Peace" and comparable to "Physiology" ("the Science of Life") and "Pathology" ("the Science of Disease"). We have colleges to teach "Polemology" ("the Science of War") but we have no real colleges or ministries of peace. The real *science of peace* is long overdue. It is my profound hope that I have contributed in some small measure to its coming.

In closing this preface I have much to acknowledge, and I do so with deep gratitude. First, let me bear witness to the patience, understanding, and assistance of my wife and family, not only during the preparation of this book, the manuscript of which my wife has helped Margaret Parton and myself to edit, but over the many years when I was writing other books and papers, seeing patients, teaching, and travelling. Also the devotion of my secretaries to their role as my assistants through the decades deserves my deep appreciation. They include Mabel Hopkins (later Mrs. Victor Jacobsen),

Catharine Thacher (later Mrs. Robert Vickery), Agnes Donovan (later Mrs. Bernard Walsh), Helen Donovan (her sister and a co-author with me of "Hearts—Their Long Follow-Up"), Dr. Florence Avitabile (later Executive Secretary of the International Cardiology Foundation), Matilda Wagner, Mrs. Margaret Thayer, and Mrs. Blanche Shaer. For many years, while my office was still adjacent to the Cardiac Laboratory of the Massachusetts General Hospital, Louise Wheeler and George Shallcross, acting for the laboratory as secretary and technician respectively, were invaluable in aiding my research, my teaching, and my care of patients.

My medical colleagues at home and abroad deserve my wholehearted appreciation, beginning with my senior associates in research, teaching, and practice, Howard B. Sprague and Edward F. Bland, and continuing with our junior successor Edgar Haber and my residents, fellows, and students, both undergraduate, and graduate. I give thanks also to my partners of the American, New England, Massachusetts, and Greater Boston Heart Associations, of the National Heart Institute and National Advisory Heart Council of the U.S. Public Health Service, of the National Research Council, and finally of the International Society of Cardiology and International Cardiology Foundation (now Federation), in the establishment and maintenance of which I have had the invaluable help of Drs. Louis Katz and Oglesby Paul of Chicago, Allan Friedlich, Florence Avitabile, and Howard Sprague of Boston, Paul David of Montreal, and Pierre Duchosal, Pierre Moret, and Carol Wehner of Geneva, and of several laymen including John Cancian and Jesse Fillman of Boston, Rome Betts of New York, and particularly Albert Baer, also of New York, chairman of our Lay Committee.

Among the other laymen who through the years have been especially helpful, one person in particular, Ben May of Mobile, Alabama, stands out as a constant source of inspiration during the last two decades or more, not only as a very

PREFACE

knowledgable colleague in the cause of public health in Washington, but even more in the support of my own role therein and incidentally of my own health and welfare.

Fortunately for me my publishers (and in particular the late Helen Everitt) have aided me enormously, especially by obtaining for me the editorial assistance of Margaret Parton of Palisades, New York. Without her help this book would hardly have deserved its printing. I am grateful for the patience shown by all concerned.

Paul Dudley White

Belmont, Massachusetts
June 30, 1970

Contents

Illustrations

Figures

Plates

The Beginning

CHAPTER I 🙾 One year before his death in 1929 my father, who had practiced medicine for almost half a century, wrote in his journal:

> When a man has lived three score and ten years he has finished Volume I anyway and whatever is added must be footnotes and appendices. One sure thing he has learned if observant is to know himself and no longer to be surprised by the animal. And yet I am more certain than ever that this body is not myself, that it is the tenement only in which I, the tenant, have taken rooms. I bow reverently before the Power and Force that started this spark of Life in this body as dumb as my watch, a lump of clay that without its occupant would be only a lump of clay and nothing more. The man, myself, the ego, the higher occupant who looks out at you as from a window is only the chrysalis of what I may yet be in some transition, for the tenement is very much out of repair and I need to move out for my own good . . . I have lived long enough to see that eventually Right and Truth do survive, that the real scientific practice of medicine is only just begun and that there must be some startling and most wonderful victorious discoveries just ahead. So I hail my descendants of only a few generations ahead as "supermen" indeed, only hopeful that they will not scorn the links in the chain that came before. We have a modest place in this triumphant Victory and grand procession; we have stumbled along; the path was obscure but we have kept our feet. . . . Thank God for the joy of my life as a doctor. [Last sentence mine—he would have welcomed this addition.]

Now that I, his son, have reached four score and more and have practiced medicine for over fifty years, I am more conscious than ever of my own place in the chain which links the generations, the chain of which my father wrote. Like my father I dare to look into the future and hopefully predict that we shall have become intelligent enough by the next century to have largely controlled in youth and middle age the great epidemic of this the twentieth century, namely, the deadly atherosclerosis of our arteries, which I shall discuss later in this book. Even more important, the study of internal medicine and other fields of human endeavor (education, music, art, business, philosophy, diplomacy, law, science, ethics of the brotherhood of man) should achieve in the next half-century much progress in the application of practical measures to establish real peace throughout the world.

Despite our inability as yet to adequately control our fate, I believe that we are in growing measure, and must become, more than we are now, masters of our destiny. We must do better than to bewail our bad luck or accept without reservation the implication expressed in the lines of Bayard Taylor's Napoleon at Gotha: "Men's lives are chains of chances and history their sum." We must control not only the deadly weapons of war but the violence in the streets, the frightful death toll on the highways, and the pollution all around us. Perhaps most important of all is a scientific application of birth control; in the last half-century the U.S.A. population has doubled, from 100,000,000 to over 200,000,000.

We cannot hope to know for certain how chance will operate in the years to come, but we can at least see how it has affected our lives and strive for a better future. I am sure that chance or fate has played a large role in my own life— which I hope to relive, if only partially, in the pages to come.

The biggest chance in anyone's life is probably that of the

genes he inherits. In this matter I am sure that I was fortunate.

My mother's father, Barzillai Dudley, was a Vermont engineer. He installed the water works in Memphis, Tennessee, where my mother was born. The family caught the last steamer up the Mississippi when the Civil War began in 1861. My grandfather Dudley was wounded when serving in the Northern army during the war and he died of his wounds a few years later, when my mother was still a little girl.

I never saw him, of course, but my maternal grandmother, Caroline King, born of Loyalist stock in Halifax, Nova Scotia, I knew well during the fifteen years that she lived with us before her death at ninety-two. Her family "returned" to Boston when she was six years old. She was a forceful though gentle character and used to tell me many stories of her younger days when she lived in the old South End of Boston. I well recall going with her by streetcar to the old Hollis Street Baptist Church for Sunday services when I was a boy. (It was largely in that church that father and mother carried on their courtship when he was a student at the Harvard Medical School and she at the Girls' High School in Boston.) Among my grandmother Dudley's memories was the cry of the Boston newsboys in the 1860s and 1870s:

> Daily Mail, Bee, and Times,
> Weekly Eagle, Weekly Bee,
> Satirist, Cactus, Olive Branch,
> Uncle Sam and Yankee!

When I was a boy I once copied this down and sent it to the *Boston Transcript*. They printed it on September 11, 1899, and I was very pleased.

My father's father, Ephraim White, and mother, Lucy Niles, were both born in New England of colonial and revolutionary stock and lived on Bunker Hill in Charlestown, a suburb of Boston. This paternal grandfather went West as a very young man in the California gold rush days. In June of this year (1970) I received in his memory the key to Sacramento, near which city he had panned for gold with indifferent success in 1851. He served in the Union army during the Civil War and eventually became a business man, manufacturing physical and mechanical aids to health—crutches and the like. He died of tuberculosis before he was forty (thirty-eight years and four months) and his wife, my father's mother, died of cholera when she was only twenty-four years and eleven months old, and my father still an infant.

Because of his mother's early death, my father, Herbert Warren White, was raised on the farm of his mother's parents, the Niles family, in Randolph, Massachusetts, south of the Blue Hill range. He was a student at the Braintree High School and graduated from the Harvard Medical School in 1880; after that he spent two years of postgraduate medical studies in Vienna, Paris, London, Edinburgh, Dublin, and at Bellevue Hospital in New York City. He then settled in Roxbury, Massachusetts, married, and began a career as a family doctor, a career which was to continue for forty-seven years. I was born on Dudley Street in Roxbury on June 6, 1886, two years after my older sister Miriam, five years before my brother Warren (who was to become first an engineer and then an orthopedic surgeon) and ten years before my little sister Dorothy. My brother Joseph Warren was named after the great patriot Dr. Joseph Warren, whose farm had been located near where we lived in Roxbury and whose statue had graced a small park a stone's throw from our home. This statue in the recent reconstruction of Roxbury was lost to sight for some years but when recently recovered was rededicated in May, 1970, on the present grounds of the Roxbury Latin School in West Roxbury. Joseph Warren himself was killed at the battle of Bunker Hill on June 17, 1775, but his young brother John helped to found the Harvard Medical School, the Massachusetts Medical Society, and the Massachusetts General Hospital, much of the development of which was the accomplishment of his descendants. The Warren Building at the Massachusetts General Hospital was named after this remarkable medical lineage.

My father must have inherited a large amount of drive, curiosity, and self-discipline from his ancestors, for he was one of the most hardworking and devoted family doctors I have ever known. He was so absorbed in the physical, mental, and spiritual welfare of his patients that our family saw little of him during the early days of our lives. He was busy day and night, Sundays and holidays, winter and summer, and we had only fleeting glimpses of him.

But through this way of life he played a large role in his community, for he was not only called for the physical ills of his many families but for advice about education, family problems, and all kinds of stress, both mental and spiritual. There were few psychiatrists in that day, only enough to take immediate care of the violently insane; I am sure that he took as good care of the psyche as he did of the body of each of his patients.

As he grew older he stole enough time from his work to travel, to read, to mingle more with his family and others outside his immediate community and to teach internal medicine at Tufts Medical School. He was one of the founders of the Baptist Hospital in Boston and an ardent supporter of the Ford Hall Forum. He continued his medical practice into old age and died in an attack of angina pectoris on his way to see a patient on a Sunday morning in the fall of 1929, at the age of seventy-one.

My mother, Elizabeth Abby Dudley, was a very gentle woman, immersed in the care of her four children and her husband, whose irregular hours must have been a great strain. But whenever she had any free time she was very active in the support of missionary work, both at home and abroad, and of homes for sick and aged women and couples. Every two or three years, when exhausted by her husband's program, the care of her children and her missionary enterprises, she would take a week off to recuperate at a pleasant rest home not far away. This custom undoubtedly helped to prevent nervous prostration and might be helpfully revived today.

Our home life was in general uneventful except for the coming of electric light in the late 1890s to take the place of our Welsbach gas student's lamps, and the installation of a telephone (Roxbury 333) to take the place of the doorbell calling father out to see a patient. My brother and I alternated weeks in mowing the lawn and stoking our hot air coal furnace, which we invariably started near the end of October and shut off about the middle of April. During the cold days earlier in October and later in April we simply wore more clothes or had grate fires in several rooms.

Transportation was mostly by our own feet and we were accustomed to walk two or three miles or to cycle even further. (When I was a freshman at Harvard I cycled the five miles back and forth all that year.) Father had a horse and buggy for his calls on patients and a "carry-all with a fringe on top" for the family expeditions on the few Sundays and holidays when he was able to escape from his practice. He used a sleigh in winter and on Saturday mornings I frequently rode with him on his rounds and held the reins while he hurried into a patient's home, thus saving him the time which might be taken by getting out the heavy weight which, swung around a post or tree, kept the horse from wandering off. Sometimes he had very frisky horses and on two or three occasions when I was quite a small boy a horse would run away with me. Once I was tossed out of the sleigh onto a snowbank, fortunately without harm. It took me years, in later life, to get over my mistrust of horses and enjoy riding them at the Dead Indian Ranch near Cody, Wyoming, where my wife and children and I used to go for a few weeks in summer.

Our family's social life was based almost entirely in the Baptist church, of which we all were members. It was ritually quite strict, which accounted for the establishment in all of us of certain habits which were helpful and of others that were not. Alcoholic beverages were taboo and so was smoking before twenty. Father and mother were teetotalers. Cards and the theater were in general frowned upon. We were not allowed to dance or to attend musical concerts except those involving religious or patriotic themes, which, later, I looked back on as a deprivation.

The religious side of such an up-bringing also had both its advantages and disadvantages. I remember arguing as a young teenager with some of the church staff about the impossibility of some of the Bible stories. But we did appreciate the beauty of much of its literature and we learned a great deal of the Bible by heart. I can still recite the names of the books of both the Old and New Testaments and also the twelve tribes of Israel and some of the Psalms and Proverbs; when I eventually went to modern Israel I found I knew them better than many of the Israelis themselves.

As I grew older, however, I found that I had less and less time for the reading of any literature, either sacred or profane, because my professional life forced me to give up most of the reading I would have liked to have continued, such as philosophy, poetry, fiction, and even detective stories. I also had to abandon the game of chess, which I, as a boy, had much enjoyed. I just did not have time for it. The need of mastering medical knowledge has been a full-time job and, happily or unhappily, has continued so right up to this day. Personally, I have found this forced neglect of cultural opportunities the most difficult aspect of a doctor's life.

Aside from the church and my family, the other important spiritual influence in my life was the Young Men's Christian Association. Early in my teens I went to the YMCA Camp Becket in the Berkshires, one of the finest boys' camps in the world, and there as a camper I learned to live with people of various faiths, color, and backgrounds, and acquired habits of exercise which have lasted me through my life. Later I became a counselor, eventually assistant camp doctor, and after an absence of some twenty years, a member and finally chairman of the camp committee. In the summer of 1968, when I was honored to have a new dining hall at the camp named for me, I suggested no strict rules of diet for these active growing boys but a dinner bell instead of a bugle and an inscription above the dining hall door quoted from Lord Byron's "Don Juan":

> That all-softening, overpowering knell,
> The tocsin of the soul—the dinner bell.

The YMCA triangle, symbolizing the unity of body, mind, and soul, seems to me to represent the whole person which I, as a doctor, have always tried to treat—not one aspect of the individual, but all three in harmony.

In today's epidemiological research into the causes of disease one of the important environmental factors in which we are much interested is the diet. The great majority of the world's populations is, I believe, malnourished—having either too little food (or protein) or too much, the latter probably true of the considerable majority of the citizens of the United States and similarly prosperous countries. Fortunately for the children and adults of eighty years ago, the average American family did not have too much to eat and what we had was not so rich as is the diet of the average family today. We did not have cream on the table and we had to freeze our own ice cream and take turns working the crank handle of the ice cream freezer on Sundays and holidays during the summer. There was no ice cream sold then in the drug stores; the only dietary hazards were at the tables of the well-to-do families, of which there were far fewer at the turn of the century than there are now. Doctors, however, were likely to prescribe excessive amounts of milk for people threatened with tuberculosis, the major scourge of the day. My father was a candidate for tuberculosis in his youth and spent the rest of his life drinking inordinate amounts of milk—which we are now sure can lead to severe atherosclerosis, as it did in his case. We didn't know any better in those days; now we know that for a baby or undernourished child or adult there need be no restriction of whole milk, but for many well-nourished children and adults skimmed milk is best.

A few years ago I wrote a general description of the illnesses of the period for the *Saturday Review*. We children, I recalled, all had diphtheria and scarlet fever, then common but now very rare diseases in New England. We escaped meningitis, polio, and empyema, which killed or maimed some of our schoolmates. We also escaped infantile dysentery, the "cholera infantum" which took a large toll and was a major cause of the high infant mortality of a long lifetime ago before the pasteurization of milk. The high maternal mortality due to puerperal sepsis or childbed fever was, however, on the wane in my own infancy when antisepsis and asepsis were already beginning to be practiced and the obstetricians and midwives of the day had clean hands.

And so we children escaped many hazards, lived a healthy life, and began going to school.

The memories of my boyhood include very strongly the intense curriculum at the Roxbury Latin School, where I spent several years under the tutelage of some of the ablest teachers in the entire country. One of my teachers in particular I have never forgotten, Clarence Gleason, who taught us Greek so that we enjoyed it. As a result, my interest in

Greece led to a first visit there in 1919 and several visits thereafter. At one time in an upper class we studied during the same year Greek, Latin, French, German, and English, along with math, science, and history.

There was not much time for play, which we enjoyed in spare moments in the famous old graveyard which bordered on our football field. I myself was always too small in weight and height to make any of the school teams but I was an active boy and played "scrub ball," ran a lot, and cycled or walked or ran everywhere I went.

And so the years passed, my childhood ended, and the time came for me to enter college. It had been a relatively simple, unexciting, but happy boyhood in a community untroubled by many of the physical, mental, and spiritual stresses of the Middle Ages, the Nineteenth Century, or the sixty years that have followed—being a hiatus in history, it seems to me, quiet, uneventful, unaware, and late Victorian. There were wars, but they were a long way off: that between China and Japan, the Boer War in South Africa, and the Russian-Japanese conflict—we were in no way directly involved.

Early Years in Medicine

CHAPTER II 🙰 My undergraduate years at Harvard, despite some interesting courses, were on the whole rather tame, as I look back on them from this distance and compare them with what was to follow. In my sophomore year I favored history as my prime interest (and as a hobby ever since), but switched to forestry at the beginning of my junior year, persuaded to do so by a friend of the family, and following Theodore Roosevelt's enthusiasm for the West. Within a few weeks, however, I lost interest, being more drawn to animals, especially the human, than to trees, and I decided to prepare for medicine; my tutorial advisor acquiesced and I changed all my courses to "pre-med." By taking Qualitative Analysis in the summer at M.I.T., I was able to enter Harvard Medical School in the fall of 1907 instead of finishing my college course with my classmates. (I was graduated in 1908 with an A.B. cum laude.)

The four years at Harvard Medical School were less routine and dull than my college course and much more interesting and challenging. We entering students were abruptly thrown into the very unpleasant atmosphere of the dissecting room, the burning of midnight oil, and the complication of the language of medical science, as difficult as any foreign tongue, but for me much ameliorated by my knowledge of Greek, which is the foundation of the great majority of anatomical and other medical terms. It quickly became evident that if we could survive those first few months, never again would we meet another professional challenge so severe.

During the first two years our class of 125 students was saturated by lecture after lecture, as was then the custom at medical schools throughout the United States. We were stimulated by some of our faculty and put to sleep by others, which is, I suppose, about par for the course. After that we greatly appreciated and enjoyed our eventual contacts with sick humanity and quickly learned that the study and treatment of the individual patient was just as important as the appraisal of his disease and often more so. We needed no detective stories to fill our spare time, for one reason because we had no spare time and for another because we had to search for clues in nearly every patient. And when we were required to follow up the patients assigned to us, in the dispensary or at their homes, we acquired more and more friends. I still see occasionally the children or grandchildren of some of those old-time out-patients of mine, and of my father's old patients as well. This has been an unexpected pleasure of my professional career. Another interesting experience, as I became exposed to each clinical specialty in turn, was to find myself deciding that that was to be my future—I found them all nearly equally appealing to me.

As we neared the end of our undergraduate medical training in 1911, we had little choice of specialties (there were very few) or of places in Boston for internships—The Peter Bent Brigham was not yet built, the Beth Israel had not yet moved from Roxbury, and the Boston University Hospital was then in a transformation from homeopathy to a mixture of that with allopathy. There were, for adult medicine, the Boston City Hospital and the Massachusetts General Hospital, for children the Floating Hospital and the Children's and Infants', and for Obstetrics the Lying-In. Some of my classmates moved away for their internships to hospitals in distant cities, and I rarely saw them except at our regular five-year medical school alumni reunions. Our last reunion was our fifty-fifth, in 1966, and was held at our home in Belmont, Massachusetts, where there foregathered a dozen members of our original class of 125—a few others were still alive but unable to attend. Two years later, in 1968, my college class celebrated its sixtieth reunion when sixty members met at the Science Museum in Boston.

My own internships were at the Massachusetts General Hospital, the first in pediatrics in 1911, when I served as the second intern in the newly established clinic of the specialty, and the second in 1912 and 1913 in internal medicine on the West Medical Service. During my hospital training from 1912 to 1913, George Minot, later renowned as a Nobel Prize winner for his discovery of the liver treatment of pernicious anemia, was, on the East Medical Service, an exact contemporary of my own on the West Medical Service. The publication of my first medical paper, stimulated and co-authored by Roger I. Lee, one of my medical chiefs, occurred in 1913. It was concerned with a new technique for the determination of blood coagulation time, a process still in use today under the name of "the Lee-White method." It was my only contribution to hematology.

What happened in June, 1913, as I was about to graduate from my medical internship at Massachusetts General, is an illustration of the part that chance has played in my life.

One day early in June, David Edsall, then chief of the Medical Services, called me to his office to ask me if I would like to receive a Harvard traveling fellowship for a year to study in London cardiovascular physiology with particular use of the electrocardiograph in man and in experimental animals (dog and cat). I would be attached to Dr. Thomas Lewis of the University College Hospital Medical School and on my return would bring back and install in the hospital one of these new machines. This would be the first instrument of the sort in any Boston hospital.

Several years before, my young sister Dorothy had died of rheumatic heart disease, and since that time I had felt a desire to learn more about heart disease—although cardiology was not yet considered a specialty. Dr. Edsall's offer therefore seemed particularly tempting. On the other hand, I had promised Dr. Richard Smith, a brilliant young pediatrician, that on graduation from my internship on July 1, I would become an assistant of his, a very desirable post indeed. Also, I was quite unsure about the value and reliability of the electrocardiograph and had heard rumors from some of my New York friends that it was a troublesome toy, always getting out of order and of little or no clinical usefulness. However, the idea of a year in London intrigued me and I was also lured by the possibility of meeting Sir James Mackenzie, the Scot who was the leading pioneer of his day in the study and treatment of heart disease.

So, still in a quandary, I went to see Dr. Smith, who gave me his blessing on this change of my career; on my return a year later I was able partially to keep my promise to him by helping in the Children's Heart Clinic of the hospital, which was eventually under my wing for a good many years.

Early in July, 1913, I set sail for Europe with a medical classmate of mine, James Howard Means, and his mother (who acted as a chaperone in case of need) to make the "grand tour" of Europe both medically and otherwise, which was still the fashion of the day. My father had done the same thing thirty years earlier but had remained longer, over two years. He had walked the wards with Lister in London and with many other notable physicians of that day in Vienna, Paris, Edinburgh, and Dublin, and had nearly succumbed to smallpox when he was in the London Pest House to which he had been taken in a hearse.

There were a few highlights of that tour that stand out strongly in my memory. By far the most important was the International Physiological Congress that met every three years. In that summer of 1913 it was held in Groningen, the Netherlands. Means and I were simply young observers who with difficulty secured lodging in a tiny attic room which was adequate except that we had to go to the Municipal Bath House to wash. We were thrilled to meet the great physiologists of the world and also many physiologically minded clinicians. My own most vivid memory of the Congress was that of the demonstration repeated by Professor A. D. Waller of London of the initial human electrocardiogram by the primitive capillary electrometer, which he had first shown at an earlier congress of the same sort in 1887, when I was one year old.

In the fall our grand tour of Europe ended in Vienna, where a hotel clerk asked us when we registered whether Boston was in North or in South America. Means left me in Bavaria to go on to Copenhagen, where he had an appointment to learn about metabolism of the human body under the renowned Professor August Krogh. I still had a week more, which gave me time to walk in the Black Forest for a few days, a most delightful adventure culminating on my last day there in meeting by chance with a young German businessman from Hanover. We strolled along the hills to the east of the Rhine and stopped for a picnic at noon. Looking west over the river into France, and freed from inhibitions by enough of the good native wine, he took a sealed envelope out of his pocket and, tapping it, said that it contained instructions telling him where he was to proceed for rifle and uniform and further instructions, upon word of mobilization for war with France. I was completely appalled for there seemed to be no indication whatsoever in the world news of the day that there was any threat of war. It was, in fact, a most peaceful scene. He added further that the Germans would capture Paris in three weeks, which a year later nearly happened, and would have, had it not been for the French taxicab army that held the Germans at the Marne.

In October, I reported to Dr. Thomas Lewis for work. He stopped for a brief moment to greet me, as he stood in his cutaway morning coat at the operating table in his laboratory, massaging the heart of a dog with one hand while the other hand held his top hat and dress gloves. Impatiently he gave directions to his "diener" (laboratory assistant) as to what to do in his absence while he was attending some official luncheon. After a short greeting my new chief paid no more attention either to me or to three others—Jonathan Meakins, a Canadian, and two other Commonwealth physicians (from India and Australia), studying in London as postgraduates with special interest in cardiovascular disease. After two weeks Meakins and I were left alone—we were obliged to remain since we had no other place to go for a year.

Despite our impatience or rather, our patience, while waiting to be accepted as graduate students and junior research colleagues of one of the great pioneers in electrocardiography and in the mechanism of the heart beat, I look back now with great sympathy for Dr. Lewis. At the very moment of his most intense preoccupation with his basic research, we were suddenly superimposed on him—ignoramuses to be trained. We were very evidently in the way and day after day Meakins and I watched on the sidelines while with his diener Thomas Lewis carried out experiment after experiment of great importance. Once in awhile we made ward rounds with him, but this side of his job interested him little and he was always in a hurry to return to his laboratory. We admired his ability, his keenness (he had the most penetrating eyes that I have ever known) his integrity and his complete concentration on his work, and we were anxious to join him in the excitement of the chase for knowledge —but for a long time he gave us no opportunity.

Late one afternoon in December Lewis suddenly asked me if I would come back to work with him that evening and of course I accepted at once. From that moment my life in London changed completely to one of intensive research day and night. On several occasions I walked along Oxford Street with Lewis back to his lodgings (he was not yet married) and then returned to the laboratory. Night after night for weeks we measured P-R and other time intervals of the electrocardiograms of cats and dogs by the Lucas Comparator down to ten thousandths of a second under various experimental conditions. I had learned earlier how to use a slide rule, which I had brought with me, and I instructed Lewis in its use, saving countless hours of mathematical calculations. This clinched my position as a devoted slave of the master; in time this relationship changed to that of devoted friend, not only of Lewis himself but of his family—Lady Lewis, his wife, and their three children, Patricia, Christopher, and Philippa.

Ten years later I brought my bride to England to meet Sir Thomas, his wife Lorna, and the children; we have continued a close association with the Lewis family ever since. At our suggestion, during the Second World War the Lewises sent their nine-year-old daughter Philippa—whom we call Pippa—to stay with us at the time of the bombing of London. She was with us for four years and we regard her as one of our family. She now has a family of her own and lives in California, while her brother Christopher practices medicine in Vancouver, British Columbia. Pat, the older daughter, her husband, Sinclair Watson, and her mother, Lady Lorna Lewis run a farm at Clearburn, Loudwater, Rickmansworth, north of London.

A very important part of my cardiological education that year in London was an occasional visit to the very special cardiac clinics of Sir James Mackenzie, where John Parkinson (later Sir John) was his first assistant at the London Hospital and where I established a lifelong friendship with them both. Mackenzie, a graduate of Edinburgh University and ᵃt first a family doctor in a colliery town in the north of England, had pioneered some most important graphic recording of the pulses in the arm and in the neck and had published a notable book on *The Pulse* in 1902, which established him as a (perhaps *the*) world's authority on the heart and had brought him to London as their first clinical cardiologist. He was a large and commanding person, and I was very much in awe of him.

One of my memories of my days in London is that as a young man I, like everyone else, traveled about on the sidewalks or in the buses, routinely every day in morning coat (cut-away) and with top hat and cane—a residual of Victorian days. Very often the cane was replaced by an umbrella, for the rain was very frequent throughout the winter from November on. The year of 1914, I remember, contained a month of March which broke all records. There were only two hours of sunshine in the entire month and I happened to be in the photographic dark room of the laboratory during those two hours! Fogs were common and often thick. One Sunday noon I left church and entered pitch darkness outside. I groped my way with my hand along the walls or fences of the houses and once I felt the base of a lamp post which had its light fully on, yet as I looked up from the pavement I could see only a very faint glimmer of light above me. Gradually the fog lifted slightly and I walked slowly home; there were no taxis or buses because of the dense fog.

The women in England had not yet won their franchise to vote and in order to get it frequently disturbed the peace during this period. Emmeline Pankhurst and her associates, the suffragettes, were on the move, and Sunday after Sunday they demonstrated with uproars and calls for "Votes for

Women" during various church services. They would chain themselves to the church pews so that it was very difficult to dislodge them. They never gave any warning as to which church or churches they would invade next and in my church-going during that year I always missed them.

The year in London after I began to work seriously, passed very quickly. Lewis, Meakins, and I published several scientific papers together, one of them in the *Transactions of the Royal Society*. All have stood the test of time. In July, 1914, with trouble beginning to brew in Europe, I reluctantly said good-bye to Lewis and sailed for home.

As I returned to the Massachusetts General with my electrocardiograph, I felt like a lonely adventurer entering an unexplored and unknown country, planning to spend my life in a new and as yet unrecognized specialty limited to the heart and blood vessels, both normal and diseased.

This was the decade before a handful of us founded the American Heart Association and two decades before we were permitted by our elders and even by most of our contemporaries to call ourselves cardiologists. It was in the dark days B.C. (Before Cardiology), when the great White Plague, tuberculosis, was still the main cause of death, and rheumatic fever was responsible for the majority of our heart patients. The wards were full of very ill patients with typhoid fever, and pneumonia was not only still "the old man's friend," but it took its high toll at all ages.

Those were months of difficult decision when those of my medical-school class who had served with me at the Massachusetts General Hospital or in other hospitals as interns but were now out in practice would chide me for "still being in white clothes," or my former medical-school teachers or hospital chiefs would warn me that I was entering an insignificant special field and would never be heard from again. Even the nurses would advise me not to study such a difficult part of the body as the circulation, which was cus-

tomarily relegated to a few back pages of the medical textbooks of the early years of the twentieth century. The infections held the limelight. The first and always the leading
chapters of the medical textbooks dealt with typhoid fever,
pneumonia, diphtheria, and tuberculosis.

In the autumn of 1914, I set up my new electrocardiographic laboratory in a small closet in the basement of the
Skin Ward, which I was given "because there was no
other place for it." I had a class in electrocardiography for
several medical professors and as a young medical resident
I rotated to a small room in the Out-patient Department and
to a very few beds in the old wards of the historic Bulfinch
Building to examine and to advise about patients who were
thought to have something wrong with their hearts. I still
used quite commonly Mackenzie's ink polygraph for the
study of the brachial, jugular, and apical pulses, not only
when the string galvanometer of the Cambridge electrocardiographic instrument would break down (it was a
delicate machine—one had to hold one's breath in replacing
the microscopic "string" between the magnetic poles), but
also to supplement it.

The electrocardiograph, with which I began to make intensive researches both in the clinic and on many of my
healthy colleagues, was still regarded as too difficult and
useless a toy to be worth much effort. But I persisted, and was
pleased when I would be invited to present some of the results of my studies to my own hospital colleagues or to meetings at the new Peter Bent Brigham Hospital, where my
lifelong friend Sam Levine was beginning to join me as an
ally in this new specialty. Gradually, during 1915, we developed the Out-patient heart clinics for adults and children,
which had already been started respectively by Dr. Joseph
Pratt and Dr. Richard Eustis. More and more I was invited
to address various hospital meetings and graduate courses in
internal medicine.

Early Years in Medicine

During the early part of 1916 I continued to develop first, our clinical and research use of the electrocardiograph (especially in the analysis of tachycardia, bradycardia, and arrhythmias) and second, the beginning of the application of Richard Cabot's classical contribution to the etiology (causes) of heart disease. This pioneer teaching of Cabot's, overlooked for many years, emphasized—as I too have subsequently urged—the first priority of prevention over diagnosis and treatment of heart disease. This viewpoint now appears in many books and articles under the common heading of "Preventive Cardiology," but in 1914, when his paper first appeared, it was a completely new idea.

Encouraged by growing recognition I began to settle into my life as a cardiologist. But once again chance affected my fortunes as I was swept into the maelstrom of World War I.

World War I and
Eastern Macedonia

CHAPTER III ⟨⟩   In describing my involvement
in the First World War, I wel-
come the opportunity to char-
acterize it as a grim and frustrating experience, the few
hours of the excitement of heroism and the drama of victory
being outnumbered a hundred thousand fold by the millions
of tragedies of wounds, illness, and deaths of the young people of the many countries involved, and especially by the ut-
ter boredom and futility of this technique of settling dis-
putes, a relic of the caveman.

Reading the manuscript of this chapter, I find it the dullest
in the book. Purposefully I have soft-pedaled the grim experiences of the horrors and violence we witnessed, which
are still presented in cold blood to the public, young and
old alike, in movies, plays, books, and newscasts as if there
were nothing better with which to educate the unthinking
viewer. On the other hand, we need to be shown that there
are still noble aims in life and happier and healthier ways
to lead us back to our senses. The publicity media have
fulfilled far less than their total opportunity and duty by
dispensing the bad news and the immorality of the times in
excess with insufficient effort to lift our thoughts and our
spirits above the level of the "yellow press." Reform in this
particular custom is greatly needed, not by glossing over the
tragedies and sufferings of the day but by presenting simul-

taneously the positive steps to eradicate them and the many generous and thoughtful actions being quietly undertaken in behalf of the brotherhood of man. This could be a major step in implementing the beginning of the science of peace (irenology), which I mentioned in the preface. Happily there are increasing signs of a more concerted effort to raise our sights. (See Appendix 2 for comment on science writers).

At the moment of the declaration of war in Europe in August, 1914, none of us young doctors at the Massachusetts General Hospital thought that it could last for more than a week, because of its great expense. Certainly the idea that it could last four years was inconceivable. We were intensely interested in the progress of the war and most of us sided strongly with England and France. In the spring of 1916, when it had become evident that the war would be a long one and might eventually involve the United States, some of us joined the Medical Reserve Corps of the Army.

In the summer of 1916 I was invited by Dr. Daniel Fiske Jones, one of the senior surgeons at the M.G.H., to join his Harvard unit (the third of a series) due to depart in early fall for three months' service at Base Hospital No. 22 of the British Expeditionary Force. This was at Dannes-Camiers, near Boulogne, on the coast of France and back of the Somme River front with its terrible trench warfare.

We were twenty-six in number, eleven physicians and fifteen nurses, destined to replace for three months' service, the second Harvard unit, which was to return home. We were briefed on the morning of August 17 at the British Consulate General's office in New York City, and then boarded the Steamship *Lapland* and set sail for England. After an uneventful voyage we arrived in London, where we remained about ten days waiting for equipment (including our British uniforms) before going on to France. London was truly a city at war, with great searchlights raking the sky at night, often pinpointing German zeppelins in their beams. One never-to-be-forgotten sight was a zeppelin on fire, an incredibly brilliant flaring in the darkness and then a few seconds later only a dim glow fading into nothing. This was the first zeppelin brought down; Lieutenant Robinson, who accomplished the feat, was the hero of the day and received the Victoria Cross.

When we arrived at our base hospital, one of many hospitals in the area, I was given charge of a medical ward of forty-eight beds and was also called in on heart cases in the other medical wards.

Another of my duties, which I found important and interesting, was that of Sanitary Officer. This required that for forty-five minutes a day I join an expert Sergeant Major to inspect all kitchens, incinerators, latrines, and drainage pits. On the second day, I remember, the camp's Commanding Officer, Colonel Sir Allan Perry, went on the rounds with us. As we approached an incinerator he stopped and said, "Lieutenant, I suppose you are very careful that no explosives get into this incinerator." I replied, "Yes, Sir!" very firmly— and at that moment there came a loud explosion from the incinerator. The Commanding Officer looked sternly at me, and I looked sternly at my sergeant.

As the fall went on we had many convoys, and they became larger and larger, and we began caring for more severe cases of illness and wounds, among them many patients with the so-called "Soldier's Heart," or "Effort Syndrome." This illness, which is still not completely understood, is not heart disease but rather a functional circulatory and nervous disorder following upon fatigue, nervous strain, or extreme exertion or anxiety. It is an illness known to British soldiers in India, to soldiers during our Civil War, and to soldiers in all the wars since then. To a lesser degree it is also known in civilian life. It has been called Neurocirculatory Asthenia (NCA) since the First World War and will be discussed in more detail later in this book.

As the weather grew worse in the middle and the late fall, those of us who lived in tents for two out on the clay cliffs had a miserable time of it, with the wind howling and the sleet and snow beginning to fall. On one occasion I can well remember, our tents blew down and we found ourselves in the middle of the night sprawling under wet canvas. Also, we had great difficulty with the rats that used to race across our beds, and ate any chocolate we happened to have handy.

But soon our interesting three months were up, and in mid-December our unit sailed for the United States, in time to be home for Christmas. Dr. George Denny of Boston, my tent mate at Base Hospital 22, and I elected to return home by ship from Bordeaux because this would include a brief stopover in Paris enroute south from Boulogne. After we had boarded our boat at the dock, about to sail, the French police entered the ship and arrested us as possible spies because Bordeaux was notorious as a center of spies and we lacked an adequate Paris visa on our U.S.A. passports. We spent the next twenty-four hours under police control until released by telegram from our C.O. We returned north and sailed home from Liverpool with our comrades of the American unit.

During the interval between Christmas, 1916, and early July, 1917, I resumed my activity as Medical Resident on the West Medical Service at the M.G.H.—not only some activity in the wards but also following up some of the research in cardiology that had been started in the two previous years.

War against Germany was declared by the United States on April 1, 1917, making this the first global struggle, whose slogan was "to make the world safe for democracy." As a member of the Medical Reserve Corps of the U.S. Army, I was ordered to active duty and was named examining and enlisting officer for the personnel of Base Hospital No. 6, eventually to be set up at Bordeaux in Southern France.

With the help of various doctors of the M.G.H. unit, I passed and enlisted 147 privates out of about 500 applicants. We knew that as an independent unit we would have to build the hospital from the ground up and therefore we enlisted many different kinds of workers. There were eleven hospital orderlies, seven pharmacists, nine mechanics and chauffeurs, five chemists and laboratory assistants, four bookkeepers and auditors, three carpenters, three engineers and firemen, two bakers, five cooks (one a captain from the Copley Plaza Hotel), two x-ray technicians, one steward, one electrician, one stenographer, one tailor, one interpreter, two embalmers, one chiropodist, one athletic director, one shoemaker, one wire man, one road constructor, two teamsters, one printer, twelve students (some of college level), sixtyone "salesmen and clerks" (because we didn't need any more specialists) and nine miscellaneous individuals. A very good crowd indeed!

Our officers numbered twenty-eight. The Commanding Officer was Colonel Frederic A. Washburn, of the Medical Reserve Corps and Director of the Massachusetts General Hospital, who had acquired a formidable military bearing from previous service overseas; the Chief of the Medical Service was Lieutenant Colonel Professor Richard C. Cabot, my own medical chief in the wards of the M.G.H. at home and a most unmilitary genius; the Chief of the Surgical Service was Lieutenant Colonel Lincoln Davis, one of our surgical chiefs at home. Colonel Larry B. McAfee was our adjutant from the regular army. There were six other regulars from the army attached to our enlisted group, of whom one was Top Sergeant and another hospital sergeant. Of the four others, two helped in the drilling and in directing the duties of the enlisted men, a third was a quartermaster, and a fourth a registrar. Our chaplain was the Reverend Henry K. Sherrill of Trinity Church in Boston, whom I also enlisted, along with our nursing staff, which numbered sixty-four, practically all M.G.H. graduates, under the charge of Miss Sara E. Parsons, Superintendent of Nurses at the Hospital. Finally we took along six civilians, five to act as secretaries and one as dietitian.

On July 9 we entrained for New York and the next day boarded the steamship *Aurania,* and sailed for Europe. Our ship docked at Liverpool, whence we went on to Southampton and crossed the channel to Le Havre. From Le Harve we went by train—a long, hot night and much of a hot day—to Bordeaux, skirting the environs of Paris on the way. There was one bit of excitement on the trip when after covering about three-quarters of the distance we were shunted on to a spur track to allow a train load of Russian officers to pass us on their way south to be interned, having deserted their place on the western front the day before. We learned that the historic Russian Revolution began in July, 1917.

For the next three weeks we officers were quartered in hotels in Bordeaux. It was a quiet, restless time, waiting for our work to begin. The nurses and enlisted men were stationed at the French Hospital No. 25, the former Petit Lycée de Talence (a small town just south of Bordeaux) which had been commandeered by the French Army. This had been in use, and was still in use when we arrived, for many kinds of sick people: French soldiers, German prisoners, Russians, and Annamites (Southeast Asians working for the French in the munition factories in Southern France). The Lycée was situated in a beautiful grove and was slowly transformed during our first two months into a large, first-rate hospital—without any damage to any trees. We officers were quartered in the Chateau Crespy nearby.

The hospital was to hold, at first, 500 patients. Before the war was over we had as many as 5,000 patients under our care.

As we began, in the late summer of 1917, to turn the Lycée into a large hospital, we welcomed the help of the specialists whom we had enlisted—the carpenters, engineers, mechanics, and other technical workers. Each of us officers had an extra job, one was head of plumbing, another in charge of painting, and so on. This was difficult because the officer had to learn from these assistants of his, while at the same time he was in charge of their work. I myself became officer in charge of the pharmacy and medical supplies, from hypodermic needles to ambulances, but after several months was able to turn over both of these jobs to qualified sergeants.

The environs of Bordeaux are beautiful. We were able to travel far and wide, chiefly on bicycle although sometimes on foot, to visit the vineyards and many historic sites. We became acquainted with many of the wines, the Medocs, the Graves, the Barsacs, and the special vineyards such as those of St. Emilion, a town to which Larry Oliver and I cycled one Sunday and from which we returned by train because we had sampled a little too much of the wine. Then there was the fine wine at the Chateau Beycheville, a beautiful spot on the river which was transformed into a convalescent officers' home and where each of the medical officers in turn spent a week. In the district there was also the Chateau d'Yquem; we never reached the place itself but we have enjoyed the wine ever since.

Occasionally tours of duty took us to other parts of France, especially to medical meetings in Paris where we were treated to bombing raids at night and to the regular explosions of shells from the German long-range Big Berthas.

When it became evident that our unit was not large enough to take care of thousands of patients, we were reinforced early in 1918 by Unit O, a group of doctors, nurses, and enlisted men from Charlotte, North Carolina. They became our friends and we often met them after the war was over.

We had, of course, thousands of patients who needed treatment for their wounds, others who had been gassed, others with infections. There were two types of infections with which we were particularly burdened, in the first place streptococcus infections resulting in rheumatic fever, which was rife. (We had in March, 1918, a large epidemic of streptococcic sore throat with rheumatic fever resulting.) Then, in the fall of 1918, came the terrible epidemic of influenza, when those of our patients who were able to be up at all were grave diggers for the hundreds who died in our hospital. We of the staff of the Base hospital had, in the spring, contracted what we called then three-day fever, or Spanish flu, which was apparently the same infection but in milder form. Therefore, none of us was stricken by the influenza in the fall when it was so severe.

The year 1918 was a very heavy one, increasingly so right up to the time of the Armistice and for some weeks afterwards. At the very time of the Armistice on November 11 we had our largest enrollment of nearly 5,000 patients. It took weeks before we were able to take care of them all properly. I remember that at one time in one convoy I received 100 new patients for my own care and I had to distribute them between my two large wards. Luckily, we had excellent orderly service and wonderful nurses. Because of a personnel shortage we had to enroll some of the convalescent soldiers to help in our wards, which proved to be very useful.

Two individuals I remember with particular gratitude for their important work in maintaining morale during the bleak spring of 1918. One was Dr. Richard C. Cabot, our medical chief, who arranged concerts and plays and his own addresses on current events. However, he was a great problem for Colonel Washburn in that he was rarely properly uniformed and on one occasion had to hide under the boardwalk of the hospital minus part of his uniform and with his arms loaded with costumes for a play to be presented that evening, just as General Pershing and Secretary of War Baker marched past over his head on one of the formal inspections of the hospital. The other was Peggy Reilly, a nurse of unquenchable courage and great cheer.

One of the most poignant memories of my life was the tremendous excitement, relief, and joy which engulfed us all, French and Americans alike, on Armistice Day, November 11, 1918, in the streets and environs of Bordeaux. We naively believed, or at least optimistically hoped, that this was "the war to end all wars."

Early in January, 1919, with demobilization in sight, there occurred another of those turns of chance which came my way. The American Red Cross Commissioner for the Balkans, to whom my name had been recommended, asked me if I would form a small unit of medical officers and proceed to Eastern Macedonia and the Greek Islands for relief work under the Red Cross. I jumped at the chance and four of my colleagues from our old unit—John Hodgson, Carl Binger, Scoville Clark, and Bob Crawford—agreed to go with me. On January 29 we said our farewells to Base Hospital No. 6, and on February 1 were demobilized at St. Aignan, a lovely town, but famous at that moment for mud. On February 3 we joined the American Red Cross in Paris and began a new adventure.

When we five assembled in Paris, the city was in a turmoil because of the peace negotiations actively going on, with many countries represented, large and small. There was much confusion, and our small mission was delayed considerably by it. However, late in February we finally got off and traveled south through Switzerland, Italy, and then to Greece, where we arrived on February 28.

Overrun for centuries by Goths, Venetians, Turks, and

others, Greece most recently had suffered invasions during World War I by Bulgarians, Serbians, and Turks. Eastern Macedonia had suffered a particularly brutal occupation and was now in the days immediately after the war, in desperate need of help.

It had been our plan at first to establish a field hospital in the middle of Eastern Macedonia. We had heard that much more than medical help was needed in that area, including supplies of food and clothing, and so we hoped that this field hospital of ours might serve as a center for this sort of activity as well as for medical and surgical relief. Before we left Paris we requisitioned a group of nurses and enlisted men, whom we knew well, from the staff of Base Hospital No. 6 to join us in Greece to make the unit a complete one for the field hospital. They never came, due to circumstances beyond our control, but our efforts to get them there illustrated our ignorance of what was really needed in Macedonia—in those days we did not have the instant communications which we enjoy today, and news traveled very slowly. Not until we reached Macedonia did we discover that almost the entire Greek army was located in the area to which we were going and that they already were operating field hospitals and centers of supply for food and clothing. What they *did* need most of all was help in the control of an epidemic of typhus exanthematicus, still raging in that part of the Balkans as it had from the beginning of the war almost five years before. In this we were able to help, although at the beginning we knew very little about exanthematic typhus which is a severe type of Spotted Fever. In contrast, we knew far more about our typhus, a mild form called Brill's Disease.

On March 7, after a twenty-one-hour train ride, we arrived in Salonika, in Western Macedonia. While we waited for further transportation to the East we walked through the city, noting the many mosques and minarets (the Turks had occupied this part of Macedonia for 500 years, and the Greeks for less than seven), the squalor of the refugees living in cellars, the ruins of the burned half of the city, and the old Citadel on the hill with its beautiful view of the harbor and of the sea beyond. Among the races and nationalities represented in Salonika were French, English, Australians, Canadians, East Indians, Zouaves, Senegalese, Italians, Serbians, Albanians, Greeks, Turks, Jews, Chinese, Austrian and Bulgarian prisoners and even a few Americans. It was such a hodgepodge of nationalities that small riots occurred now and then, and of late the city had acquired a very unsavory reputation for murders, usually of drunken soldiers at night. During the two previous months seventy-two British soldiers had been found dead in the streets of Salonika.

The sun was bright and the Aegean Sea very blue. The climb up the tortuous narrow streets gave us a new scene every moment, especially of the people: Turkish women with their veils; pretty Turkish children playing; Macedonian peasants with their bright red sashes, baggy trousers, and trim blouses, trudging along with their little mules loaded with brushwood; Jewish bakers with their small bakeshops open on the streets; boys on the hills flying their kites; refugees squatting in front of their hovels searching their clothes or their neighbor's goods for vermin. Such a kaleidoscope I had never seen before.

But our destination lay farther to the east, at Kavalla, a beautiful headland reaching out into the sea just north of the island of Thasos. We reached there on March 7 and immediately set to work, in cooperation with Greek army medical officers, on the epidemic of exanthematic typhus. Our relationship with them was excellent.

The city of Kavalla was divided up into districts with medical inspectors like ourselves assigned to the various districts. We had Greek medical officers assigned to us as interpreters and coworkers and I was particularly fortunate in having the help of Dr. Alexander Moutoussis, who later became the dean of the Medical School of the University of Athens. We became great friends; in 1948, after the Second World War almost thirty years later, I was happy to be able to work with him again on another mission, and we reminisced about the hillsides of Kavalla as we had known them in 1919.

We American doctors lived in a comfortably furnished apartment on the top floor of a tobacco warehouse, which was said to contain the only bathtub in Kavalla. For the three weeks we were in Kavalla we "were in clover," with good beds, hot baths, splendid meals, a cozy lounge with an open fire and gramophone, all quite different from what we had expected— which was that we would live out in the fields in tents. In Drama, to which we moved on April 3, and later in Serres, a badly afflicted and ruined town, we had adequate accommodations, but none like the comforts of Kavalla.

I was given an additional area to inspect in Serres in the malarial Struma Valley after John Hodgson had been infected by bedbugs with typhus—an illness from which, though at first very ill, he eventually recovered. This was in the ruins of the city where several cases of typhus were discovered every day, even in the cleanest of the houses. The sick would be transported to the quarantine hospital where they would remain; their houses would be posted and put under guard to prevent the spread of the disease. Since the typhus is spread largely by lice, the entire population had to be deloused at regular intervals, at least once a week, and they had to carry with them a certificate of delousing, properly dated. Delousing included the clipping of the hair close to the head, which process was carried out at the entrance of special baths where the cleansing process went on. The mortality from typhus, which had been high during the war, had been reduced to less than ten per cent, so the danger was not as bad as it had been, though still bad enough.

The work was always interesting. One day, for instance, I

was sent to retrieve a young girl who had escaped with a Greek officer from a quarantined house. I found them living in a house at the opposite end of Serres and had quite a time forcing her to take a delousing bath and then return to her quarantined home. The next day, with a gendarme to help me, I forcibly escorted twenty-four dirty Tsiganes (whom the Greeks considered to be the worst gypsies) from one of their many lairs in the Katakaminika section of town to the public bath. While these gypsies were on their protesting way to the bath, we passed one of the frequent religious processions chanting its way through the town to scare away the pestilence. Priests were in their glittering robes, and crowds of people trudged along, carrying lighted candles (in broad daylight), and holding banners and relics. At each door along the street stood a table with candles lit and incense burning before pictures of Christ. Today, looking back at these ceremonies, I think they were almost as helpful as we were, for although the quarantine helped some, we had no specific treatment for the disease. It was only when the natives whitewashed their houses in the spring and took their annual baths, that the typhus began to decrease in its extent and severity.

Greece·was not alone in suffering the epidemic. I still have in my possession a 1919 clipping from a French newspaper:

> There die in Russia every month about 85,000 persons sick with exanthematic typhus. Moscow occupies in these statistics the first place, with more than 10,000 deaths. The municipality of that city has had to monopolize the manufacture of coffins, of which 10,000 were ordered from the cooperatives of Riazan at the price of 700 roubles each.

This was a forerunner of what was to come the following year when, at the height of the destitution following the revolution and the war, uncounted millions of Russians died of typhus and starvation, or often of both together. It was almost impossible for anyone to get into Russia during those days, so the rest of the world learned little of what was happening there, and therefore paid little attention to the appalling statistics and suffering.

By the end of May, the time had come for me to leave Greece, but when I arrived in Athens I was asked by the Department of Hospital Services in the Greek Red Cross division of the American Red Cross if I would be willing to spend a few weeks longer inspecting the hospitals of Thessaly and of the Peloponnesos, on behalf of the American Red Cross and the Ministry of the Interior of Greece. I agreed, and for the next three weeks was very busy traveling, inspecting, sight-seeing, and doing a little amateur archeology on the side, aided by advice given me by the Greek widow of Heinrich Schliemann, the noted German archeologist who had excavated Troy and Mycenae. When I called on her at her home in Athens she took down from her mantelpiece, to show me, some of the gold cups and other treasures which she had helped her husband to excavate at Mycenae—later of course they were put into the museum in Athens. My first stop was at Corinth where the great American archeologist Carl Blegen put me to work helping to find prehistoric graves on a mountain hillside after I had inspected the local hospital.

At each of my hospital visits, I would carefully note down the needs of each of the hospitals and report them later to the authorities in Athens. What the hospitals needed most, aside from better internal structure and repairs to the buildings, were instruments for surgical operations and anesthesia, and other supplies, particularly medicines. Unfortunately, aside from a few dressings and surgical kits, we Americans had very little left over from our recent war experiences in France to give them. The Red Cross shipped out from Paris and Marseilles great boxes of supplies, but so far as I could find out most of them contained only pajamas. These we did distribute throughout Greece and for years after we were there, many Greeks were dressed in American pajamas as one of their chief costumes.

At the end of June two events took place that were momentous for me. On June 28 peace with Germany was signed by all the Allied Nations. And at midnight on June 30, my official duties in Europe ended.

July was spent getting to Paris, partly through the Balkan countries. I was asked by the American Red Cross to carry mail, as an armed courier, up through the Dardanelles, into the Black Sea and up the Danube to Bucharest, to deliver to some of our American personnel who were still there. After two days in Istanbul (where I saw the last Sultan of Turkey ride, on a Friday, to his mosque) my boat went on into the Black Sea, carrying hundreds of prisoners of war back to Bulgaria and Rumania. They were a happy lot, joyous to be going home after months, and sometimes years, of captivity.

When I finally came into Bucharest by train, I found that there was a taxi strike and the only vehicle I could find to transport my heavy bags of mail was a wheelbarrow. In the course of loading it one of the bags split open and a blizzard of letters spilled into the street. Friendly bystanders helped me to collect them and I finally arrived at the Red Cross headquarters with all of the mail.

On arrival in Paris, I found a telegram from Athens, informing me that the Greek Government's Silver Cross, Order of the Redeemer, had just been conferred on me and would be delivered in America. This was the beginning of repeated visits to Greece initiated by the excellent courses in the Greek language and history to which I was exposed at the Roxbury Latin School.

On August 7, 1919, I sailed for home on the Holland liner *New Amsterdam*, which also carried 1,400 returning American troops. On August 16, we docked in New York, and the first thing I did was to seek out a nearby drugstore where I greedily devoured three chocolate ice cream sodas in a row after over two years of abstinence. The next morning I reported to the Red Cross office, received my discharge, and took the train for home. It was twenty-five months since I had left Boston to go to war. Now at last, I thought with relief, we are through with wars. How wrong I was.

The Decade of the 1920s:
The Beginning of Cardiology

CHAPTER IV   As I review the manuscript of this chapter I realize that much of the text is likely to interest the medical historian much more than the layman, but I also know that the general reader today has become more interested and knowledgeable than his predecessors of a generation ago in the advances of medical science, particularly since heart disease has become so common that it has seriously affected members of nearly every family. Therefore, I have omitted little of the chronological course of the evolution of the new specialty of cardiology.

In my absence abroad, during the war and afterwards, Miss Mabel Hopkins, who had joined me in 1916 as a skilled technician, carried on with the electrocardiograph and occasionally sent me prints from the glass plates and thus helped to keep up my interest in the special field that I had entered. On my return to the hospital in the fall of 1919, I served again as West Medical Resident, concentrating in cardiology, before starting a more or less independent career in the fall of 1920. Thus that decade of 1911 through 1920 was one of preparation first in pediatrics, then in general internal medicine, and finally in cardiology—except for the interruptions caused by World War I.

In 1920, there were neither undergraduate nor postgraduate courses in the subject of cardiology, except toward the end of that decade, and there were only occasional individuals, including especially Mackenzie and Lewis, who not only were pioneers but were able teachers in the field. Some of the professors in Boston, although not specialists, were interested in heart disease; they included Henry Jackson, Joseph Pratt, Richard Cabot, and Timothy Leary. But for the most part we were all beginners together and were rather regarded by our contemporaries as a little strange for taking on something "so impossible" or "of such little importance."

As I look back on the decade of the 1920s I find that it consisted of ten years of intense activity in my chosen field, as it did in many other pioneering branches of medicine. In 1920 I finished my residency, became a teaching fellow at the Harvard Medical School, and began my practice and teaching. I have always enjoyed all three aspects of my own medical program, namely, research, teaching, and practice. It would be very difficult at the present time to carry on such activity as I did then, because of the tremendous development of the total field. It would be like spending eight hours a day on research, eight hours a day teaching, and eight hours a day in practice; but in those years when I was beginning, I spent about four or five hours on each of the three aspects of cardiology, and thus every day was a long day. I had already done some clinical research during the decade before, but it was much intensified during the 1920s.

At the beginning of this decade my ECG laboratory was still in the basement of the Skin Ward at the M.G.H., but I was able shortly after to move it to a very small suite on the ground floor of the Bulfinch Building, located under the eastern flight of outside steps leading to the Treadwell Library and the medical wards on the second floor. There we had our hilarious moments, improvising space, privacy, and repair of the delicate parts, especially the strings of our primitive galvanometer, which were always getting out of order. When in the middle of that decade Howard Sprague became my resident and later my senior associate he took great pleasure and showed much skill in the care of our instruments. In fact, later he himself invented the first practical combination stethoscope which went by his name, the Sprague-Bowles.

In the fall of 1920 I left my quarters at the hospital and went to live with several colleagues in a house at the corner of Marlboro Street and Massachusetts Avenue. This was about a mile and a half away from the hospital; sometimes we walked to the hospital, sometimes we drove, and on a clear day in winter we would skate down the Charles river, less polluted than now. In the early 1920s three bachelors, Arlie Bock, Joe Aub, and I, became roommates and established luxurious quarters at the Brimmer Chambers.

Although our lives were strenuous, we managed from time to time to take time off for fun and relaxation. In 1922, for instance, one of my roommates, Joseph Aub, and I decided to take two and a half months off during the summer and to travel on the European continent and in Great Britain.

We went by train to Quebec, where we boarded one of the Princess ships for Southampton. Just before we sailed we met on the dock the famous actor, Otis Skinner, and his wife, who were seeing their daughter, Cornelia, and her companion Emily Kimbrough off for a summer in Europe; the Skinner parents were planning to travel by a faster ship and to meet the girls when they arrived in England. Soon after sailing, we were assigned table seats for our meals, and Joe and I found ourselves placed at the Captain's table alongside the girls.

Just before we reached the French port of Cherbourg, en route to Southampton, they asked our advice about an acute febrile illness that had suddenly attacked Cornelia, one which involved her throat and mouth, and skin, and eyes; she had fever and much malaise.

She told us that shortly before sailing she and Emily had made a brief visit with Mr. and Mrs. Skinner to a school for the blind, where there had been a recent epidemic of measles. With this clue, we looked for so-called Koplik spots on both the mucosa of the mouth and the skin. They were easily identified, and so the diagnosis was clear—measles. Then what to do?

Our first inclination was to call the ship's doctor, but then we found on inquiry that if the authorities discovered her illness Cornelia would be quarantined and then taken to a hospital at the ship's final port of call in Germany. Since her parents were to meet the girls on the dock in Southampton, this seemed an undesirable course of action; we decided at a momentous conference among the four of us to conceal the disease in some way, despite its very obvious manifestations, and to smuggle Cornelia into England, where I promised to stay long enough to see her through her illness. (Joe Aub was to disembark the next day at Cherbourg, leaving me and the girls to carry on the plot.)

As a matter of fact it was not an easy decision, for two reasons. In the first place Cornelia's own health was in hazard. She had rather high fever, was very ill, and looked miserable with spotted skin and mouth, and inflamed eyes. In the second place, we were breaking all the rules, and importing a highly contagious and sick person secretly into England. The morning we docked, Cornelia, with Emily's help, made herself up convincingly, and with paste and powder and rouge and a most concealing veil, procured from I know not where, she looked almost the picture of health, as, on my arm, she walked past the ship and shore doctors to disembark. It was a critical moment and although she looked rather odd in her elaborate make-up no one suspected anything wrong.

Meanwhile, Emily had disembarked ahead of us to tell the Skinners what was happening. When Otis heard the news he shouted aloud for all to hear, "What! Measles!"—but no one knew what he was talking about and Cornelia and I soon joined them and we all hurried to a nearby hotel where reservations had been made. Cornelia was put to bed with curtains drawn. There she convalesced during the next week, happily free from complications such as pneumonia, which we had feared because of the hazard associated with those few hours of disembarkation. Otis and I became well acquainted and walked the streets of Southampton together, playing a game of seeing who could spot the most amusing shop sign. We tied the score together when we suddenly saw a sign on a ladies' store which read "Hipps, Limited." After this adventure we went our various ways again but were reunited in Paris, where Joe rejoined us and we had several pleasant days together.

One day in the early 1940s I was on a train going to a medical meeting in Chicago. To relieve the pressure of my medical absorption while on the ride, I picked up a copy of *Reader's Digest,* and as I was thumbing through it I suddenly encountered my name. As I read on I was dumbfounded to find a detailed account of how I had smuggled Cornelia into England. The wicked deed set forth for all the world to read! The girls have always claimed that they had notified us of their intentions, but my first realization that the girls had actually written and published "Our Hearts Were Young and Gay," came to me from the abstract in the *Reader's Digest.*

I was appalled. Just as I was beginning to attain an authoritative position in the medical profession, I appeared in print as a youthful playboy, and as if that weren't bad enough, I was distressed to think of what the legal consequences might be. So when I got home I consulted Joe Aub and together we confronted the girls. They, of course, expressed great innocence and announced that their book would improve our reputations rather than the reverse. In England we were regarded as "Innocents Abroad," and all our friends at home envied and flattered us.

I might add that some other secrets of the adventures of the girls became known to us only on reading their book (which went on to be a best-seller). One of the new things we learned was their concern that we might have been conscious when we danced with them on ship board of the swinging and bumping of their money purses, which were suspended from their belts, as was apparently the custom of the day. As a matter of fact, in the course of my own absorption in my non-existent dancing technique I don't remember that I was conscious of this impediment of theirs. And I have long since forgiven them the revelation of our reprehensible behavior.

To return to the chronology of my personal life during the 1920s: in 1924 I was married to a lovely and intelligent girl named Ina Reid, whom I had met at Smith College when I went there in 1923 to give my first lecture at the Smith College Graduate School for Social Work. She had graduated from Smith the previous year. Later Ina was transferred for her winter program to the Social Service Department of the Massachusetts General Hospital, and there we renewed our acquaintance and became engaged to be married; the ceremony took place on June 28, 1924. We spent three months abroad on our honeymoon, and I took Ina to many of the places I had visited earlier—to England, Ireland, France, Germany, Austria, Switzerland, and Italy.

The other personal event of the 1920s was the death of my father, who survived a heart attack in 1928 but died in 1929. (My mother died of pneumonia in 1948, at the age of eighty-eight.)

As I turn now to the professional activities of the decade of the 1920s, I want to refer to the intense preoccupation that fell upon me during those years and which has continued right up to the present time. I have been trapped by this striking and dramatic unfolding of medicine, of health and disease, the lure of patients, researches, teaching, and of public health. Through most of these years I have had very little time for outside social activities. I have often felt very sorry about this, but I could do little about it. I have worked day and night. Not infrequently I would come home from my office (which at first was at the hospital, then later on Beacon Street, where it still is) at seven o'clock, have a rather quick dinner and then go off to see a patient in consultation or settle down for three or four hours of reading and writing in the evening. Frequently I stayed up into the early hours of the morning. This still goes on but at a somewhat slower pace.

During this decade, as in the others which followed, I was active in several professional events that were related to, but not directly involved in, my work. While a member of the American Medical Association in the early years, with several colleagues I studied the effect of drugs—namely digitalis, quinidine, squill, apocynum ("Canadian hemp"), and convallaria ("lily of the valley")—on the heart and on the electrocardiogram. We reported on these drugs and their effects at the annual meeting of the American Medical Association. Over a period of a few years in the early twenties, I became Secretary, later Vice-Chairman, and finally Chairman of the Section on Pharmacology and Experimental Therapeutics of the American Medical Association; and in the 1950s I received the annual Distinguished Service award of the AMA.

Several health exhibits were held in Boston in the early years of the 1920s; among these we had individual exhibits, in a large area of the old Mechanics Building, devoted to the heart. They were concerned with all sorts of techniques, such as taking blood pressure without a mercury column but with water that was colored red, or the taking of electrocardiograms of the sightseers themselves. This led to the further development of the New England Association for the Prevention and Relief of Heart Disease. We really did think a good deal about prevention of heart disease, particularly rheumatic heart disease, even in those early years, but we were too busy taking care of sick people to spend much time on the prevention of their diseases.

In 1924, the newly organized New England Association for the Prevention and Relief of Heart Disease joined four other similar groups in the country in establishing the American Heart Association. I was the first Treasurer, for two years, and eventually became President in 1940 and 1941. When I looked over my small notebook recently, I found that the Association's budget for the whole country that first year was about $2,500, and for the second year approximately $10,000. In the past two decades the budget has been in the millions (forty million in 1969) and the membership in the thousands. I have been kept busy through most of these years in the support of the Association and just recently (in the spring and summer of 1969) visited eighteen states on behalf of Heart Association drives.

In 1920 Doctor David Edsall, then dean of the Harvard Medical School, invited me to become his assistant dean, but I believed that I should not accept because I had other more important original work to do. I was also invited to serve as assistant editor to Doctors David Edsall and John Howland, Professor of Pediatrics at Johns Hopkins, on a new journal called *Medicine*. For two years I carried on that duty, but I finally retired from it because of other activities more interesting to me.

In our cardiovascular program of the 1920s I had attached to me as assistant usually one so-called cardiac resident or fellow and sometimes two or three other graduate or undergraduate students, so that often we were five or six together. We had a wonderful time carrying on studies in this unknown field of cardiology, including electrocardiography and various types of heart disease and especially disturbances of rhythm. I first became interested in arrhythmias in London in 1913 and 1914 (see Appendix 2), and I continued this interest in

45

the next few years when I was a resident at the Massachusetts General Hospital, also during the First World War and immediately afterwards. During the 1920s we added to our studies a number of other subjects, including especially rheumatic heart disease with the various deviations and complications thereof.

Early in my career I was sent by Richard Cabot to study the out-patient departments of hospitals here and there in the United States. I returned to take over the dispensary, that is the Out-patient Department (O.P.D.) of the M.G.H., to revise it, to bring it up to date and thereby to improve it. I took over the Adult Heart Clinic myself and assisted in the Children's Heart Clinic, which later on I also took over. With our work in the clinics of the O.P.D., as well as on special bed cases in the wards, our group concentrated on our clinical investigations. We would not infrequently have for study and treatment five or six cardiac patients in the wards, and at the same time, several other patients in the O.P.D. every week.

One of the most important papers published in this decade of the 1920s (with the help of Merrill Myers of Iowa) was that on the Classification of Cardiac Diagnosis, emphasizing the fact that the etiological diagnosis should come first, that is, the cause of the heart disease, followed by the abnormal pathological findings, and finally the functional condition— a threefold diagnosis. Heretofore, causes had not been considered particularly important, but as we studied them we became more and more convinced that *prevention* of heart disease should in this way be emphasized as of prime importance.

Another very important subject during the twenties was that of the fitness of the cardiac patient to do physical work. Beginning in 1921 we made and published studies of cardiac patients in industry and the ability of the cardiac patient to work. We felt then that patients could be rehabilitated sufficiently to return to work and to be useful for years to come. The repetition of this same advice thirty years later, when I helped care for President Eisenhower, was based on this early work of ours in the 1920s.

Several other subjects were of much interest to us during that decade in cardiology. One of them was again the electrocardiogram, its form and its relationship to the electrical axis of the heart. From 1920 to 1921 Sidney Burwell, my first resident (who later became dean of the Harvard Medical School), helped me in studying the electrical axis in space, which we reported at the meeting of the "Young Turks" in Atlantic City in 1921. This was more than ten years before it became utilized practically, in the form of the so-called chest leads with electrodes placed on the chest wall. We used chest leads to make this determination, but we did not use them long enough to realize their important clinical value.

We studied other relationships of the electrocardiogram, for example, with Dr. Howard Sprague, the atrial T waves, representing the time of the muscular contraction (systole) of the atria (the two upper heart chambers whose function it is to receive the blood coming back to the heart, the right atrium from all parts of the body except the lungs and the left atrium from the lungs, and then both atria to pass the blood along to the two ventricles—the large muscular chambers of the heart which pump the blood on, the right to the lungs and the larger left to all the rest of the body). Before this we had been paying all our attention to the T waves of the ventricles, but now we studied the T waves of the atria. Later, Seeley Mudd of Southern California and I studied the determination of the length of systole as measured from the Q wave to the end of the T wave. We reported on this in 1929. (See Figures 1 [circulation] and 2 [electrocardiogram].)

Among our other studies was included one on diphtheria, "The Effect of Diphtheria on the Heart." Diphtheria, when severe, can affect the heart and cause death, as was evident in the South Department of the Boston City Hospital where, in that decade, there were many patients with diphtheria. How-

ever, when we studied the patients who had survived diphtheria, and made a report in 1927 on 100 such cases, there was
no evidence of any serious residual effect. We found not a
single case of heart block, which some of our colleagues had
prophesied we would find. However, there are very rare cases
of the sort, but almost all diphtheritic patients who developed
high grade heart block during their acute diphtheria died
quickly.

We found and studied interesting and puzzling conditions,
including the fascinating illness formerly called "Soldier's
Heart" and now most commonly "Neurocirculatory Asthenia"
or "Effort Syndrome." This condition, which I had studied
in World War I and have mentioned in Chapter III, is common in civilian as well as in military life if nervous (emotional) stress and fatigue are severe enough. The exact mechanism, probably biochemical in nature, responsible for the
curious combination of symptoms (sighing type of shortness of
breath, left breast aching, palpitation, tendency to faint or to
feel faint, morning fatigue, and easy exhaustion) is still elusive. But since the condition, though often very disagreeable,
is never dangerous, it has not been so extensively or intensively studied as have other more serious disorders and diseases. It is still a puzzle and it is still often mistaken for heart
disease itself.

We studied the heart in high blood pressure and nephritis,
and reported the findings in a paper toward the latter part of
the decade. We began also to study congenital defects of the
heart as early as 1921. Later we published the report of a
"blue baby" who lived for nearly sixty years. He was Henry
Gilbert, the composer, whom I saw myself when he was in
his mid-fifties. He was still very blue and very limited in his
activity. I shall describe him in detail in Chapter X.

After Mr. Gilbert died, we did a study of his heart and
found he had one of the extreme types of congenital heart
disease. The reason for his blueness (cyanosis) was that the

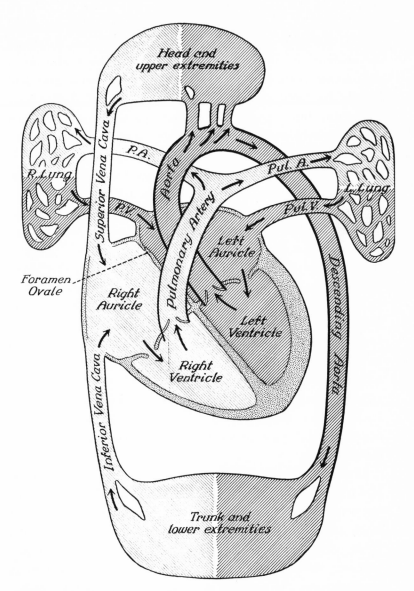

Figure 1. In the normal circulation, the blood from the right auricle passes into the right ventricle and out by way of the pulmonary artery to the lungs, where it is oxygenated. The oxygenated blood is returned from the lungs by the pulmonary veins to the left auricle; thence it passes to the left ventricle and out by way of the aorta to the systemic circulation. The blood from the head and upper extremities is returned by the superior vena cava to the same auricle. There the cycle starts again.

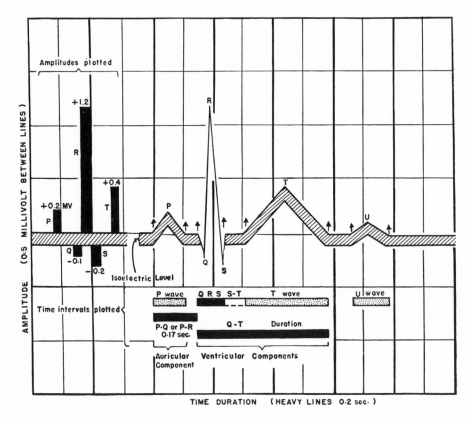

Figure 2. Diagram of normal electrocardiogram showing the individual complexes with special reference to amplitude and time duration. P = atrial deflection; QRS = first ventricular deflection; ST segment and T wave = remainder of ventricular activity; beginning of Q to end of T = duration of systole (contraction of ventricles); end of T to beginning of Q = duration of diastole (resting phase of ventricles).

blue (that is, unoxygenated) blood in the right side of the heart was in major part shunted directly into the aorta which was misplaced to the right directly over the septum between the ventricles, the upper part of which was missing. Only a small part of the blood went through the lungs to be oxygenated. Mr. Gilbert has been, I believe, the most famous of the "blue babies," including those operated on later by Drs. Blalock and Taussig in Baltimore. Now such defects as his can be almost completely corrected by open heart surgery; in olden times they rarely allowed survival beyond the age of twenty.

During the twenties we also made an important study of family incidence (in part hereditary) in rheumatic heart disease. We visited many of the crowded areas in the slums of Boston where some of our Out-patient Department cases with rheumatic heart disease lived. We examined the relatives of the patients themselves in their homes, and we found that about fifty per cent of the families of patients we had seen in the hospital had some other member of the family affected by rheumatic heart disease or rheumatic fever. Since then, this has been our general finding in the poorer areas of the city. In other more prosperous suburbs of Boston, where families lived comfortably, we found that there was far less rheumatic heart disease (acute or chronic) among the children—actually only about twenty-five per cent of the number found in the poorer sections. Certain families (perhaps five per cent) seem to be susceptible to the hemolytic streptococcus, with rheumatic fever as a sequel. In such cases there first appears a sore-throat infection, a "strep throat," which later on in the course of eight or ten days gives rise to rheumatic fever. Now that it is possible to protect against rheumatic fever by using antibiotics, especially penicillin, to control the streptococcic infection, we have and shall have in the future very little rheumatic fever and the rheumatic heart disease that follows.

We studied syphilis in relation to heart and aortic disease (the aorta is the great artery arising from the heart and carrying the blood to all parts of the body except the lungs—see Figure 1) and made a report of the rarity of involvement of heart or aorta in children with congenital syphilis. But the disease in adults was still an occasional cause of aortic and heart disease (four to ten per cent of all cardiovascular cases at that time). It is now, happily, very rare.

Other studies concerned the important effects on the heart of thyroid disease, both overactive and underactive, including exophthalmic goitre, that is hyperthyroidism, and myxedema due to a serious decrease or absence of thyroid secretion.

Another condition which we studied was failure of the heart, due to weakness of the heart muscle from strain of one kind or another. The strains were due to disease or deformities of the heart valves, or to prolonged and at that time uncontrollable overaction of the heart from thyrotoxicosis, or to uncontrolled high blood pressure, or to severe coronary heart disease with large heart muscle scars (called infarcts). All these conditions can cause failure of the heart muscle, and that was what we did not know how to treat adequately in that decade. Although foxglove, that is, digitalis, helped a lot, we had no adequate diuretics, and we did not know enough to limit the salt intake.

We also studied signs and symptoms, including murmurs of one kind or another, like the one first described by Dr. Graham Steell a hundred years ago. Among them was the venous hum in the neck, which is sometimes wrongly interpreted as a sign of trouble but is simply due to the flow of blood rushing down the jugular veins in the neck toward the heart, especially in a very young person when in the upright position. (See Appendix 2 for further comments on murmurs.)

In this decade I also took especial interest in the sighing type of breathing, which is often noted in neurocirculatory asthenia when there is no heart disease itself, but rather nervous exhaustion. We differentiated this type of breathing from "cardiac asthma"—a much more important symptom.

We presented, at one time, a classification of heart pain, distinguishing the different types of pain, especially angina pectoris, which means literally "choking of the chest," a heavy pressure under the breastbone on effort, due to lack of oxygen in the heart muscle when the coronary arteries are too much narrowed by disease.

In this period we studied functional tests of the heart which were rather unsatisfactory, since most of the tests of exercise were breath-holding and demonstrated the general unfitness of the individual, emotional as well as physical, rather than disease of the heart.

Another subject concerned the heart in pregnancy. When the Boston Lying-In Hospital was on McLean Street in the old West End, before it moved to its location near the Harvard Medical School, Dr. William Breed and I made a study of the pregnant women who had symptoms and signs which suggested trouble with the heart. About half of these patients did not have any heart trouble at all but were fatigued by the burden of pregnancy and had symptoms typical of neuro-circulatory asthenia. On the other hand, some had rheumatic heart disease of a moderate type. Once in a while patients with more severe mitral stenosis would become pregnant and then there would be trouble, but this was not the common finding. When the hospital moved from McLean Street to its present abode, Dr. Burton Hamilton, a colleague, took over its heart clinic and published a book on heart disease in pregnancy which was followed a decade or so later by one written by his successor, Sidney Burwell, together with Dr. James Metcalf, on the heart in pregnancy. Both these books marked useful steps ahead in this field. The study of heart disease in pregnancy is now well established, but prevention of heart disease is more important than its treatment or diagnosis—as some of us have maintained for a great many years.

In 1926 and again in 1928, Dr. T. Duckett Jones and I published papers describing our studies of the prevalence and incidence of heart disease and disorders in New England. The 1928 paper consisted of an analysis of 3,000 cases—1,000 of them from my own cardiovascular practice, 1,000 from the wards and the Out-patient Department of the M.G.H. and 1,000 from ten practitioners of medicine—that is, family doctors or internists outside the hospital. In this analysis, rheumatic heart disease accounted for about half, hypertension for another third, and then there were coronary heart cases, congenital heart cases and other types. In the 1950s, when Duckett Jones and I reviewed similarly another 3,000 patients we found quite a shift. Coronary heart disease had become first, hypertensive still was second, and rheumatic heart disease third and going down. One other important change was the greater frequency in our figures of congenital heart disease, though we doubt that there was any important increase in the amount of it; more children with congenital defects were brought to us then by parents who would never have come to the large cities or clinics like ours unless they had known that some help could be given to them. So when surgical procedures came into play the frequency with which we saw congenital heart disease suddenly changed from 1.5 to 7.8 per cent. This was not a true increase in frequency, but the increase was due mostly to the public's growing knowledge of available help, although our growing diagnostic ability also played a role.

In the early years of the 1920s and in the years before that, the most important type of all as now seen in 1970, namely coronary heart disease, could not have been very common. I base this assertion on the fact that of the first 100 papers I published, only two, at the end of the 100, were concerned with coronary heart disease. If it had been common I would certainly have been aware of it, and would have published more than two papers on the subject—and I already knew its chief symptom, angina pectoris, and its chief objective evidence in the electrocardiogram.

In 1924 Henry Marble (a surgical colleague) and I reported on the confusion in diagnosis between a "heart attack" (coronary thrombosis) and a gall stone attack. Two years later Louis Wolff (my cardiac resident) and I reported a series of cases of acute coronary occlusion, that is, coronary thrombosis or heart attack. These two papers were the first two on this important subject to appear among my first 100 papers. However, we began to publish near the end of the decade other papers on the subject, for example, the prognosis (future) of angina pectoris and coronary thrombosis or occlusion, and on angina pectoris in young people due to coronary insufficiency. We had begun to suspect that the prognosis of patients with coronary thrombosis was not as bad as was first thought. It had been believed from experience in the first decade that angina pectoris and coronary heart disease were very serious indeed and would not allow long survival, a few years at best. But we had been following more and more patients since the early twenties and had learned much. I saw my first case of a heart attack with that diagnosis established in January, 1921, during the first year of my private practice; by the end of the decade we realized that some of the patients had not only recovered but were in good health and back at work. Early in the next decade I was able to report in Memphis, Tennessee, in 1932 on "Optimism in the Treatment of Heart Disease" with particular reference to this group of recovered patients with coronary heart disease.

Reviewing my other papers, it is evident that during the twenties we had great difficulty in controlling dropsy (abnormal accumulation of serous fluid in various parts of the body) due to congestive heart failure. One of the techniques used in order to try to clear away the congestion that appeared in the legs was to insert little silver Southey tubes into the tissue of the legs through which the fluid drained into bottles.

We would sometimes get two or three quarts of fluid out of a patient in a few hours; this helped some patients but it was a very crude method indeed.

In 1928 there came a big change in my life; I received a traveling fellowship to go abroad for a year, primarily to write a definitive book on heart disease. (This book, which became the standard textbook on the subject for several decades, first appeared in 1931; the fourth edition was published in 1951. It was translated into Italian and Spanish and was also printed, in English, in Japan.)

My wife and I sailed for Europe in the late summer of 1928 and went for a month to England, visiting old medical friends in London and getting their latest ideas about cardiology. Among them I saw John Parkinson, and together we decided to prepare a paper on our discovery of the so-called Wolff-Parkinson-White syndrome, the W-P-W syndrome, which is now well known. This is an anomaly due to a more or less normal variation of the conduction tissue of the heart which gives rise to an electrocardiogram in which the P-R interval is short and the QRS waves are wide and of unusual shape. There is in this anomaly a tendency for the heart to beat fast at times, that is, with paroxysmal tachycardia, although not all cases show that disturbance of the rhythm. This mechanism is probably due to an extra bundle (a sort of short circuit) which connects the two auricles or atria of the heart, the receiving chambers, with one of the two ventricles, the pumping chambers of the heart, while short-circuiting the other. In April, 1970, I chaired a panel discussion of this oddity in a three-day symposium on "Cardiac Arrhythmia" at the Hamlet Hotel in Elsinore, Denmark. At that discussion, I reported on the current good physical health of Case Number 1, discovered at the age of eighteen in 1928, and of an even earlier case, recorded in 1917, eleven years before we made the discovery.

In 1928 we went on from London to Paris for a month, doing more or less the same things we had done in England. Then in Vienna we settled down for two months; there I studied pathology under the great Professor Erdheim and roentgenology under the brilliant young Hugo Roessler; these were weak spots in my own training but subjects in which the Viennese excelled. We would have spent the whole winter and spring there if it had not been so bitterly cold. Vienna at this time was very poor, the public buildings were closed because of lack of heat, and the cafés were full of people trying to keep warm. The Danube was frozen over for the first time in many years. Fortunately for us we received word that we could rent a delightful little villa on the island of Capri in early February and so we fled south to the Casa Surya.

We spent four wonderful months on the slopes of Monte Solaro at Caprile on the edge of Anacapri. We worked hard on my manuscript every day, but also had some leisure time to climb the mountain, to go down to the sea to swim, to take walks all over the beautiful island, and to enjoy our terraced garden of flowers and vegetables.

We saw some friends there, but we were mostly secluded. Others who were doing writing on the island in that area were either novelists or poets. I suppose I was the only person writing a serious scientific work. It took about a week for us to get adjusted, because this seemed too much a paradise in which to write anything serious, but after the first week we managed to settle down to work.

This delightful villa was the property of two Dutch artists, Sara de Swart and Emilie van Kerkhoff. The latter had gone to Bali to paint, but Miss de Swart remained in a little house in the garden which we helped her tend. She had been a pupil of Rodin and was now living as a peasant and teaching English to the children of Anacapri. She had been much influenced by her visits to Bali. Someone in Holland is now collecting material on her life in preparation for a book concerning her place and influence on art in Holland in the early part of this century.

After the day's work we would walk down the famous old Roman steps to the piazza at Capri itself, have an aperitif, or tea or coffee, and wander over that part of the island and down to the shore on the north, called the Marina Grande, or the one on the south, the Marina Piccola. It was a very beautiful place. We remember it with great pleasure and have revisited it several times since then. Capri has been known since Roman times for its pure, invigorating air, and we got so that we could climb as easily as goats.

We were interrupted pleasantly a few times by friends who were visiting other parts of Europe, and some stayed with us. Maude Abbott, for example, came for a week. She was the famous Montreal (Canadian) pathologist who was the world's expert of that day on the pathology of congenital heart disease. This was the beginning of a long-treasured friendship with that remarkable woman, so intelligent and warm and so hilariously funny. (When she eventually died, Helen Taussig of Baltimore received her mantle and became a very important person in following up the work Maude Abbott had started and in developing the clinical side of it.) Another delightful visitor was Fuller Albright, one of the most brilliant medical pioneers of our time.

In concluding this chapter on the 1920s I see that there were for me three major features: first, the environmental changes that affected all of us in the United States and especially those of us who lived in New England; second, the medical scene in which I was beginning to play a role; and third, my personal life.

The First World War was over and we physicians who had been involved in the military life of the previous decade were beginning to get back into our civilian responsibilities in the medical field, affected as were all other Americans by the dark days of the economic depression which began at the very end of the decade. In New England, the Boston police strike led to the elevation of Governor Calvin Coolidge to the presidency.

This last event reminds me of an incident concerning President Coolidge's father, an incident which led eventually to my first dinner at the White House.

On the first day of May of the year 1925, an old gentleman, Colonel John C. Coolidge (the President's father) came down from his home in Plymouth, Vermont, to consult Dr. Arthur Chute, noted senior urologist in Boston, and me, a pioneer though still young cardiologist, about a serious cancer involving his prostate gland, and his equally or probably more immediately serious heart failure with high blood pressure, coronary heart disease, and high grade heart-block. It was obvious that he was dangerously sick and under ordinary circumstances should have been hospitalized. However, when we had completed our examinations and advised him to enter the hospital at once, he firmly refused. "I have never spent a night out of Vermont in all my more than eighty years," he said. "I certainly don't intend to start now." Thereafter we were obliged to resign ourselves to telephonic advice more or less daily to his doctor at home, up to the time of his death a few months later.

A few days after Colonel Coolidge's visit and while attending a medical congress in Washington, Dr. and Mrs. Chute and my wife and I were invited by the President to dine at the White House and discuss his father's illness with him. Though very taciturn during dinner and annoyed that his doctor had forgotten to bring the dog into the dining room to be fed there, when we three men were assembled later in the oval room upstairs, the President suddenly changed and talked entertainingly about many things. That was my first visit to the White House, and was followed by a personal letter from the President about his father and asking me to send him (the President) my bill which was quite a small one.

The second main feature of my professional life in that decade was my exciting participation as a pioneer in the new medical specialty of cardiology (literally, the science of the heart), still considered by most of the medical leaders of the day as trivial preoccupation and not likely to amount to anything but rather a waste of time and a revolt against their medical leadership. Despite this heavy condemnation of our efforts, a few of us throughout the country—including in New England Samuel A. Levine and myself—struggled along and by the end of that decade could see the light ahead. Also, in those ten years coronary heart disease began to loom as a rival of the then still preponderant and devastating acute and chronic rheumatic heart disease. Tuberculosis, diphtheria, typhoid fever, dysentery, and syphilis were on their way down, although still serious threats.

Above all, I had learned by the end of the twenties that despite our increased knowledge there was still a great deal more that we did not know, still many mysteries about the heart which we did not understand.

Finally, my personal life was evolving, with my marriage in 1924 (a bit late, but a happy change) and, as the older son, my additional new role as pater familias upon my father's death at the end of the decade.

The History That Went Before

CHAPTER V   Like my physician father, I have always been deeply conscious of "the links in the chain that went before." For many years medical history has been one of my principal interests and I am constantly aware that my work in cardiology would not have been done had it not been for the work of many men who preceded me, in some cases by decades, in others by centuries. It is for this reason that I would like at this point to turn aside briefly from the story of my own life's work and describe that of a few of my favorite predecessors, whose work was important to humanity's growing understanding of the human heart.

In the preparation of the first edition of my textbook *Heart Disease*, I began to include in certain chapters important quotations from the classical writings of cardiological pioneers of times gone by, long before the specialty itself began. In the first edition of 1931 there were thirty-three such quotations, which added greatly to the enjoyment as well as the edification of my readers. In securing most of these quotations and in checking the accuracy of the bibliography of my individual chapter references, I consulted the first editions of these noted authors and became enamoured of the historical volumes which I found in the major medical libraries of this country and abroad.

With my own background as a student of history in college, I began to acquire a fine collection of first editions, largely by studying catalogues or visiting the shops of dealers in medical classics, mostly in European capitals. In the 1960s I presented this collection to the Countway Library at the Harvard Medical School.

Some of these books were very old, in fact a few were incunabula ("in the cradle"), which means that they were dated before 1500 A.D. Some were of interest for other reasons such as the great medical botanical classic of Leonhard Fuchs, published in 1542. The copy that I had was of considerable historical interest aside from its intrinsic value, since it had evidently been in the possession of a church or religious library. This book was written during the Inquisition. Fuchs was a heretic and lived in the city of Basel in Switzerland, which was a strongly Protestant city of the anti-Catholic revolution. On the title page of the book the name of Fuchs as the author is heavily crossed out with red ink, as it is elsewhere in the book. On the title page is written in red ink *Autore damnato et nomine expurgato* ("The author has been damned and his name has been expurgated"). The name of the city of Basel is scored with red ink wherever it appears and many lines in the introductory pages are similarly disfigured. On the back of the title page, however, there is a portrait of Fuchs which is untouched—apparently in order not to destroy the appearance of the title page.

This is a quarto volume and the pages are large. Every plant that was being used in medicine, or had been used up to that time, is represented by a woodcut of a large size, and the opposite page describes in Latin the details of the plant and what it was used for. Incidentally, it is for this German botanist that the beautiful fuchsia is named.

Interestingly, at the very end of the book there is an appendix which consists of the insertion of two more plants that had been forgotten and came to light too late for the regular press run. One of these two plants is a member of the mint family called Ocimastro, of which little has been known or said of late. The other is the famous digitalis, or foxglove (given its Latin name by Fuchs himself), which was used in the sixteenth century as an emetic and which continued to be used for this purpose for over 200 years, until William Withering confirmed scientifically the important empiric discovery that a small dose of the leaves of the foxglove was beneficial to a patient with dropsy due to heart failure. Some thirty years ago I was given a first edition of Withering's volume (1785) by a former pupil and good friend, James Faulkner; along with the Fuchs quarto and all the others, it is now at the Countway Library.

Two other books which were also published in the 1540s and were prime items in my collection were the 1541 English translation of the Regimen of Health of the Medical Faculty at Salerno, composed early in the twelfth century, and a first edition of Andreas Vesalius' great Anatomy with woodcuts by his friend and fellow Belgian, Van Kalkar, a student of Titian in Venice.

The latter book, which I obtained from Davis & Orioli in London, has a most interesting history. When Hitler entered Austria in 1938, various libraries were confiscated and that of the monastery at Melk on the Danube River above Vienna was removed by the monks before the Nazis arrived, and hastily sold. For this reason, the London book dealers were able to acquire the Vesalius Anatomy. It is a fine original copy with the original binding and tooling on pigskin over boards. Its anatomical woodcuts are magnificent. Centuries later, the original blocks of these woodcuts were discovered in Vienna, I believe. (See figure 3 for one of the fine Vesalius woodcuts.)

As my interest in old books developed, I also became fascinated with medical history, particularly where it concerned the heart. Early in the thirties I prepared a historical chart which was privately printed, the first edition appearing in

1933. It was labeled "The Evolution of our Knowledge of the Heart and Its Diseases," and covered all of medical history from B.C. up to the time of publication. Heart disease as such was noted to have been recognized only in about the year 1500 A.D. The large pages of the chart covered two periods of a thousand years up to 1500 and after that by decades for each century up to 1900, following which the growth of our knowledge increased to such a point that the subdivision was by five-year periods.

I would now like briefly to describe the high points of this development of our knowledge.

Although the heart and blood vessels of mammals, including man, were known to the ancients (as witness the Egyptian papyri, the Bible of the Israelites, and the writings of the schools of medicine of the Greeks—all before the time of Christ), *diseases* of the heart were not recognized for many centuries thereafter, actually not until 1500 A.D., largely because until that time dissection of the human body was considered a sacrilege.

The pulsation of the heart and arteries was not only known to the ancients quite naturally by personal observation, but some observers became especially interested, as evidenced by Aristotle's discovery of the beating of the chick embryo's heart in 384 B.C., and the many writings of Galen in the second century A.D. concerning all sorts of variations of the human pulse. But the circulation of the blood throughout the body was not proved until more than 1,500 years later, by William Harvey, early in the seventeenth century.

When human postmortem examinations (autopsies) began to be legalized by the church about 1500 A.D., slowly it was discovered that the heart could show deformed valves and other abnormalities without causing death. Before this time it was thought that if the heart were damaged in any way (as in war) death would come at once, but most deaths were

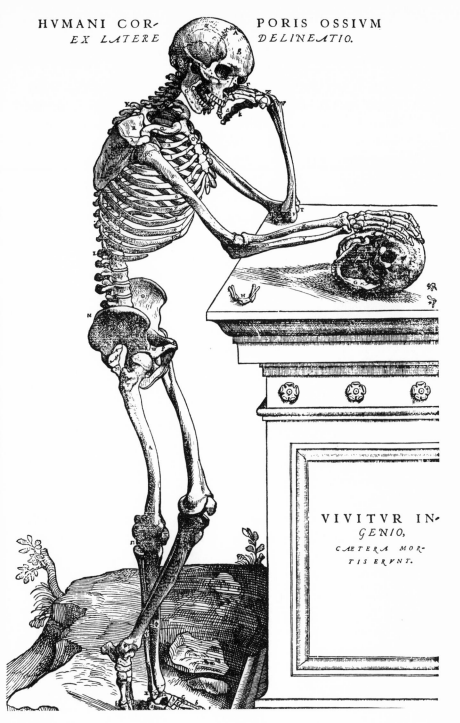

Figure 3. Vesalius woodcut with motto, "The spirit lives; all else is mortal."

Members of the Graduate Course in Cardiology at Massachusetts General Hospital on the steps of The Bulfinch Building in August, 1940. Front row (left to right): Reno Porter (Richmond, Va.), Bernard Walsh (Washington, D.C.), Earle Glendy (Roanoke, Va.), Paul Dudley White, Howard Sprague attributed to the will of God or quite rightly to epidemic plagues or physical injuries. Benivieni in Italy in 1507 was the first to publish case histories of autopsies, but it was Théophile Bonet who, in his large collection of autopsy reports in his *Sepulchretum* in 1679, demonstrated a wide range of diseases of the heart and blood vessels. This was expanded in his second edition in 1700, which became the basis for the magnum opus of Morgagni, entitled *De Sedibus et Causis Morborum* ("concerning the sites and causes of diseases") in 1761. In 1670, Kerckring had been the first to point out that blood clots (thrombi) in the heart were neither worms nor polyps (new growths). But it was not until nearly two centuries later that the German pathologist Rudolf Virchow established in 1857 the existence and significance of thrombosis (blood clots) and embolism (traveling blood clots).

The slowness with which medical and other knowledge, too, developed through the Dark and Middle Ages can be attributed to several factors: (1) the short life of the investigators themselves, laid low by the plague and other pestilences and even by more violence than that of today, (2) the labor of copying everything by hand (even when printing came along in the fifteenth century medical knowledge spread very slowly), (3) the difficulties of travel and communication, and (4) the heavy censorship, both political and religious.

Clinical cardiology, the study of the cardiac patient while still alive, had a much slower start than that of diseases discovered after death. It took years, decades, or even centuries to differentiate the various causes of *symptoms* such as dyspnea (shortness of breath) and chest pain (including angina pectoris), and of *signs* on physical examination, such as various heart murmurs, irregularities of heart rhythm, cyanosis (blueness), and râles (bubbles) in the lungs. I shall mention a few pioneers who did make such a differentiation. Vieussens in 1712 explained that shortness of breath and pulmonary edema in mitral stenosis (narrowing of the mitral valve opening) was not due to so-called congestive heart muscle failure but to the severe limitation of the air space in the lungs by swelling of the small vessels with blood which could not get past the obstruction caused by the narrowed valve when the heart was beating fast—a shrewd discovery in his time. Lancisi in 1728 described the fulness and pulsation of the jugular veins in failure of the right ventricle. Heberden in 1768 coined the term "angina pectoris" for the particular oppressive pain due to coronary heart disease and insufficiency, but it took Jenner, a colleague of his, to discover the cause some years later. Cheyne was joined later by Stokes, another Irishman, in describing in 1818 the unusual kind of respiration (periodic heavy breathing alternating with no breathing at all) which goes by their names. Another Irishman, named Adams, was also joined later by Stokes in describing in 1827 the fainting attack due to the very slow pulse of heart-block (the Adams-Stokes syndrome). Da Costa, a Philadelphia physician who served in the U. S. Civil War, was the first to describe (in 1871) the so-called "Soldier's Heart" which we now know as Neurocirculatory Asthenia—not a disease of the heart but a nervous reaction of the circulation to extreme fatigue. Lian in 1910 in France differentiated very early the separate failure of either left or right ventricle, a discovery which was not accepted by English and American doctors until much later. And it was James Herrick of Chicago who, in 1912, first put on the map the clinical picture of coronary thrombosis, the most prevalent disease in the United States today. One might cite many other physicians who through the last two or three centuries have made contributions of value, but they were of lesser importance than those I have cited.

The third category of advances in cardiology that deserves special note, after those of pathological findings post-mortem and the clinical analysis of symptoms and signs, is that of techniques or methods of study.

In 1707, around the time that watches were being intro-

duced, Sir John Floyer suggested that the minute hand might
be useful in comparing the pulse rate of an ill person with
that of the same person in good health; this was one of the ear-
liest astute observations of the need for recognizing the importance of the wide range of the normal.

A second technique of examination, emphasized first by
Albertini in 1726 was palpation of the chest (feeling the
heart beat with hand placed over the chest wall overlying
the heart). And a third was percussion, or tapping with the
fingers on the thorax and abdomen, introduced by Auen-
brugger in 1761 to discover the dullness of fluid or the tym-
pany (resonance) of air. A fourth advance was made by the
Frenchman Laennec, who in 1819 announced his invention
of the stethoscope to make auscultation more convenient by
the use of a long wooden tube rather than by applying the ear
directly to the chest over the heart; for the first time physicians could listen more scientifically and comfortably to the
heart for its sounds and murmurs and to the lungs for bubbles
or râles or for consolidation as in pneumonia.

A fifth advance was the introduction of the sphygmograph
(pulse tracing machine) by Vierordt and Marey, in 1855
and 1860 respectively. This was later perfected by Mackenzie
about 1902. A sixth was the invention by Roentgen in 1895
of the x-ray tube, which was immediately applied to the
heart by Williams and has been of fantastic importance in
cardiology ever since. A seventh was the development of the
sphygmomanometer (blood pressure machine) by a series
of investigators just before and after the turn of the century.
Actually, the blood pressure was first measured in a mare in
1733, by Stephen Hales, an English clergyman more interested
in physiology than in theology, who described his experiments
in a book called "Haemastaticks."

An eighth technical advance was the invention of the string
galvanometer for clinical electrocardiography, by Einthoven
in 1903. And a ninth was the introduction of cardiac cathe-

terization and angiocardiography, by Forssman and Castellanos in 1929 and 1931, respectively. Their pioneering has evolved into the present-day technique of introducing a long thin rubber or plastic tube (catheter) into an arm vein or leg artery, threading it into the heart to test the blood pressures and blood gas contents in the various heart chambers and great vessels and then taking x-ray photographs of opaque material injected through the catheter into the heart. This technique has revealed deformities, either congenital or acquired of the heart chambers, the valves, and of the blood vessels, big and small.

I shall end this chapter with a summary of important advances in the treatment of diseases of the heart and blood vessels, first medical and then surgical.

One of the three therapeutic measures for practically all diseases carried out by man ever since antiquity was to cause bleeding from an arm vein (venesection). It was still used vigorously at the final illness of George Washington in 1799 and may have contributed to his death. Like the other two popular measures used through countless centuries, namely purgation and vomiting (emesis), its continued application was doubtless supported by the very small minority of patients, less than a very tiny fraction of one per cent, who were obviously benefited. These were persons with acute edema of the lungs due to heart failure or to mitral stenosis (narrowing of the mitral valve); the decrease of the volume of blood in the body relieved the congestion of the lungs. The application of venesection to relieve severe dyspnea (shortness of breath) was pointed out by Celsus of Rome early in the first century A.D. and emphasized centuries later by more modern observers like Vieussens and Senac, specifically for pulmonary edema.

A good many drugs now in common use and valuable in treatment have come from so-called medicinal plants originally introduced for their properties to induce vomiting or purgation. Probably the most notable of all these was digitalis (foxglove), introduced by the botanist Leonhard Fuchs, in 1542, as an emetic. As I have said earlier, it continued to be used for that purpose until in 1775 William Withering discovered its beneficial effect on the heart in relieving certain kinds of dropsy. After ten years of testing, he published his experiences with the drug in 1785. It is of interest that the first active principle of the foxglove was introduced over a century ago (in 1845) as digitaline (digitoxin) by Nativelle.

Dietary advice has also played a part in the history of heart therapy. It is, for instance, an important feature of the "Regimen of Health" composed around 1100 A.D. by physicians at Salerno, Italy, the first medical school established in Europe. At the request of King Henry VIII, the regimen was translated into English in 1541. The first verse reads as follows:

> The Salerne Schoole doth by these lines impart
> All health to England's King, and doth advise
> From care his head to keepe, from wrath his heart.
> Drinke not much wine, sup light, and soone arise,
> When meate is gone, long sitting breedeth smart;
> And after-noone still waking keepe your eyes.
> When mov'd you find your selfe to Nature's Needs,
> Forbeare them not, for that much danger breeds,
> Use three Physicians still: first Doctor Quiet,
> Next Doctor Merry-man, and Doctor Dyet.

The matter of diet was, however, little recognized in the treatment of heart disease until 1866, when the Russian Karell presented the famous diet named after him for the treatment of heart failure. It consists of four feedings in twenty-four hours of 200 milliliters (c.c.) of skimmed milk. This remains one of the best of our therapeutic measures in emergency cases of heart failure over a period of days, being low in sodium, water itself, bulk, and calories. The value of the low sodium intake in congestion was later clearly pointed out by Widal and Lemierre in 1902, but was not accepted in this country as a routine measure of treatment until forty years later.

Returning to drugs, we find two important medicines for angina pectoris: amyl nitrite, introduced by Lauder Brunton in 1867 and the more practical nitroglycerine by Murrell in 1897. The next two drugs in cardiac therapy were both accidentally discovered. The first one was quinine for arrhythmia, introduced by a patient of Wenckebach in 1914. He was a Dutch East Indian merchant who found that when he took quinine to control his malaria, his cardiac arrhythmia was also controlled. This drug, which is extracted from the bark of the cinchona tree, was later replaced by an isomer, quinidin introduced by Frey in Germany in 1918. The second was a mercurial injection (Salyrgan) given for syphilis in 1920 but discovered to be the first of the potent diuretics which have greatly eased the lot of edematous cardiac patients during the last generation.

I shall soon stop, since further developments in medical therapy took place well within my own time and will be discussed in future chapters. But before I stop this part of the discussion, I would like to pay tribute to the pharmaceutical industries and the pharmacological departments of the universities, for their researches, which have in the last few decades quite changed our hit or miss, almost always accidental, discovery of useful medical therapy in heart disease to an organized biochemical program improving many fold our treatment today.

Since almost all the successful surgical treatment of cardiovascular disease has come in my time, the early pioneers were few and can here be presented very quickly. Since I have already described venesection as an essentially medical measure I shall not repeat it now, although I must admit that it was the province of the so-called "barber-surgeons." I am sure, however, that many of the medical professors in many emergencies performed it, although they surely thought it beneath their dignity.

A more difficult and more special surgical procedure was, however, paracentesis (tapping with a needle) a pericardial effusion (fluid around the heart) by Romero in 1819. Evacuation of pleural and peritoneal fluid effusions by needle has been common practice during the past century. In 1877 Southey introduced the little silver tubes named for him to drain fluid out of the edematous legs and scrotum of patients with congestive heart failure. This was, of course, before the days of the powerful diuretics which we now possess.

Farina in Italy and Rehn in Germany were pioneers in 1896 in operations on the heart injured traumatically, and in the First World War such surgical repairs were occasionally made. In 1898 Delorme of France was the first to suggest cutting away the stiff constricting pericardium from the heart's surface to give relief for the congestion that resulted, but years passed before Sauerbruch of Germany actually initiated the procedure in 1913. Churchill in 1928 carried out the first highly successful operation of the sort in the United States and perhaps in the world, including the pioneering by Sauerbruch. This was in the case of Catherine Southworth, a patient of mine, who survived for forty-one years afterwards in good health, and finally died of unrelated lymphoma.

In 1902 Alexis Carrel introduced the delicate suturing of blood vessels—a routine measure today, but not then or for years after. In the same year Matas did the first surgery on an aneurysm. In 1916 Jonnesco did the first sympathectomy for angina pectoris, later tried in this country with indifferent success; that was more than two decades before Smithwick carried out his successful thoracolumbar sympathectomy for high blood pressure in 1940. In 1924 intracardiac surgery on the heart valves was attempted by that bold pioneer, Elliot Cutler, but he was, alas, nearly twenty-five years ahead of his time (though one case by Souttar was successfully carried out in London).

I end with my hat off to the pioneering of my host of friends among the cardiovascular surgeons all over the world. They have done a wonderful job, but I have every hope that eventually we epidemiologists (that is, physicians primarily interested in preventive medicine) may very materially reduce the need for corrective surgery by preventing the diseases that at present make it necessary.

The Decade of the 1930s:
New Diagnoses

CHAPTER VI 🙰   As the 1930s began, the pace quickened. Not only were we (one or two research fellows and myself) in the heart unit at M.G.H. intensively involved in our clinical researches in cardiology, but we were also very active in our teaching, for which our ward and dispensary patients volunteered as subjects. I had developed a busy private practice in addition, affording me much more material to teach with, especially in a long follow-up. The great majority of my private patients were delighted to serve as subjects. Our teaching in the field became much more involved with postgraduate students than with undergraduates, who were not expected to enter specialized fields before graduation. Now and then, however, a fourth-year student would join us for a term or two and this custom grew as cardiology gradually became, during the thirties, a more recognized specialty.

Our summer courses for graduates begun in the 1920s became a routine practice throughout the 1930s and we enjoyed them very much. They lasted as a rule one month, either July or August, and some years we had two such courses with twenty to thirty doctors in each. These were at first privately organized but later were under the wing of the office for graduate teaching at the Harvard Medical

School. During each course we arranged on a weekend a picnic at our place in the country at the town of Harvard where we would begin with a softball game in the pasture with a keg of beer at third base for the refreshment of the batter who succeeded in reaching it. It was at one of these games that I myself successfully stole home in an effort to tie the score, but sliding to the plate I was buried by both catcher and batter and in addition to the run came up with a broken leg. Following the baseball game we would partake of a barbecue feast and finally in the evening retire to the barn where I passed around the treasures from my collection of notable cardiovascular volumes of past centuries.

An especially interesting development in the 1930s was an increasing frequency with which we were beginning to see patients with coronary heart disease, not by choice but by necessity. An indication that heart attacks were not, in the 1920s and earlier, the order of the day, as they have become in succeeding decades, is the fact that the first time my name appeared in published papers on the subject of coronary disease was in my seventy-seventh paper, printed in 1924. And among my first 100 papers, only one other concerned coronary heart disease.

During the 1930s my house staff included eleven fellows or residents who are now scattered throughout the country. There were also twenty-two graduate and undergraduate students who were associated in our clinical researches and in our long follow-up. A number of these associates had begun to come to us from abroad: Hugo Roesler from Vienna, Oscar Brenner from Birmingham, England, Jorge Salcedo-Salgar from Colombia, Aristotles Brasil from Brazil, Alberto Taquini from Argentina, Trevor Cooke from England, John Spillane from Wales, Teofilo Ortiz from Mexico, Donal Murnaghan from Ireland and Noboru Kimura from Japan, a forerunner of others who were to come from the Orient.

We published a good many papers and a few books during

the decade. In 1931 my large volume *Heart Disease,* which I had written in Capri in 1929 and proofread in Jamaica in 1930, was published by the Macmillan Company. (There was a second and much amplified edition in 1937.) Also in 1931 my senior colleague, Howard B. Sprague, joined me in publishing a paper in honor of Professor Samoiloff of Kazan, U.S.S.R., entitled "Our First 10,000 Patients Electrocardiographed at the Massachusetts General Hospital from 1914-1931." It was published in Russian in the *Kazan Medical Journal.*

A few years later I wrote a small book called *Heart Disease in General Practice,* at the request of Dr. Morris Fishbein. This book, however, was quickly lost to sight because of the failure of the evanescent publishing house. I regretted this, because it was planned for the general practitioner and could, I believe, have been quite useful.

Late in the decade Ashton Graybiel and I, then neighbors in Chestnut Hill near Boston, combined our efforts in a volume called *Electrocardiography in Practice.* It was an early book on the subject and was published by W. B. Saunders Company.

During the twenties and early thirties I had discovered for myself the relaxing tranquilization of a pleasant degree of physical fatigue in counteracting the nervous stress and strain of my medical work with patients, students, and researches. I became convinced of the beneficial effects of exercise on the heart as well as on the general health, and in 1937 I put this conviction into words in an article called "Walking and Cycling," which appeared in the American Medical Association's lay magazine, *Hygeia.* Two years later the same ideas on prevention were put forward in a column entitled "The Heart and Heart Disease," which I wrote for the 1939 *Encyclopedia Britannica.*

During the decade I wrote editorials and *in memoriams* to a number of great physicians who happened to be my medical teachers and friends, including Professor Alexander Samoiloff, pioneer in electrocardiography in the U.S.S.R.; Jean Heitz of France, an eminent pioneer in clinical cardiology; Louis Gross of Montreal, a leading figure in cardiovascular pathology, killed in an airplane accident when very young; Richard Clark Cabot, our noted teacher and one of the great doctors of New England; James Esler, a fine young colleague of mine who died young of cancer; Herman Frank Vickery, one of the medical leaders of the staff of the M.G.H. and translator of German textbooks on medicine before Osler; and Henry Jackson, who was the first president of the New England Association for the Prevention and Relief of Heart Disease, after whom an annual lectureship is named under the direction of the Massachusetts Heart Association.

My wife and I went several times to Europe in the thirties. The highlight was a visit to England in 1935, to deliver the St. Cyres Lecture at the London Hospital. This lecture and a clinic at Guy's Hospital in which I took part shortly afterwards concerned chronic constrictive pericarditis, with apparently hopeless dropsy (edema), which was the malady affecting Catherine Southworth, the first successfully treated case in America, and a healthy survivor for forty years. At Guy's Hospital I referred to the fact that this disease had been described twice by their own staff in the previous century, but that these pioneer observations had not been recognized even by the Guy's Hospital staff itself. When I called attention to these two papers, one by Chevers in 1842 and the other by Sir Samuel Wilks in 1870—both of which had appeared in the Guy's Hospital Reports— they were reprinted in one of the 1935 Reports.

In addition to my absorption in medical literature during these decades, I developed, greatly stimulated by Sir William Osler, Oliver Wendell Holmes, and the Concord authors of the nineteenth century, an interest in non-medical literature as medical therapy, particularly poetry and outstanding prose. When I was asked to help dedicate a medical library in Maine in 1938, I wrote a paper on "Doctors and Books," which was published in the *New England Journal of Medicine*. The next year at a hospital directors' meeting I presented a paper entitled "Medicine and Literature"; this was published in the journal *Hospital*.

The 1930s were important to us, personally, because it was in the middle of that decade that my wife and I adopted an infant girl, whom we named Penelope. Four years later we also adopted an infant boy, whom we called Alexander. We have greatly enjoyed, although often with apprehension, the excitement of their lives to this very day, with the crises that are common in most families.

It had been in the 1920s that we found the lovely town of Harvard, Massachusetts, some thirty-five miles northwest of Boston, where we have now summered for over forty years. At first we lived in a beautiful old colonial farmhouse with a big barn on Prospect Hill, which was called Makamuche-kamuk by the Indians. It overlooked the Nashua valley and on its slope there were several historic places. Clara Endicott Sears had owned much of the hill for many years, and the title included the original house called Fruitlands, a farm owned in the early 1840s by Bronson Alcott (the father of Louisa May Alcott). He and his family walked there from Concord and for seven months he presided over his unfruitful colony of transcendental philosophers. This was written up later by Louisa in an essay called "Transcendental Wild Oats." One hundred years later a house was moved over from the nearby Shaker colony to join Fruitlands on the hillside; later an Indian museum containing many arrowheads and artifacts that had been found in the valley was opened, and finally a building to house the works of itinerant portrait painters of colonial days was erected.

We enjoyed the view from our farmhouse for some years, until improved road paving brought crowds of Sunday and holiday visitors to the museums, visitors who would often picnic on our front lawn. So in 1938 we moved away to a quiet little place on Poor Farm Road, where we still spend our summers. We have a few acres with a pleasant pine grove, vegetable and flower gardens and a sense of remoteness much as if we were far off in Vermont or New Hampshire. Yet we are near enough to Boston for me to commute to my hospital and office four days a week during two summer months, following our regular fortnightly vacation in early July. This refuge has been very important for the health of our bodies, minds, and souls, and we have all enjoyed it greatly.

Our 1725 cottage has old fireplaces where the cooking was done, and a well room with a hook where the meat was hung, a well wheel and the original well which was the source of water for the families who had lived here for 200 years before us. The well still has water, although sometimes woodchucks fall in, but when we moved to the house in 1938 we drilled an artesian well on the hill above us and for years our water was pumped into a large tank by a windmill, one of the last of its kind functioning in this part of the country. Recently we have added an electric pump; since August is often without wind, the gardens dried up and we had to carry water from a well at the roadside. The tank is high enough above the house so that water flows into the house by gravity. For many years we had no telephone or electric lights, but as we grew older we finally succumbed to these comforts of modern life.

As I sit here at the window of my room in the attic, writing this chapter, I look out at my wife's flower gardens of lovely design and at the vegetable garden where I am growing some beans, corn, squash of different kinds, tomatoes, cucumbers, and a few other vegetables. Within sight are blueberry, raspberry, and blackberry bushes.

For years we had depredations from woodchucks (ground hogs) and raccoons, even though we shot or trapped them, and we still have raccoons who live in our attic during the winter. We are only the summer visitors. These raccoons have been very destructive of any property left in the shed, throwing jars of food from shelves onto the floor to break them and then devouring the contents. Finally we put up a four-foot-high wire fence which goes a foot and a half into the ground, and this summer we have added an electric wire on top. Now we shall have no trouble in growing our vegetables. We have had to cover our berry bushes with nets to save our crops from the birds.

In view there are also a few fruit trees. When we lived on Prospect Hill we did have a considerable orchard, which bore delicious apples and did not require so much spraying as is apparently necessary today. We even used to sell some of those apples. But although we have few fruit trees here on Poor Farm Road, we do have many lilacs and wild flowers, and the woods are not far away. One of our favorite walks is a trail through the woods behind our house where, about a mile away, we come to the old Shaker Village which housed a Shaker colony from about 1790 to 1914, when the few remaining Shakers moved away to settle in New Hampshire with other colonies.

Now I come to some of the special professional subjects which interested me during the thirties and which resulted in medical contributions by our growing staff.

I suppose that our most important claim to medical fame was our work on pulmonary embolism with the discovery of what we called the acute cor pulmonale, a condition of dilatation and failure of the right ventricle, resulting from massive embolism (clots moving through the veins to the heart, and thence to the lungs, mostly from the leg veins) and thereby obstruction of the pulmonary arterial circulation. This really came to light as the result of an important research by Oscar Brenner of Birmingham, England. Dr. Brenner was a student of mine who in 1933 examined in detail microscopically and macroscopically the lung circulation in 100 consecutive patients autopsied at the M.G.H. On going over this material we discovered that one of the important findings, often unrecognized clinically, was embolism and thrombosis in the pulmonary arteries. Brenner himself later published this important work in detail in the Archives of Internal Medicine, but as early as 1933 we published together a paper summarizing the findings and emphasizing the importance of this particular discovery. Two years later, Sylvester McGinn and I published a paper entitled "The Acute Cor Pulmonale," which showed that we had found distinctive changes in the electrocardiogram, changes which were sometimes confused with coronary thrombosis which massive pulmonary embolism can mimic up to a certain point.

This interest in pulmonary embolism continued because of our finding through the years of that decade that pulmonary embolism was more common in the medical wards of the hospital than in the surgical wards. Hitherto it had been considered to be a common complication post-operatively and in obstetric cases after childbirth due to thrombosis in the leg veins as the result of stasis (inactivity) during hospitalization. But then we found that the stasis imposed on cardiac patients, or in fact on other medical cases, resulted in leg vein thrombosis with complicating pulmonary embolism. The embolism to the lungs would frequently cause what we call infarcts,* that is, consolidation of areas of the lung which had been often confused with pneumonia; we rather quickly found that pulmonary embolism with or without infarction was the chief cause of death in heart failure of any type, and not the failure itself.

This condition had been called hypostatic pneumonia or

---

* Infarction or an infarct, which will be referred to occasionally in future pages of this book, is defined as an area in any organ or tissue of the body which has been acutely damaged by cutting off its blood supply; as it slowly heals it leaves a scar of variable size depending on the amount of tissue destroyed.

just plain congestive failure. An interesting error made by a leading cardiologist of New York, an important contributor to our knowledge of cardiovascular disease in other respects, was his statement made about this time that congestive failure might be attended by fever; in our findings it was quite obvious that the fever was due to the pulmonary infarction following embolism and not to the congestive failure per se.

What this means in layman's terms is that we discovered that if a human body—and particularly the legs—is completely inactive for a period of time, ranging from several days to weeks or months, there may develop (through the lessened flow of fluid through the body) a blood clot, or thrombus. The clot may then move through the blood stream to the heart and lungs, and cause death.

Our study of pulmonary embolism continued into the next decade and still interests us greatly. Pulmonary embolism continues, despite all that has been done, to be one of the most troublesome diseases of man, and is aggravated by the sluggish leg circulation of a large proportion of the citizens of this country today. At one time I tried to get the Boeing Company of Seattle to put some simple technique of exercise of the legs at every seat in their airplanes—a sort of spring mechanism by which travelers would exercise their legs off and on during a long flight—but my persuasion was not adequate. I also had suggested that a standing bicycle near the pilot's cabin might be very useful in maintaining the health and alertness of the pilots themselves, who, during long flights, might use the exercise bicycle one minute every hour. Once again the response was negative, and now the pilots are threatened by hijackers and are not even allowed to walk into the passengers' quarters.

Unfortunately, prevention of disease has attracted much less attention than its diagnosis and treatment. It obviously deserves the first priority, but it is less dramatic than surgical procedures, is rarely asked for by the not-yet-educated public, and the doctors are overworked simply taking care of sick people. However, there has been some improvement in prevention counseling recently, particularly in the warnings against the danger of smoking.

I suppose that the second in importance of our works in clinical investigation during the thirties concerned coronary heart disease. Our labors culminated in 1937, when Drs. J. Kenneth Mallory and Jorge Salcedo-Salgar joined me in studying the speed of healing of myocardial infarction (heart muscle scar) and showed quite clearly that with the average-sized infarct, the healing of the muscle damage required about three weeks, a time period somewhat similar to that of the healing of a broken bone, and that by four or five weeks the scar was pretty well set and moderate activity could be resumed safely in the average case.

Almost equally important was the discovery that young men could have coronary heart disease. My first paper on that subject was in 1935, and was entitled "Coronary Disease and Coronary Thrombosis in Youth"—it was an analysis of four cases under the age of thirty years, twenty-one under the age of forty years and 138 under the age of fifty.

The next paper, even more important, because of the larger number of very young patients, published in 1937 by R. Earle Glendy, Samuel A. Levine, and me, was called "Coronary Heart Disease in Youth," and was a comparison of 100 patients under forty with 300 patients past eighty. Ninety-six of the 100 were males and most of them were "robust." Further analysis of this group was prevented by the Second World War, but this study stimulated us to make a more complete research a decade later.

Another important aspect of our coronary studies through the decade was that of prognosis (outcome). In 1931 Dr. Edward Bland and I established the beginning of a long follow-up series of 500 patients with angina pectoris, and 200 patients with coronary thrombosis. Our final report of these groups twenty years later, when all but three of the coronary thrombosis group had died, has been one of the authoritative clinical studies of this generation and is frequently referred to. By and large, the prognosis of our cases was far better than had been expected in the 1920s. This improvement in prognosis, or at least in our ideas of prognosis, was already becoming evident in the late 1920s and was the chief reason for an important paper which I presented in Memphis, in 1932, entitled "Optimism in the Treatment of Heart Disease," already referred to in an earlier chapter. In other words, our studies had shown that, contrary to previous beliefs, coronary heart disease could allow long survival in many cases.

In 1932, incidental to our optimism in the treatment of heart disease, we were also interested in occupational therapy and in the ability of cardiac patients to return to their regular activities on recovery. We published two papers on this subject.

Trauma (from the Greek, meaning "injury" or "wound") of the heart and blood vessels, although observed earlier during the First World War, began to interest me more particularly in the 1930s. Often I came upon actual physical injury to these structures, which might be bruised, perforated, or ruptured by accidents in civilian life, either industrial in nature, home injuries, or automobile accidents.

Many individuals who were hurt or killed had accident insurance policies, but many did not and so became medico-legal problems, especially when certain unethical lawyers tried to push claims in situations in which actually there was no proof, on physical examination, x-ray study, or electrocardiogram, of any actual injury except to the feelings or psyche. A favorite source for fraudulent claims was the so-called steering wheel injury, which caused a blunt blow to the front of the chest, infrequently injuring the heart itself but sometimes fracturing or bruising ribs or cartilages. The heart is a very movable organ and not easily caught between sternum (breast bone) and spine. Dr. Earle Glendy, then a fellow of mine at the M.G.H., worked with me in 1936 to help outline rules about the diagnosis of these traumatic lesions; the following year we wrote a chapter called "Nonpenetrating Wounds of the Heart" for Brahdy and Kahn's book *Trauma and Disease*.

My continued interest in the subject brought me into contact with Law Professor Hubert Smith, who taught first in Boston and later in Texas. I took part in several of his medico-legal courses and eventually we published together a classic paper in the *North Carolina Law Review*, entitled "Scientific Proof in Respect to Injuries of the Heart." This led to the establishment of a Committee of the American Heart Association, set up to examine the effect of strain and trauma on the heart; later the difficult subject of emotional stress was included. The committee was made up of cardiologists, industrial physicians, pathologists, insurance physicians, lawyers, and the dean of the St. John University Law School, Professor Harold McNiece; in 1961 Professor McNiece—backed by a grant from the American Heart Association—published an important book entitled *The Heart and the Law*. After repeated meetings every year for nearly a decade, this committee made its final reports, which in summary advised first, that doctors and lawyers try to understand each other better and second, that much of the excessive litigation in the courts be transferred to the more sensible realm of health insurance. A continued interest in the subject was evidenced by the American Heart Association, which in 1968 reopened discussion of this difficult medico-legal problem at a symposium in Chicago, and, as a matter of fact, I have been asked to speak on the same subject as recently as 1969 and 1970.

We made several other interesting but less vital studies during the decade. One of them was a comparative study of identical twins, from the standpoint of electrocardiography and of heart size as shown by x-ray. Such a study has great value in the analysis of the effect of environmental factors on health or in sickness, since the important influence of heredity is no longer a factor. In this study we found by x-ray that the heart size and shape were identical, but that electrocardiograms showed as much individuality as do fingerprints.

Many of these twins were young, and I have followed some of them ever since with helpful conclusions about the occurrence, for example, of coronary thrombosis in a pair of adult males—with long survival of nearly thirty-nine years in one who had his thrombosis relatively young, and of rapid death in the other, whose thrombosis came a decade later, when his coronary arteries had doubtless become too extensively involved. At one time the case of a pair of identical twins whom I have followed for the last twenty-five to thirty years suggested an attempt to determine the effect of smoking on the ultimate prognosis and longevity. One twin had not smoked at all, but finally we advised the twin who *was* smoking to stop; by this time we had had scientific proof, through other studies, of the harm of smoking.

Subacute bacterial endocarditis (inflammation of the thin serous membrane lining the cavities of the heart) was still a great problem, and we struggled hard to do something about it. We tried, for example, to immunize a donor whose blood might be transfused into a patient, but this was ineffective. We also tried the sulfonamides, especially sulfa-pyridine, which made the patient sicker than did the streptococcus itself, and although we did have a slight reduction in mortality it was still nearly 100 per cent and remained so until penicillin came into use in 1944.

Valvular disease was a constant source of study. We published several papers concerning aortic stenosis (narrowing of the aortic valve opening). The apparent disappearance of mitral stenosis was an important contribution in 1935, when heart murmurs resembling those of valvular disease in acute rheumatism disappeared as the rheumatic myocardial process and the resulting dilatation of the heart cleared up. Incidentally, Duckett Jones, his sister Jean Jones Perdue, Edward F. Bland, and I arranged the transportation of children with rheumatic fever to Florida to determine, if possible, the benefit of a milder climate in the winter. We found that, although they were better, they were not cured by such therapy. For one thing, the streptococcus exists in Florida much as in New England, and secondly, the families and children were inconvenienced by the expense and family difficulties incident to transportation to the South. We found the same difficulty when we sent rheumatic heart patients to Mexico.

The important conclusion that either ventricle can fail alone, with the other still working adequately, was not thought possible by some of the leading cardiologists at this time. But we confirmed the old report of unilateral ventricular failure by Camille Lian of Paris, published in 1910, and our researches indicated that it was possible; in 1933 I wrote a paper, "Weakness and Failure of the Left Ventricle without Failure of the Right," which was published in the *Journal of the American Medical Association.* In 1936, we took a further step forward and wrote "The Commonest Cause of Enlargement of the Right Ventricle," which we showed was due to chronic or recurrent failure of the left. William P. Thompson and I published this paper in the *American Heart Journal.*

Congestive heart failure was still with us and although

digitalis helped, it was often inadequate and we still had to cope with dropsy. We still used the little silver Southey tubes (trocars) to relieve the dropsy of the legs and even of the scrotum, since the powerful and effective diuretics of to-day had not yet been introduced and the importance of decreased sodium intake was not yet understood. This predicament we were in applied to pulmonary edema as well as to dependent edema of the extremities and liver. But despite the frequency with which we saw heart failure followed by edema of the legs, we also found that much of the edema of the legs was local and dependent, due to faulty venous return of blood and stasis therefrom. In a study that we carried out in 1940 on the clinical significance of bilateral edema of the lower extremities, of 100 instances we found that in ninety per cent heart failure was not responsible, but rather some other factor, especially obesity, inactivity of the legs, and faulty venous circulation, sometimes with thrombosis.

The effect of causes other than heart disease itself in changing the electrocardiogram, occasioning errors in diagnosis, was a subject of much interest to us in the 1930s. We reported a number of studies showing "abnormalities" in the QRS and T waves due to change in position of the heart in the body resulting from respiration and from changes in body position. Also we noted that in a sensitive person the smoking of a cigarette could invert the T waves temporarily and that the same change, even in a perfectly normal young man, could happen to a subject not expecting it, from excitement due to the experimental discharge of a gun, during the taking of an electrocardiogram. It had already been shown by others that the drinking of ice water could have the same effect (although there is nothing wrong with this, unless the cold water causes distress). These were some of the bases of interest which resulted in my paper "Errors in the Interpretation of Cardiovascular Symptoms and Signs," published in the *Annals of Internal Medicine* in 1936.

Symptoms were an interesting subject and included the frequent complication of heart disease by gastrointestinal symptoms, especially "cardiospasm" or irritability of the esophagus and stomach. Another symptom of interest was that of tenderness over the heart. This, so far as we could discover from a special study in 1932, was never due to heart disease itself, even when there was myocardial infarction, but rather to the sensitivity of the individual. Most persons who have sensitivity over the precordium (left breast) have had an injury to the chest or have neurocirculatory asthenia as an important underlying diagnosis. Neurocirculatory asthenia was of constant interest through this decade. A revival of the interest came at the time of the Second World War in 1941, because it had been a considerable cause of semi-invalidism during the First World War.

Toward the end of the decade I became interested in the relationship of climate and mode of life to heart disease. One of my graduate students, Dr. Aristoteles Brasil of Bello Horizonte (Brazil) made an interesting study on the relationship of the weather in New England to certain cardiac conditions. This comprised a study of patients seen in practice during the previous ten years and was published in the *Transactions of the American Clinical and Climatological Association* in 1936. In this study the temperature, barometric pressure, humidity, wind velocity, and wind direction for every day for ten years was charted against attacks of angina pectoris, coronary thrombosis, paroxysmal tachycardia, and sudden death, in my own practice. The only constant relationship found was that angina pectoris due to insufficiency of the coronary blood supply to the heart muscle was much more common in cold weather, but that coronary heart attacks and important disturbances of the heart rhythm were not particularly related to the weather.

Arrhythmias of all kinds still interested us, in particular high grade heart block and uncomplicated atrial fibrillation and flutter for which we had as yet in many cases inadequate therapy.

But appearing on the horizon to herald the beginning of a new era in the surgical treatment of heart disease was the pioneering closure of patency of the ductus arteriosus in two cases, both in Boston, the first of which failed in 1937 and the second of which succeeded in 1938. The latter patient's story will be presented in Chapter XIII.

Finally, already interesting to us was the connection between the individual's heart and his way of life. I discussed this subject in particular in an address near the end of the decade which I gave at the New York Academy of Medicine. My talk consisted largely of a plea to study the relationship of individual ways of life—involving such habits as overeating, underexercising, and tobacco smoking—on the health and in particular in the production of diseases of the blood vessels, the lungs, and the heart. At that time we had not yet developed any solid information, though our experience strongly suggested that the influences were important.

From this beginning concern there stemmed, a decade later, a large share of my medical interest in the epidemiological (causative) population investigations throughout the world, a part of international cardiology of which I shall speak in later chapters.

And so the 1930s came to an end with a serious depression at the beginning, the Second World War at the end, and much advance in medical diagnostic techniques and accomplishments in between.

Elephants and Whales

CHAPTER VII 🐘 Now I turn away briefly from the chronological story of my medical life to a subject which has been of great interest to me, not just for a few months or years but for decades: the study of the heart in animals other than man, especially in the larger mammals.

Man, top dog in the animal kingdom, makes use of all other living things in the fields, in the forests, in the seas, and in the air. He does this not only for his food, for clothing, and for labor, but also, and perhaps most importantly, for his health. During the past generation or two man has increasingly studied the physiological functions of other living species, their reactions to diseases and injuries that affect man, and how they respond to man's curative efforts, both medical and surgical. At least half of all the great medical and surgical advances of our time have been made possible by animal experimentation.

It happened that during my year with Thomas Lewis in London, he took me occasionally to the London Zoo in Regent's Park, where he studied various animals, and obtained their hearts, when they had died, for anatomical scrutiny— with a special interest in the elaborate and fascinating makeup of the specialized muscle system that conducts the electrical stimulus that causes the actual heart beat. Some of these hearts he fixed permanently in paraffin, a technique that I followed later in Boston. I have in my museum at home the mitral and tricuspid valves of a sperm whale which I prepared in 1916 and which are still in perfect condition for handling and studying more than half a century later.

Returning home in 1914 from that year in London, I applied to the City of Boston for a position as medical examiner at the Franklin Park Zoo. Although there was no such post, aside from the necessary care of the animals by veterinarians, one was created for me and I occasionally visited Franklin Park to study the circulation of sick animals and to obtain their hearts when they died, as in the case of a deer, a swan, and their pet elephant, Molly, who died of a stroke at the age of about sixty in 1921. Dr. C. Sidney Burwell, later dean of the Harvard Medical School but at the time my first resident in our new cardiology department at the M.G.H., went out to Franklin Park with me on a cold winter morning to get Molly's heart. Her body was a strange sight, with her back to the ground and her legs extended in four directions, securely fastened to stakes driven into the frozen soil. The thorax had been opened, and two park employees wearing rubber boots, rubber coats, and rubber hats were in the thorax hunting for the heart with the distended lungs ballooning out around them when we arrived. Other persons were there, too, from various institutions waiting to receive portions of the carcass for study or exhibit; Molly's skeleton, for example, was later put on display at the Peabody Museum of Natural History at Harvard University.

But years before this, actually in the fall of 1915, during my second year as resident in medicine at the M.G.H., I had learned that Captain Cleveland of New Bedford was about to make his final whaling voyage, as the last whaler from that famous whaling city. He was sailing into the

South Atlantic, and I asked him if he would obtain for me the heart of a sperm whale. When he consented, I sent him full directions for its preservation, and a check for forty dollars. This canceled check is today in my museum at home.

When six months later a keg of alcohol arrived in my office, I had forgotten all about this commission and, to my surprise and pleasure, I found that the keg contained the forty-eight-pound heart of a young sperm whale in excellent preparation for our study, both macroscopic and microscopic. (Naturally, the heart weight of the whale varies greatly according to the kind of whale, the age from birth to maturity, and the size of the adult. An adult beluga's heart weighs only about 10 pounds, while that of a gray whale of thirty-five tons weighs about 300 pounds, and that of the blue whale 100 feet long and with a weight of 100 tons, the largest animal that ever lived—and is still extant—1,000 pounds. This is approximately 0.5 per cent of the body weight.)

During that fall of 1916 William Kerr, later to become Chief of Medicine at the University Medical School in San Francisco but at that time completing his interneship at M.G.H., joined me in the dissection and description of the intricate anatomy of the heart of my sperm whale. The beautifully elongated cells of the electrical conduction system of that whale's heart remained engraved in my memory and eventually helped to induce me and my companions to obtain the first electrocardiogram taken of a whale, in Bering Sea in Alaska nearly four decades later. In the interim, we were so absorbed in the new cardiology of man himself that we postponed further thoughts about whales.

The next chapter of my involvement in comparative anatomy and physiology pertaining to the largest mammals came late in the 1930s, when James Jenks, president of the Sanborn Company, which made spirometers and electrocardiographs and was then located in Cambridge, and Fran-

cis Benedict, head of the noted Carnegie Metabolism Laboratory, located near the Harvard Medical School, invited me
to join them in a project to study the electrocardiogram of
the elephant. The first crude record of the sort had been
taken seventeen years earlier by Alexander Forbes of the
physiological department of the Harvard Medical School,
but we felt that further studies with our improved techniques
would be of value.

Our new records were made from female elephants, by
name Clara, Juno, Lizzie, Modoc, Myrtle, Pigmy, Queen, and
Tillie, all of Barnum and Bailey's Circus, which was then entertaining the children of Boston and their parents at the
Boston Garden. Good records were easily obtained, since
these elephants were well trained and simply stood gently
on the electrodes.

I was especially glad to accept this invitation inasmuch as
we were, at the time, trying to establish the upper limits of
normal for the time intervals of the human electrocardiogram.
We knew very well that the intervals between (1) the
electrical action current of atria (upper chambers of the
heart) and that of the ventricles (lower pumping chambers)
and (2) the duration of the first ventricular complex, called
the QRS wave, varied greatly with the size of the heart. But
the upper limits were still obscure and so we welcomed the
information to be derived from the hearts of mammals
larger than man. Also it was of interest to learn the heart
rates of larger mammals. The human baby's heart rate at
birth is about twice the average heart rate of the normal
human adult—for example, 140, compared with 70—and
its time intervals are about half as long, but whether the
heart of a large healthy human as well as the enlarged heart
of a sick person may exceed the upper limits of the so-called
normal in time intervals, was the question. Incidentally, the
heart rates of the smallest mammal, the shrew, and of the
hummingbird, have been recorded at about 1,000 per min-

ute, while the heart rate of the relatively small beluga whale which we recorded at sea in 1952 was only 15; to explain such a slow rate, a factor called the "diving reflex" enters in, as well as the heart size, which is not very large in the beluga.

In the sequence of events, the next happening was the publication of the electrocardiograms of the elephants by Benedict, Jenks, and myself, along with a companion paper on the anatomical findings of the hearts of Molly, our Franklin Park elephant and of Tusko, a male which had been studied in Seattle by Dr. Robert King, who later became President of the American Heart Association.

These two papers appeared together in the *American Heart Journal* in December, 1938, and ordinarily they would have excited relatively little public interest had it not been for the curiosity of an Associated Press reporter, who was browsing in the Boston Medical Library and was attracted by the unusual titles of these two papers in a journal primarily concerned with the human heart and its diseases.

He promptly came to see me to inquire more about the reasons for our interest and when I answered that it was the size of the heart that mattered, he asked why we did not seek the electrocardiogram of the largest mammal of them all. I countered as excuses that the elephant was large enough, that the whale would be too difficult, and that we were too busy. A few days later, however, a note appeared in several of the newspapers throughout the country saying that a Boston doctor was interested in obtaining a whale's electrocardiogram, but needed advice as to where to find the whale. Thereupon letters began to reach me from various coastal areas, offering their own kinds of "excellent" whales encountered off their own shores, particularly the Carolinas and California.

Most of these suggestions were impracticable, but one seemed possible, and James Jenks and I decided to go ahead with it. The plan came from an Oregon salmon fisherman who went every summer to Kodiak Island of the Aleutian chain and whose ship was regularly visited by several friendly gray whales; he was confident that if we came with him we would be able to obtain their electrocardiograms. We accepted and, when we invited him, so did Dr. Robert King of Seattle, who was already interested in large mammals. I enlisted the aid of my old friend and medical classmate Ernest Gruening (then Governor of Alaska and later to become a United States Senator), who promised to lend us a coast guard cutter; the Bureau of Fisheries agreed to develop for us harpoon electrodes of the right size for a thirty-foot whale.

This was early fall of 1941, and our preparations for the trip, which we planned to make early in the summer of 1942, were complete. But at this point a confidential letter came from Governor Gruening saying that Japanese submarines had been sighted off the Alaskan shores and that none of his coast guard cutters could be spared; Pearl Harbor happened two months later, and that was the end of our whaling schemes for a good many years.

Another decade went by and we had almost forgotten about whales when we received a message from Bob King that he and Jenks and I had been invited by a patient of his who was an officer of a salmon canning company with a large plant at Clark's Point on the shores of the Bering Sea to come the next August at the end of their canning season and utilize their facilities and expert harpooners to obtain an electrocardiogram of the beluga (white) whale. Despite the fact that this was a small whale, smaller than an elephant in both body weight and heart, we decided that it would at least be good practice in preparation for recording the electrocardiogram of the much larger gray whale, and so we accepted.

Jenks and I flew to Seattle on August 3, 1952, to join King, and then we all flew up to Anchorage, where we consulted some experts * of the U.S. Bureau of Fisheries about our plans. From there we took off in a small plane for Clark's Point, where we were guests for a week in the luxurious quarters of the company management.

The first day at Clark's Point was a busy one; harpoon electrodes were constructed in the machine shop and we became acquainted with our assistants and their scouting plane and our mother ship, which was to tow our whale boat. Four or five of us could be installed in the whale boat to carry out the maneuver; they were skipper Joe Clark (an Indian), our harpooner, nicknamed Jeff Davis, and the three of us—Jim Jenks, with his Sanborn electrocardiograph protected by oilskins from the spray, Bob King to aid the skipper and the harpooner, and myself, with movie camera.

The weather was stormy, and so we were grounded the second day and explored the neighborhood, which included an Indian-Eskimo village and an ancient cemetery with gravestones of early Russian and Norwegian sailors and settlers. On the third day the sea was not so rough, although there was still a chill rain falling. We donned oilskins and rainproof hats and set out to sea.

About an hour later our plane signaled to us and we started off in search of a small school of whales, which we soon overtook. But our technique was faulty; the wire embedded in the head of the harpoon, which Jeff Davis had accurately placed in the torso of a beluga, broke under the stress of the struggles of the whale to escape from us. We had a wild ride in a small boat through a stormy sea until we released the whale and returned to shore to revise our technique. That night three harpoons were prepared, one without any wire connection, but strong enough to hold us to the whale, while the other two were fitted with wires for attachment to the electrocardiograph.

---

* In particular, Lawrence Irving, who discovered that the act of diving reflexly slowed the heart rate of marine mammals.

The next day dawned with clearer skies, but there still was a rough sea. We started out more hopefully and our hopes were justified. A new school of belugas was sighted by the plane and the whale boat started off with its outboard motor at top speed. The boat was soon anchored to a whale and the motor was turned down, allowing the whale to supply most of our horsepower. One wire was immersed in the sea and was supposed to return a record from the sea water close to the whale, but there was no response. Then, at an appropriate moment, the third harpoon with its electrode was inserted in the back of the whale.

Jenks' head and his precious machine were hidden under a tarpaulin, but I heard him shout with joy. An electrocardiogram had been obtained—the first ever taken of a whale (*circulation, 8:387*). That night, which happened to be his birthday, we properly celebrated the unique occasion.

The story of our success appeared in several newspapers, and with it the report of our desire to obtain the electrocardiogram of a larger beast, the gray whale. As a result a few days after our return from Alaska, Dr. Snodgrass of the Scripps Oceanographic Institute at La Jolla, California, telephoned me one evening and offered the facilities and services of their Institute to us for the pursuit of the gray whale, which was one of their own special interests. This interest of theirs was largely because early every winter a procession of gray whales swam day after day and night after night past Point Loma nearby, on their way from Alaska to "hibernate," to breed, and to give birth to their young in the warm waters of the lagoons of lower (Baja) California. This most courteous invitation of the staff * of the Scripps Institute we accepted at once and so in January, 1953, we "three musketeers," with improved harpoon electrodes, assembled in La Jolla. We quickly discovered that our har-

* One of the most interested and experienced of the staff in the life and habits of the gray whale was Ray Gilmore, who was very helpful to us.

poons were useless, for we could not get anywhere near the gray whales with either big boats or small, because of the noise the boats made and because of the fast speed and rapid change of direction of the gray whale when submerged. So we remained but a few days, to return the next winter better, but still inadequately, prepared.

During the summer of 1953 Jenks and I devised a crossbow with electrode wires connected to the arrows, and after some practice we became quite expert in hitting targets at short distances, but the arrows could not travel far. Meanwhile, Bob King had practiced with a gun which also shot wired arrows, and with these new instruments we met again at La Jolla in January of 1954. Once more we were aided by the Scripps boats and further helped by a naval subchaser from the San Diego base. Several times we were very near our prey, but each time they eluded us and it became evident that the whalers of old, with their sails and muffled oars, had a great advantage over us who used noisy, even though much faster, transport. Again we returned home empty-handed.

We might have ceased further efforts, had not Sir Richard Fairey (a pioneer aviator, a maker of planes in England, and a patient of mine) put us in touch with a friend of his, Donald Douglas of the Douglas Aircraft Company. Mr. Douglas, who lived in Santa Monica, thought that further efforts to secure the gray whale's electrocardiogram might be successful if carried out in Scammon's Lagoon in Baja California (Mexico), called in Spanish the *Laguna de l'Ojo de la Liebre* ("Eye of the Hare"). Scammon, a marine biologist and also an expert whaler of a century ago, published in the early 1870s a most interesting volume entitled "The Mammals of the West Coast of North America." It is still the standard work on the subject. In the lagoon named after him, Mr. Douglas pointed out, hundreds of whales would be quietly assembled and would probably not be as elusive as they were on their steady move south.

And so again, an invitation came to us from an unexpected quarter and again we accepted. In February, 1956, King, Jenks, and I joined Mr. Douglas, Sr., and his son Donald, Jr., Mr. Frederick Conant, vice-president of the Douglas company, and Mr. (Captain) Charles Langlais who was an old friend and fishing companion of the Douglasses, aboard the Douglas boat *The Dorado,* and sailed south to Scammon's Lagoon, which we entered somewhat precariously at flood tide. I served on the dawn watch with Mr. Conant and shall never forget his rich quotations from Kipling as he navigated down the coast with the help of radar and sonar and his own vast experience with the sea.

The Dorado, with its small boats to be used later on for whaling, was supplemented by planes and a helicopter, which used the salt flats nearby and the hard beaches as landing strips. We also had the support of the National Geographic Society and the active help of Samuel Matthews, a writer on the staff, and their photographer, Roberts; they joined me in a National Geographic story of our expedition later that year.

The lagoon itself is a large body of water indenting the western coast of Mexican California, about halfway down, and stretching for miles with many cul-de-sacs and arms reaching into the desert and with a mountain range in the distance. As our ship entered the lagoon we saw many whales spouting far and near, and rising half their lengths out of the water to look around (a procedure called "spy-hopping") and ending in a great splash as their bodies fell back to the water's surface. During the week that followed we must have counted close to 500 whales, males, females, and babies.

Based on the mother ship, our three small whale boats took off each day to explore the various waterways of the lagoon, but again failed to get close enough to use harpoon electrodes or arrow guns. However, when oars were tried instead of motors, it was possible to approach much nearer. When this was discovered, Donald Douglas and Fred Conant wired the spears which they were accustomed to using on large fish at sea and set off with their skipper and with Jim Jenks and Sam Matthews. Not adequately acquainted with geographic details of the lagoon, which that evening we all learned too late from Scammon's book, this boatload of adventurers headed for disaster and made its way into the arm of the lagoon called "the nursery" by Scammon. "Keep away from the nursery," he had warned.

Cruising up one side of the estuary, the whalers saw a gray whale coming down the other side and decided that it was to be their subject for study. The skipper therefore headed the boat toward the whale, which was some hundred yards away. They had covered half the distance when suddenly they saw that there was a baby whale alongside its mother. At once it was obvious that danger loomed large ahead and so the whale boat turned tail and with motor at full speed, tried to escape.

Quickly, the infuriated mother overtook the boat and ploughed into it with a shock that tore away the rudder, broke the shaft and the propellor. A second blow stove a large hole in the bow where Jenks was seated with his precious electrocardiograph. Water poured into the boat and everyone bailed furiously; the mother whale departed; had she returned to attack again the whalers might have been killed or seriously injured, as so often happened in early whaling days.

At the time of the whale's attack, the skipper sent out a call for help by walkie-talkie and those of us who had remained on the mother ship lowered a rescue boat. Meanwhile a second boat that had left us earlier to follow the harpooners came rapidly to their rescue.

The whale boat was beached, and later repaired and used again, but with far more caution. A few more attempts were made during the next two or three days, but again without success. A gray whale which would submit to an electrocardiogram was beginning to seem as elusive as Moby Dick to Captain Ahab.

The next year I took part in the most elaborate expedition of all, and one that almost succeeded. It took place in February, 1957, and was organized by the two Donald Douglases with the help of friends and a quota of the U.S. Air Force, which established a small camp on an island in the lagoon. We had to secure permission from the Mexican minister of defense to "invade" Mexico; when this permission was slow in coming because of the red tape involved, I telephoned an old friend, Professor Ignacio Chavez, in Mexico City, and asked his help. It just happened that the minister had visited the professor's office that very day for a checkup. I rang off and an hour later word came from the minister giving us permission to fly the planes over Mexican territory. This was certainly a stroke of good luck. I have had many such during my long life.

With planes galore, whale boats, specially trained pilot and marksmen in a helicopter, stations on shore and on ship to receive radio transmission of any electrical activity in the gray whales' bodies—the maneuver got off to a good start. This was the intended technique: as the whale was beginning to awake in the early morning, a helicopter hovering over it would shoot into the whale a light arrow with wire attached to a small telemetering sled, which was dropped upon the water simultaneously with the shot and which would then be pulled along by the whale as it submerged and sped away from the helicopter. With one electrode in the salt water of the lagoon and a signal recorded from the mast on the sled every ten seconds, it was hoped to deliver the electrocardiogram to the shore and ship stations.

But we encountered two major difficulties: in the first place, the gray whale was largely covered and protected by a coat of thick barnacles which deflected the arrows unless they were perpendicular to the surface of the whale, and this deflection became the rule; secondly, the electrode was far from the heart, which is close to the ventral surface of the body, while our electrode could only be in the far-off back. When we did obtain a tracing, it was evidently caused by a very regular and rapid skeletal muscular action resembling "flutter" in a human heart, but clearly too rapid and monophasic to be an electrocardiogram.

Whether we would have succeeded (as in Alaska with the beluga) by entering two separate electrodes simultaneously, by placing one electrode in some manner very close to the heart, or by inserting a newly developed electronic device which would transmit the whale's electrocardiogram directly by radio to receivers on ship and shore, we did not have time to find out—all of us were busy men and could only spare a week for this adventure. So once again the gray whale had defeated us.

As far as I am aware, there has been only one occasion to date when a good electrocardiogram of a large whale has been recorded. This was made by Dr. Alfred Senft, of the Woods Hole Oceanographic Institute in Massachusetts, who, one cold night in December, 1959, learned that a forty-five-ton finback whale had been grounded the day before on a beach at Provincetown—at the other end of the Cape from his home in Falmouth. He knew that a whale this long out of water would soon die and would, in any case, be removed in the morning by the coast guard, so with his wife and two young children he made the long night drive, found the whale, managed to place the copper rod electrodes accurately, and obtained an excellent heart record of the finback. The electrocardiogram was published in the medical journal *Circulation*, and showed a heart rate of 27, doubtless abnormally rapid for a healthy whale of this size, and showed also, as was to be expected, prolonged time intervals. The whale was, of course, beginning to suffer from asphyxia, which caused its death a few hours later.

The final episode of this tale of mine consisted of a fascinating expedition organized in 1967 and carried out by the Mason Research Institute of Seattle, Washington. It was headed by Dr. Merrill Spencer, a friend and colleague of Dr. King, who had told him of our efforts to obtain the electrocardiogram of a gray whale a decade and more earlier. Jenks and I had almost forgotten this old interest of ours when we were invited along with Bob King to accompany Dr. Spencer to Scammon's Lagoon to join the Seattle team of young researchers, engineers, medicos, aviators, and boatmen. We elderly "three musketeers" were given a tent to ourselves with cots on which we placed our own sleeping bags, for it was still cool in the lagoon in February. We were in large part simply observers and historians, but we were treated most courteously and were well fed by one of the scientific team who was an excellent cook; as compensation in part, I read aloud each evening after dinner instructive and entertaining passages from Scammon's famous book, emphasizing his warning about the "nursery"!

This team, although it also failed in its primary objective, was the most important of all. Its first aim was to obtain an electrocardiogram of a large whale, using an improved technique which might include the insertion under anesthesia of an electronic device to transmit an electrocardiogram later on, after recovery from the tranquilizer. A second aim was to determine the proper dose of sedative to be injected by a syringe attached to an arrow into the back of the whale and shot from a helicopter. The first trial was to be with a dose that had been found effective in East Africa, where elephants and other large mammals had been sedated so that they could be transported elsewhere from areas to be flooded. It was, however, believed that larger doses would be needed because of the larger size of the whale, but this was to be determined by trial.

The third objective was to study the blood and the metabolism of the whale, to be obtained when the animal was emerging from the anesthetic. Blood samples were to be drawn from the flukes (tail) or elsewhere, and an airtight mask was to be placed over the blowhole to collect the respiratory gases.

When we arrived by air at the lagoon, the team had already tried their hypnotic on four whales. The first two trials, employing the dosage which had been used on the animals in East Africa, were without effect and so, too, was a third trial which doubled the previous dose. The fourth, which tripled the ineffective double dose, was fatal.

Two days after our arrival, another trial was made, using a dose midway between the ineffective double dose and the largest dose of all. This was obviously a satisfactory amount, for in the course of the next half hour the whale became first excited and then somnolently beached herself on a low sand bank a mile or so from the camp. We had feared that the drug might so affect the whale that she would settle to the depths and drown, but evidently whales that are drowsy or ill know enough to keep their blowholes out of water, either on land or at sea.

At the very moment that the helicopter and the whale boat were prepared to set off for the study of the whale, a northwest gale in full fury hit us and prevented any possibility of navigating or flying. The gale lasted all night, and in the morning the whale was gone. And once again, our time was up—the team had to return with Dr. King to Seattle, while Jim Jenks and I had work to do elsewhere.

And so we await the next chapter, possibly a renewed effort by Dr. Merrill Spencer and his team, who have already helped to expand our horizon of the study of the large mammals of the sea. This is especially important, in view of the fact that man in his approaching need of utilizing the sea for food, for minerals, and for underwater life, must learn in every possible way how our distant cousins, the whales, have adapted themselves to an element that covers more than half the surface of our earth.

Hopefully, I may yet be able to add a footnote to this history, for at the moment we are contemplating the possibility of one more possible trip to Scammon's Lagoon, to be made in 1971 or 1972.

The Decade of the 1940s: The Wide Range of the Individual Both in Health and in Disease

CHAPTER VIII 🙰 Much as the first decade of my professional life from 1911 to 1920 was a critical stage in my development, so too the decade from 1941 to 1950 was an important turning point in my career. The second and third decades, that is, the 1920s and the 1930s, as I have recalled them, passed as rather smooth ten-year periods of intense activity in my chosen field of cardiology. Before I take up the details of my daily life in teaching, clinical research, and practice in the 1940s, I would like to mention several major events that occurred during that decade.

The first was, of course, the Second World War, which began for the United States in December, 1941, at Pearl Harbor. This war we accepted without reservation as a very necessary crusade against a cruel dictator. For me, like the First World War, it was another hideous but essential experience. A science for peace was still nonexistent. I was turned down for active military service because of my age, but I was asked to serve as chairman of the Cardiovascular Committee of the National Research Council, which met frequently in Washington. This was a very efficient committee that served for the next four years. One of the first things we had to do was decide what the criteria were for admission to the armed services, so far as the cardiovascular system was concerned. These criteria included such things as the presence of murmurs, the electrocardiogram, the blood pressure, and the size of the heart—to be determined if necessary by x-ray—and so on. The most difficult question was that of the blood pressure. How high can the blood pressure be and still allow the subject to be acceptable for service? There was a good deal of discussion about that. For example, should the maximal acceptable blood pressure be 150 millimeters of mercury systolic and 90 diastolic, or was that too high? There was a difference of opinion. At one time a small voice in the background from a doctor connected with the Veterans' Service said, "Aha, but if you take on individuals who are at the upper end of 'normal'—that is, with 150 systolic and 90 diastolic, which most of us consider too high for young people—then we will receive them later on as patients in the Veterans' hospitals, when they will have higher pressure, real hypertension, and the results from all that, namely strokes [that is, apoplexy] or heart attacks."

Then another small voice answered and said, "On the other hand, don't we want an efficient army rather than a long-lived one? It may well be that those who have their blood pressures in the higher range of normal are stronger and more resistant to fatigue than those with low blood pressures, who would be very acceptable for life insurance." This question of blood pressure remained the puzzle during that time and afterwards too, because of the wide range of the normal even in the same individual under different conditions.

I would like now to digress from chronology and discuss for awhile this question of the range of the normal.

Although from time immemorial a common maxim has been that no two persons are just alike and that two individuals with very different characteristics can be equally healthy, we physicians (especially those who do not see private patients) tend to pay only lip service to this idea. We like to emphasize averages, or the mean, particularly in statistical analyses, and we make general rules to be applied to diagnosis, treatment, and even prognosis, and are surprised when we find so many exceptions to these rules. This is one of the reasons why everybody should have his own private physician, be he family doctor or specialist, who has become well acquainted with him.

I was taught none of this in medical school, except in my last year, when two or three teachers did discuss a few of the exceptions to the average rules in diagnosis and treatment. I had to learn the hard way, which may have been the best, although I doubt it.

Two early physiological experiences which have been invaluable to me illustrate normal variations. The first concerned the heart rate. On April 19, 1917, I drove out to the start of the annual Boston Marathon Race in Ashland and, with the permission of the management and of the entrants as well, counted the pulse rates of ten of the several hundred contenders a few minutes before the race started, and received further permission to record the pulse rates of these same runners at the finish. I had been careful in my choice of these ten men, accepting the advice of experts in the sport, and was fortunate in including the winner. These ten men had pulse rates at the start, before they had run a step, ranging from 60 per minute to 118. If a heart rate of over 100 had been a criterion for excluding participation in the race we would have rejected the winner, who finished this long race easily and comfortably with a pulse rate of 108 at the finish. The answer is, of course, that he was nervous before the race started and doubtless apprehensive as to his plans and their success. This is just the opposite of many, probably the majority, of long distance running champions whose heart rates are very slow when in training. At the time of the Second World War, I wrote a letter, published by the *Journal of the American Medical Association* in 1942, telling of four authentic distance running champions whose heart rates were under 40 per minute, but with normal rhythm. One was McMitchell the mile champion of the day, another a two mile champion, and a third a marathoner.

The second experience in normal physiological variations concerned the great differences in blood pressure that may exist not only in different healthy young persons but also in the same person at different times of the day and night. This I investigated during the First World War at Base Hospital No. 6 of the American Expeditionary Force. In both categories there would be differences of as much as 30 to 40 millimeters systolic and of 10 to 20 diastolic between two convalescent but otherwise healthy soldiers actively up and around at the same time of day, for example, 140 to 100 systolic and 90 to 70 diastolic, and the same differences in a single individual at different times of the twenty-four hours, for example, at noon and on first awakening early in the morning. These differences were commonly present.

When I continued my cardiovascular investigations both in healthy and diseased individuals after the First World War, I found similar and often striking ranges of the normal in electrocardiograms, x-ray shadows of the heart and aorta, in heart sounds and murmurs, and in reactions to the stress of exercise, excitement, coffee, tobacco, and injury. Although I was aware of these normal variations and mentioned them in appropriate chapters of the first edition of my textbook on heart disease published in 1931, I was so distressed by the errors that were constantly being made by inexperienced observers, often to the great detriment of the patient's morale and actual health, that in my second edition in 1937, I added a new chapter early in the book and called it "The Range of the Normal." I had already written and published an important warning on the errors which could occur in the interpretation of cardiovascular symptoms and signs, and another on the common mistaken diagnosis of cardiac enlargement by x-ray when a triangle of fat at the apex of the heart is included in the measurement.

During the last thirty years, many errors in diagnosis have continued to pile up with each new technique that has been introduced, because of the inadequate knowledge of the range of the normal. It sometimes takes years before we learn of the wide range of the normal and it is often wiser to give the patient the benefit of the doubt when we are uncertain about an individual case, rather than to label him as diseased—which on occasion has resulted in his retirement from work, or even worse. Borderline findings should, of course, be followed up, but not to cause constant apprehension of the individual. The few errors of omission are in most instances excusable in contrast to the host of errors of commission, which can alter the entire life of thousands and thousands of persons.

Of even greater importance is the need for knowledge of the great range of reaction of patients not only to their diseases, but especially to their symptoms and to their treatment. Some persons are so insensitive that they barely feel the discomfort of angina pectoris accompanying effort or excitement, while others feel the symptom as an excruciating pain which on rare occasions can even cause syncope (fainting). A considerable number of patients will go through an episode of acute coronary thrombosis with or without myocardial infarction (heart muscle scarring) and regard it as a grippe attack or a minor indisposition, while a much greater number are seriously prostrated by the same degree of heart involvement. This explains the majority of the patients with so-called "painless" heart attacks. Some persons will be unconscious of occasional premature heart beats while a few will find every one very disagreeable and often acutely painful. Much judgment is needed in the appraisal and treatment of both extremes.

Finally, one of the most interesting and important of all

my medical experiences has been the variety of reactions of my patients to their treatment. Some crave just plain rest in a hospital bed or at home and others abhor it; the happy mean is hard to find or indeed to carry out. Here much judgment is needed. The same is true of reactions to diets, to drugs, and even to surgical operations. The sensibility, as well as the biochemical response, is to be judged. Some persons who are very unhappy with strict limitation of sodium (salt) intake may be helpfully allowed a little increase with a similar slight increase in the diuretic administered. Some patients are made easily toxic by average or small doses of digitalis; others need three or four times the "average" dose every day to have an adequate therapeutic effect free from symptoms or signs of toxicity. (William Withering pointed this out in 1785.) Some patients can take powerful diuretics with ease, while others are exhausted by them.

And thus, we must not try to fit all persons into the same mold, not even identical twins, as we have found out. General overall rules are helpful and some, such as the advice not to smoke, are widely applicable. We must realize that when we are concerned with individual humans we must study and treat them as individuals and not necessarily as average units in an overall health survey. We shall always need plenty of practicing physicians who can fill this essential role.

To return to the early 1940s: we had a further chance to study the mysteries of blood pressure when General Hillman of the Medical Corps of the Army joined us on the Cardiovascular Committee of the National Research Council, to help us study the records of many thousands of army officers who had had blood pressures which were either high or borderline, and also those army officers whose pulse rates tended to be "too fast," or who were overweight. These reports, which we published in the *Journal of the American*

Medical Association during the next few years, are a source of basic information that is still being consulted, or at least should be. Among our findings was the significant fact that those officers with doubtfully high blood pressures, fast heart rates at rest, and obesity had shorter lives than was the expectation and usually died cardiovascular deaths.

Another important study that we carried on during the war took place in five cities—New York, Philadelphia, Chicago, San Francisco, and Boston—and consisted of the re-examination of 5,000 cardiovascular rejectees who had been turned down by the examining boards because of some trouble with their circulation. These troubles had included rheumatic heart disease, hypertension, congenital defects, and arrhythmias. We wanted to see how many of these men could go into service after all, because some of the murmurs were merely physiological, some of the blood pressures were borderline or even normal after some rest, when their temporary excitement had passed, and sometimes their heart size had been exaggerated by a horizontal position of the heart (a common error). Out of the 5,000 cases examined in these five cities we found that we could rehabilitate into service about 1,000. It was an interesting experience, but not very profitable, because there were enough soldiers otherwise; however, if the war had kept on much longer we would have had to scrape the bottom of the barrel and take some individuals with minor cardiovascular defects of one kind or another, but fortunately we did not have to do so.

Now I would speak of the extra work that those of us who remained at home had to do when the young men of the various hospitals of this country went into service with their respective base hospitals or elsewhere. The M.G.H. unit went to North Africa and then to Italy with Dr. Edward Bland, my younger associate, as its cardiologist. I missed him badly. Also we greatly missed Dr. Howard Sprague, who joined the Navy and was in the Pacific for the duration of the war. Fortunately there were some young doctors who were turned down for service because of some defects, often not very serious, but enough to permit them to stay with us or to join us.

Not infrequently we burned the midnight oil, and one of the things which it was necessary for me to do in 1943, in preparation for the 1944 third edition of my book *Heart Disease,* was to sit up from midnight to three in the morning, for months on end, revising and editing the text. I found that I could do this, although the first week was difficult; I would still get up at seven o'clock in the morning, and carry on until three the next morning, day after day. I don't advise doing this, but I found that it could be done, even by a man of fifty-seven years of age.

The next item of interest was that graduate students from Latin America came to us during the war when they could not go to Paris as they had done for generations for their postgraduate training. We became well acquainted with a great many of them and now, twenty-five years later, they are in the saddle and the kind of medicine that is practiced in Latin America is generally of our type, instead of French or German, which it had been previously. As one result of this graduate teaching of Latin Americans, I have had a great many patients from the countries of South and Central America ever since.

Another experience has been interesting in our relationship with Asia and the Pacific. It happened right after the war that many young doctors came to us from the Pacific area, from the Philippines, Japan, India, Thailand, Singapore, Pakistan (after it became independent in 1947), and other places, and they have been our friends ever since. It was with them that I helped to organize the Asian-Pacific Society of Cardiology in 1956. A result of our acquaintance with them and of their now becoming senior in their professional life is that I have had many patients referred to me from Asia and the Pacific and have made many friends in that part of the world. I welcome these friendships very much, not only for themselves but because of my great interest in international relationships, which I hope will eventually promote world peace.

Another extremely important event was the passage, on June 15, 1948, of the National Heart Act by the United States Congress. This Act set up the National Heart Institute, a new body of the Public Health Service, and the National Advisory Heart Council. Up to this time there had been only scattered small funds available from the government for any work in cardiovascular disease in this country. We had most of our help from our patients or from small foundations, and a little but not much, from the American Heart Association. A small group of people in New York City, mostly laymen (including in particular Mary Lasker and James Adams) persuaded Congress to pass the National Heart Act, which set up these two new bodies and which accounts for much of the great increase of our knowledge by research and by training for research in the field of heart disease.

Near the end of June, 1948, when I had returned from a medical mission to Italy and Greece, I was visited by T. Duckett Jones, and that changed my career—another link in my chain of chances. Dr. Duckett Jones had been my resident at the M.G.H. in the late 1920s, and in the 1930s he had worked at the House of the Good Samaritan, studying rheumatic fever and rheumatic heart disease; he subsequently established himself in New York as the director of a program in the same field. Duckett came to Boston that June of 1948 to tell me of this new Act of Congress just passed on the fifteenth, which I had not yet heard about. He told me that it would be very desirable if I would go to Washington and join in the effort to make the new Institute and Council important organizations. He thought I should go and talk with the various full-time doctors in the Public Health Service who were responsible for setting them up. My response was that I was not interested in going to Washington or getting mixed up in any way with the government, and that as a New England Yankee I had always tried to keep away from the politics of Washington. But Duckett was so insistent on the importance of this job and the importance of keeping the Institute and the Advisory Council out of politics, that I finally agreed, and early in July I went down.

To my surprise I was quickly convinced that he was absolutely right, that it was a duty and an opportunity, a really wonderful opportunity, in which I should become involved. However, I did not want to go to Washington to live, and finally I made an agreement with the Institute people—who were most able, devoted, and not at all political—that I would join them and spend about one-third of my time in Washington and also in traveling to other medical centers throughout the country, to help establish the work of the new Institute and Council. Thus I became executive director of the National Advisory Heart Council for the next four years, and at the end of that period served for another two, and after that I acted as consultant.

Starting from scratch, the National Heart Institute, with the help of the National Advisory Heart Council, has obtained from Congress increasing allocations of funds—now up to $150,000,000 and more every year. However, it took time and a lot of education, and of that I shall speak later. Here I might just note that the fact of the strong financial support of our work, with our many cardiovascular centers, is one reason why this country is so far ahead of all the rest of the world in this field. There are centers of other types, too, concerned with cancer, mental health, infectious diseases and so on, all due to the forward-looking group of laymen who started these National Institutes of Health way back in the 1940s.

At the same time that our government was establishing the

National Heart Institute and Advisory Council, the American Heart Association was going through a metamorphosis. This was the private organization of doctors, which was started in 1924; I served as its first treasurer for two years and as its president in 1940 and 1941. The new idea, initiated in large part by my old friend and colleague, Dr. Howard Sprague, was to take in nonmedical, that is to say, lay persons, as members—educators, scientists, businessmen, lawyers, other professionals—who would be able from their knowledge of life in general and of our government and industry in particular, to be of great help to the doctors. This has proven to be valid. Through the laymen who joined the American Heart Association, the support of our campaign against heart disease has increased from almost nothing in 1949, when our annual drives began, to $40,000,000 in 1969.

In order to be able to find time and space to carry out my new work for the Public Health Service I had to alter my life to a considerable degree. I resigned my post at the M.G.H., still continuing, however, to meet with the heart group. Dr. Edward Bland became my successor in 1949, at which time I moved out of my office and laboratory at the hospital to my present office at 264 Beacon Street. For over thirty years I had had my headquarters at the hospital, hardly ever emerging until after dark, and now for the last twenty years privately on Beacon Street, enjoying my relative freedom. I retired also as clinical professor of medicine at the Harvard Medical School, but continued to take part in graduate teaching during the next decade or more.

I greatly increased my attendance at meetings all over the country, both in the way of teaching missions and also in constantly learning a great deal from my colleagues at these congresses, conferences, symposia, and panels: about the interpretation of symptoms, technical advances, new and old drugs, surgical progress in the treatment of diseases of the heart and blood vessels, and statistical analysis of possible causative

factors behind heart disease in studies of populations throughout the world. We learned more about the causes of heart
disease and the beginning of ways to control it, as well as
better ways to diagnose and to treat it.

The next major subject I would take up concerning the
1940s is that of *medical missions abroad.* During the last
twenty years this has been one of my chief activities, affording me most interesting opportunities to become acquainted
with peoples throughout the world.

In 1946 I was asked by the Unitarian Service Committee to
go to Czechoslovakia for a two months' visit with the medical
profession of that country, as chairman of a mission of sixteen
medical professors from twelve different American medical
schools and universities. We represented medicine, surgery,
obstetrics, pediatrics, dentistry, physiology, and biochemistry,
and we all found the occasion a fascinating experience.

This mission was a resumption of relationships between the
Czech medical profession and the American, which had been
severed with the closing of Charles University during World
War II, first by the Nazis and then by the Russian Army.
1946 was one of the few free years for Czechoslovakia until
the Communist coup in 1948, which almost cut the country
off from the West.

We spent our two months first in Bohemia in the west, then
in Moravia in the center, and finally in Slovakia in the east.
We talked to doctors and laymen, patients and people at
large, grateful that our dental expert spoke fluent Czech.
In the larger cities we would usually travel as a total team of
sixteen, but often we divided up into two teams of eight, four
teams of four or eight teams of two. We visited every city
and town of any size or importance in the whole country, and
we became acquainted with practically all of the doctors and
many laymen too.

In general, we found a high level of medical science and
practice in Czechoslovakia, undoubtedly the highest level in

Eastern Europe. Their hearts and blood vessels were the same as ours and their diseases also. In some medical accomplishments they were a step ahead, but they needed new equipment since their own had been sadly depleted during the war. Most of all, they needed freedom to travel and to study abroad—precisely what they have found it very difficult to do.

My wife and I have visited Czechoslovakia several times in the years since my 1946 mission and have followed its developments with great concern and much affection for the people. The 1968 invasion by the Russian troops was a blow to us as well as to the Czech people. Many of our friends are still active there, including some who are still associated with Prague's Charles University, a teaching institute founded in 1348.

My first revisit to that country was on the occasion of the six hundredth anniversary of Charles University in 1948. The Communists had taken over the university two months earlier and the country was under martial law. Still, a celebration was held, and in the Aula of the university I received an honorary degree. President Conant of Harvard, knowing that I was planning to visit Prague, gave me a beautiful document engraved on parchment, sending in Latin the greetings of Harvard University on its three hundred and twelfth year to Charles Univeristy in Prague on its six hundredth year. But in Paris I received a cable from President Conant saying "Please destroy that document because Harvard, Yale, Princeton, and a few other institutions in the U.S.A. are not going to send any representatives to Czechoslovakia because of the Communist coup. You may go at your own risk." This is also what our Ambassador in France told us, but nevertheless I believed that it was our duty to go, since I had so many friends in Czechoslovakia.

I went to see an old Parisian friend, Professor Réné Leriche, a French surgeon of note. He was also scheduled to receive an honorary degree, and so I asked him what he planned to do and what he thought I should do. He said "You and your wife come along with my wife and me and we shall go together." So we did. And as it turned out, he and I were the only two physicians to receive Doctor of Medical Science degrees at the ceremony. A Russian named Professor Orbeli was to have been there, but he was not allowed to come since he opposed the currently official biological nonsense of the political dogmatist Lysenko. As for our side of the iron curtain, some of our American and British colleagues who should have been there were not allowed by their universities to accept. A few American universities and colleges were represented, however, and responded when they were called. One of these was Boston University, representing eastern New England in place of Harvard.

We shall never forget those days. We heard the last speech of President Eduard Beneš, the great Czech nationalist and statesman, who had had a stroke and indeed was to die a few months later. When he entered the Hall of the Knights in Hradčany Castle to give Charles University a new charter, the audience of Bohemians, Moravians, Slovaks, and others who were present, wept to see him, quite aware that this would be his last appearance and that they were in for a difficult time themselves.

In his speech President Benes spoke of the distress and difficulties that had happened to Charles University and to Czechoslovakia every hundred years since it was founded in 1348, and he pointed out that these years happened in every case to be the forty-eighth years of each century, in 1448, 1548, 1648, 1748, and 1848. "And now," he said, in closing, "it is 1948, and Czechoslovakia is again having difficulties."

The great success of our 1946 medical mission resulted in the Unitarian Service Committee's asking me in 1948 to chair another mission, with twelve professors from various medical schools in the United States visiting Greece and Italy. I accepted, and so from the stirring events of the anniversary celebrations in Prague, I flew to Rome and then on to Greece, while my wife stopped to visit friends in England en route home.

In Athens our mission first visited the old university, conferred for a few weeks with the professors there, held clinics, lectures, and conferences, and renewed old acquaintanceships. We went on after that to Thessalonika (Salonika in English) in the north of Greece, near where I had been stationed for the Red Cross in 1919, and where a new medical school had recently been established. Here we did the same things that we had done in Athens, except that we had two days off and used them to visit Mt. Athos, with the help of a Greek destroyer which took us to several of the monasteries.

These old monasteries on Mt. Athos are medieval and resemble little walled cities, the walls to protect them from the bandits of the Middle Ages. (At the time we were there some Communists were still up in the hills and we had an armed guard of Greek soldiers to protect us.) An interesting part of our visit was to see the treasures in each of the treasure chambers opened for us by the monks; jewels, robes, tapestries, beautifully hand-illuminated medieval manuscripts. We also saw many old men who seemed to spend most of their time praying and drinking ouzo—quite different from the scholars of previous centuries who had created and preserved these treasures.

This whole experience at Mt. Athos was fascinating, not only because we were suddenly transported back to the Middle Ages, but also because of the dramatic architecture of the monasteries, perched as they often were high on the mountainside or on cliffs overlooking the sea, because of the rare treasures in their strongholds, and because of the primitive life of the monks themselves. We spent one memorable evening examining the monks by candlelight in their black robes and tall black hats, in one of the monasteries where we spent the night. We found that except for occasional broken bones and cancerous tumors they were extraordinarily healthy, with normal hearts at an advanced age. However, we brought back with us to the hospital in Salonika a few of the more seriously ill or crippled monks.

Following our mission to Greece we spent a few weeks similarly in Italy, having a conference at the Vatican with the Pope, visiting hospitals, attending clinics, giving lectures, and meeting with Italian doctors. Thus we renewed the acquaintanceship between the American and Italian medical professions after the war.

One of my strongest beliefs has always been in the importance of just such an exchange of information between doctors of all nations. I was therefore enormously pleased when the Foundation for a World Congress of Cardiology was established in the 1940s.

From small beginnings in the 1930s, international cardiology began in major form in the 1940s with two meetings in Mexico City. The first was in 1944, when in the presence of the world's leading cardiologists the National Institute of Cardiology was inaugurated by Professor Ignacio Chavez, one of the world's pioneers in cardiology. There was a very fine program to inaugurate the Institute, including some discussion at that time of establishing an international council of cardiology. Two years later, also in Mexico City, such a council was established. It was then decided that an international meeting, a congress of cardiology, should be held as soon as it could be arranged. A preliminary meeting was then held in Chicago in 1948, under the supervision of Professor Louis Katz of the Michael Reese Hospital, and it was decided to hold the First World Congress of Cardiology in Paris in 1950.

In several parts of the world during the 1940s physicians were still having trouble in making cardiology a specialty. In 1947, for instance, Professor Nylin of Stockholm asked me to write a paper backing up the efforts of the few internists in

Sweden who were encountering difficulties in their desire to specialize in cardiology. It was published there with the title "Cardiology as a Specialty," and I understand that it helped them a good deal in their campaign. At any rate, Sweden was able by 1950 to send a good delegation to Paris for the First World Congress. Now the picture is completely changed of course, and cardiology has become the most sought after specialty in most of the countries of the world.

I suppose that the most important special subject in which I was interested in the middle of the decade was the reversibility of hypertensive heart disease, which had heretofore been thought to be slowly, but almost invariably, fatal. Dr. Reginald Smithwick, first at the M.G.H. and later at the Memorial Hospital of Boston University, proved that a continuous reduction of high blood pressure could be achieved by lumbodorsal sympathectomy (cutting the sympathetic nerves in the thorax and lower part of the back to dilate the arteries of the pelvis and legs); he and I and our colleagues showed that such an operation often had a very important and favorable effect on heart size and on the electrocardiogram. Now of course we can accomplish the same result by medicines without operations, except in rare cases.

This high blood pressure type of heart disease was the last of several kinds of heart disease which by the mid-forties had been shown to be reversible either by nature or by man. I consider that this proof of the possibility of reversibility of all kinds of heart disease (at least in a certain percentage of cases of each kind) has been a high point in the history of cardiology, in which many cardiologists have collaborated.

The next most important of the particular advances with which I became involved during that decade was the introduction of penicillin for the treatment of subacute bacterial (also called malignant or streptococcus) endocarditis, with which we had struggled for many years. Until 1944 practically every patient who had subacute bacterial streptococcus viridans—endocarditis—died. There was a 99+ per cent mortality even with the trial of various so-called antibiotics like the sulfonamides (in particular sulfapyridine). Finally in late 1944 we tried penicillin. Our first patient showed a good initial response, but then died because our supply ran out. Our next patient, even though given what we know now to be usually an inadequate amount, survived.

From that time on, penicillin has saved most of the cases of subacute bacterial endocarditis, although there have been some failures. Penicillin has also proved to be a specific for the streptococcus sore throat, and this has greatly reduced the prevalence of rheumatic fever and rheumatic heart disease. It has also been found to be a cure for syphilis, a major reason for our triumph over that dread disease and the serious "tertiary" sequels of aortic aneurysms and aortic valve regurgitation and of tabes dorsalis (damage to spinal cord)—despite occasional flare-ups from time to time, as recently has happened in the environment of promiscuity among many of the youth of today.

The next important advance in that decade was the realization that a low sodium intake in the diet would help very much in congestive heart failure, when too much fluid accumulates in the body. By limiting the sodium chloride, by cutting down every type of sodium, including sodium bicarbonate, and sodium benzoate (used in the preservation of food), as well as the sodium chloride in the food itself or in the salt shaker, we were able to improve very much our treatment of congestive heart failure. It is of interest that actually this idea had been discovered by two Frenchmen, Vidal and Lemierre, way back at the beginning of the century as noted in Chapter V; for nearly forty years their discovery had lain fallow until it was finally rediscovered early in the 1940s. By the middle of that decade we were using this therapeutic measure in full force. We have since had to be careful not to get the sodium too low or to allow, along with it, a serious loss of potassium. Today, almost invariably, we give potassium when we prescribe strong diuretics.

I was still interested in symptoms and signs, that is, in discussing what the patient felt; in studying physical signs as well as electrocardiographic and x-ray evidence, there was a good deal of advance during the 1940s. The establishment of clues and the recognition of errors was very important. We had to realize through the decades that no two normal individuals were alike and that we might misinterpret and call some of our findings disease rather than extreme ranges of the normal—in dealing, for example, with the pulse rate, the blood pressure, the heart size, the electrocardiogram, and so on. As I have said earlier in this chapter, in 1937 I had to add a new chapter in my textbook on heart disease on the range of the normal heart, and at that time we began to write about errors in over-diagnosis of conditions which were unimportant and within the range of the normal. We began to collect clues which later developed into a textbook, *Clues in Cardiovascular Diagnosis and Treatment,* a useful volume that was translated into five languages, Italian, Spanish, Yugoslavian, Japanese, and Russian.

During the 1940s we continued our studies of pulmonary embolism, which we recognized as being very common. It has been very common ever since, no matter what we have done about it, though undoubtedly it has been less severe because of the use of anticoagulants and surgical occlusion of the leg veins. Not infrequently we found that a precipitating factor in heart failure was the occurence of pulmonary embolism, which often, in previous decades, had been unrecognized. (This effect is due to a blood clot traveling from a thrombosed leg vein to block the circulation in the lungs, sometimes quickly or slowly fatal.) In 1943 Drs. Murnaghan and McGinn joined me in an important follow-up paper, "Pulmonary embolism With and Without the Acute Cor Pulmonale" (the latter being acute dilatation and often failure of the right heart chambers due to a sudden massive pulmonary embolus). I also wrote a chapter entitled "The Cor Pulmonale" for Henry Christian's new edition of *Oxford Medicine* in 1943.

Coronary heart disease by this decade was in full bloom. It had become much more common and serious than it had been thirty or forty years earlier and was attacking younger and younger patients, mostly males. Dr. Bland and I carried on the study of the prognosis of nearly 500 cases of angina pectoris and 200 cases of coronary thrombosis through that decade and into the next. What became very evident was the natural tendency for recovery to occur in these coronary cases through the establishment of an adequate collateral circulation, already pointed out by Herrick in 1912 and clearly confirmed by Blumgart and Schlesinger in the 1930s.

Another study of coronary heart disease showed that rupture of the heart in acute myocardial infarction (severe heart attack due to coronary thrombosis) occurred much more commonly in mental patients than in the average patient in the general hospitals. This was doubtlessly due to the fact that the attack in these mental cases was not diagnosed early and they were too active in the very first week of their myocardial infarction—when the heart wall ruptured, and before the scar had a chance to heal.

We continued to be interested in structural changes in the heart, and we saw a good deal of rheumatic heart disease. In one paper with Dr. Bland we reported on several cases of mitral stenosis (narrowing of the mitral valve opening, causing congestion of the lungs) found after the age of eighty, which was very surprising but evidently still possible. Another structural defect which we studied was that of senile ectasia (stretching and weakening of the aortic wall) in old women, causing rupture of the aorta and sudden death at a very old age.

Among the many papers on various aspects of cardiology which we wrote during the 1940s, the most important one came at the end of the decade. This was my Wesley M. Carpenter Lecture, on "Heart Failure," presented before the Academy of Medicine of New York City, and published in the *Bulletin of the New York Academy of Medicine*. In this lecture, I emphasized a belief of which I had become more and more deeply convinced throughout the decade, namely, in the priority of the prevention of heart failure over its treatment. The emphasis on preventive medicine was to become my major interest, and possibly my major contribution during the latter half of my career.

Before I leave the 1940s, I must express my great gratitude, and that of my cardiological colleagues, to the bold pioneers who firmly established cardiovascular surgery in that decade. A few rather isolated successes had antedated the 1940s, as noted in Chapter V, but it was now that the skill and courage of a considerable group of surgeons all over the world became manifest. I have already spoken of Robert Gross of Boston and his success in the surgical closure of the patent ductus arteriosus in 1938. His next notable contribution, made simultaneously with that of Professor Crafoord of Stockholm, was in the correction of congenital coarctation (narrowing) of the aorta in 1945. News of this Swedish success was brought to me by Gunnar Biörck (later to become chief of medicine of the Serafimer Lazarettet of Stockholm), when he came as a graduate fellow to spend a few months with us at the M.G.H. in Boston. It happened that Dr. Gross was, that very evening, to present an address on this new achievement of his at the Boston Medical Library. I took Dr. Biörck to the meeting and in the discussion period after the lecture I introduced him. The audience was thrilled to learn of the independent pioneering of these two surgeons.

Meanwhile in the mid-forties Alfred Blalock and Helen Taussig of Baltimore were introducing their spectacular, though not yet definitive, surgical treatment of the so-called congenital "blue baby." This treatment brought to Baltimore hundreds of these congenitally cyanotic children, generally afflicted by the Tetralogy of Fallot (for this complicated deformity of the heart, the reader is referred to Helen Taussig's textbook). So many of these youngsters came early from France that Dr. Blalock decided to go to Paris to instruct the French surgeons in the technique.

Shortly after this, Dwight Harken of Boston, and Charles Bailey, then of Philadelphia, who had come back from the Second World War where they had had much experience in the surgical treatment of wounds of the chest involving both heart and lungs, opened a new surgical era. They had found that the heart was not after all such a delicate organ, and could usually be handled with safety, as in the extraction of shrapnel. They simultaneously began to work on patients with mitral stenosis (narrowing of the valve opening through which blood flows from the left atrium into the left ventricle), the result of rheumatic fever in childhood. They split open the tight mitral valve either with the gloved finger or a tiny knife introduced into the left atrial appendage. The technique was variously called "mitral valvulotomy" and "mitral commissurotomy" (the commissures are the minute spaces between the two valve cusps of the mitral valve).

Through the 1940s, surgical treatment of diseased blood vessels, both arteries and veins, was making progress in clearing clots and other obstructions and for varicose veins. Réné Leriche of Paris was a noted pioneer whom I met several times. He introduced for general use the special technique called endarteriectomy, in which the obstruction blocking an artery was mechanically removed, allowing restoration of the blood flow through the artery. This was especially effective in the legs, where pain in the calves on walking, called intermittent claudication, could thus be relieved. Pain in the thighs on walking has been called Leriche's Syndrome.

Those years of the 1940s were certainly ones of hard work and great progress! The war added greatly to the stress of overwork and undoubtedly slowed the progress of medical science, but it promoted two great therapeutic cardiovascular advances, one, the rapid development of antibiotics and, two, the beginning of surgical treatment of lesions *inside* the heart.

Spring of 1929: The Whites outside their rented villa on the island of Capri, where they spent four months working on Dr. White's book on heart disease.

Cartoon depicting the author's 1956 expedition to Scammon's Lagoon in Baja California, Mexico. With James Jenks and Dr. Robert King, and the help of Donald Douglas, Samuel Mathews and The National Geographic Society of Washington, D.C., Dr. White attempted to obtain the electrocardiogram of the gray whale.

A mural of "Modern Cardiology," painted in 1941 by Diego Rivera, in the entrance hall of the National Institute of Cardiology in Mexico City. On the opposite wall is "Ancient Cardiology" (not shown here). Dr. White appears near the top of the picture, below Drs. Einthoven and Waller. *Courtesy of the National Institute of Cardiology in Mexico City*

Dr. White with Pope Pius XII at the International Medical Conference at the Vatican in 1956. This second meeting with the Pope concerned plans for psychosomatic research sponsored by the new hospital at San Giovanni Rotondo in southeastern Italy. From left to right: Professor Pierre Duchosal of Geneva, Pope Pius XII, Paul Dudley White and Professor Gustav Nyliu of Stockholm.

Swollen Ankles

Some thirty years ago in the Out-patient Department of the M.G.H., we found in studying 100 individuals with swollen ankles that in ninety per cent of the patients the swelling was due to local difficulties with the circulation and in only ten per cent to diseases of the heart or kidneys. This finding was, at that time, directly contrary to general belief.

The most common local cause of the swelling of the ankles is a sluggish circulation in the legs due most often to stasis in obese or physically inactive people, especially if they sit or stand for any great length of time, and also as they grow older. For example, an older person riding in an airplane for five or six hours without getting up from his seat is bound to have some swelling of the ankles at the end of that time, and yet he may be quite healthy in every other way. Other common causes, but also quite frequent ones, are varicose veins, and thrombosis or blood clots in the veins of the legs. Clotting of blood in the veins may also occur from stasis or sluggish circulation in persons whose blood tends to clot easily, or it may come from injuries, for example a sprain or a strain of a muscle or a joint. When the cause is thrombosis, it tends to spread to the other leg so that although the injury may start in one leg, we frequently have bilateral thrombosis of the leg veins.

In 1540 an Italian named Canano discovered valves in the veins of man. (In anatomy, a valve is a membranous fold or structure which permits body fluids to flow in one direction only.) This discovery of Canano's was almost as important as that of the circulation of the blood in the next century. In fact, the discovery of the circulation of the blood by William Harvey (presented by him in 1628 in a very important treatise "De Motu Cordis") was largely due to the discovery by the Italians of the valves in the veins, both anatomically and physiologically. Canano made the first anatomical discovery, but it was Fabrizio d'Acquapendente who gave an excellent presentation of these valves in 1603, in a book called "De Venarum Ostiolis." The valves were found in the veins of the arms and of the legs, especially in the leg veins, where they play a much more important role than in the arms. William Harvey, the English physician, came to northern Italy for his postgraduate education, and worked and studied from 1599 to 1603 in Padua with Fabrizio and with other medical scientists of the day. When he went back to England he gradually put together the puzzle of the circulation of the blood, as illustrated in his famous work of 1628.

To understand what nature has done as an engineer we need to go back to prehistoric times, many hundreds of thousands of years ago, when man became a biped and needed the valves in the veins to prevent his blood from settling in his feet, therefore with none, or very little, going to the brain. At that time valves had already developed in the veins so that he could be viable. When the valves don't work very well because of injury or when we are just static, that is, sitting or standing without moving our legs, blood can leak past these valves, and swelling of the legs can occur. I want to put in a very strong recommendation for the use of the leg muscles by exercise such as walking, or swimming, or running, or tennis or golf, or any such activity or sport. As we know, when the leg muscles contract they squeeze the veins and the valves in the veins prevent the blood from going down, and thus the blood is pumped up toward the heart and thence to the brain. This observation is of the utmost importance, the equal of any other to be found in this book. I hope that it will help many of the readers to establish a better program of exercise in order to have better circulation throughout the body. The heart is not the only pump, although it is the most important one. We have several other mechanisms in the circulation that are very helpful, and one of them is vigorous action of the leg muscles. This is not only physiologically beneficial, as I have already stated, but also the fatigue of the leg muscles, which are the largest muscles in the body, has a very pleasant, relaxing effect. Undoubtedly, also, an active circulation through the veins helps to prevent blood clots from forming. There is a certain amount of evidence that exercise, especially of the legs, and thus in the use of the leg muscles, may have a retarding or even preventive effect on the early development of atherosclerosis, that is, the disease of the arteries which is now the most common and important serious disease in this country today.

The difficulty of our way of life is that man no longer labors much, and so must substitute exercise for the former necessity of working hard physically. In this connection I would like to cite an important article in the July, 1966, number of the journal called *Circulation Research*, which presented for the first time clear proof of the muscle pumping action of the circulation in the dependent leg. Dr. H. F. Stegall observed the peripheral circulation in healthy, sedentary males by measuring calf circumference, muscle pump ejection velocity, intrathoracic and intra-abdominal pressures, and power of the leg muscle pump. Measurements of pressure, flow velocity, and volume changes in the dependent venous beds of healthy young men demonstrated that during running in place (walking also has much the same effect) the abdominal muscular contraction necessary to fix the pelvis did raise inferior caval pressure, that is big vein pressure, and impeded venous outflow from the legs, but that the leg muscles themselves were capable of effectively pumping blood past this functional obstruction. By doing so these peripheral pumps contributed more than thirty per cent of the energy required to circulate blood during running. I might add also that free use of the diaphragm, which is a muscle involved in the process of breathing, makes of the thorax (the part of the body between the neck and the abdomen) a suction pump, and in this way also helps in the circulation of blood.

A patient, Charles Thiery, whom I saw first when he was one hundred years of age, is a case in point. He was perfectly healthy and was brought to me by a friend who thought I should see a healthy man one hundred years old, as well as patients who were sick at a much younger age. He was of Huguenot ancestry, but born in Cambridge, Massachusetts; at the time of my acquaintance with him he lived in Belmont. His story is recorded in a book I wrote which was published several years ago, *Hearts: Their Long Follow-Up*, put out by the Saunders Company. In this book I wrote:

> Mr. T. gave a history of being almost fatally ill with pneumonia at the age of two years (and I might add now that he finally died of pneumonia at the age of 107½). He had had the usual childhood diseases and also chorea and scarlet fever, and had fractured his arm. At the age of twenty he had had "slow" (probably typhoid) fever, but after that he had very little illness except for occasional colds and attacks of "grippe." Also for many years he had had "nervous indigestion" which prevented him from eating as much as most of his friends (who had died much earlier in life). His only other complaint was that he was somewhat hard of hearing. He had always been a very active man, walking long distances in his youth—at one time he walked 25 miles in five hours—and riding a horse, especially

when in military service in the cavalry. Even in his old age he continued to walk a great deal and he averaged one to two miles a day during the last few years of his life. He had never married. He did not smoke or drink, and he thought his long life was favored by his avoidance of tobacco and alcohol. He ate well but sparingly and was never obese. He did not like eggs but ate a good deal of ice cream and liked butter, milk, cream, and pastry. He started his first job in silver—and gold—smithing under his father's tutelage at 11 years of age and retired at 93. His father had died at 79, a brother at 92, and a sister at 85. His mother died of "Bright's disease" at the age of 39 and a second sister of the same disease at 21. (It seems likely that these relatives had had scarlet fever, or something of that nature, which had caused serious illness prior to that.)

Physical examination showed him to be a healthy appearing, elderly man with white hair, beard, and mustache. His height was 63 inches and his weight 115 pounds. He was a little hard of hearing. His eyesight was good with normal pupils and no arcus senilis. His heart was normal in size and sounds, the second doubled at the base. There were no murmurs. There were occasional premature beats at a rate of 68. His blood pressure was normal at 140 systolic, 70 diastolic. He had a good arterial pulse in the ankles.

The electrocardiogram showed slight left bundle branch block.

After that we examined him semiannually with the same findings.

In the winter of 1953 to 1954, when he was 103 years old, he had a prolonged respiratory infection, undoubtedly a type of influenza. During his convalescence, while he sat all day in a chair, there developed considerable soft, pitting edema (swelling) of both legs equally to his knees, and he thought that his end was approaching. However, his heart was still normal in size, his neck veins were not engorged, and he had no shortness of breath. *We were therefore quite certain that the edema, or swelling, of the legs was due to local stasis from the effect of gravity since he had spent day after day sitting inactively. There was no evidence of heart failure or of phlebitis. So we advised him to begin to walk again, which he did daily, and within a fortnight the edema entirely cleared and never returned. His leg muscles had pumped all the swelling away.* [Italics mine]

A still more dramatic illustration of the need of the proper interpretation of the significance of swollen ankles appeared in the person of Admiral Jesse B. Oldendorff, who came to my office for examination on September 27, 1943. He was an Admiral in the U.S. Navy on duty in the Pacific, and had been brought to me by two young naval doctors because of a diagnosis of heart failure causing swollen ankles. His retirement had been advised, but he had requested one more consultation, which is how I happened to see him.

Following a detailed history, physical examination, x-ray study, and electrocardiogram, I disagreed with the diagnosis of heart failure and advised that he not be retired, and so he was allowed to remain on active duty.

The history he gave me was that he had always been active physically and mentally, but that early in August, nearly two months previously, he had been salmon fishing on a Newfoundland stream, and had slipped on a rock, injuring his right ankle. A week or so later his wife noticed that his right ankle was swollen. Slowly both legs began to swell each day until on September 8, two weeks before I examined him, he called on his doctors, who found pitting edema, or swelling, of both legs to the knees, more on the right, and a questionable electrocardiogram. He was referred to the hospital for study. With rest and other treatment the swelling of the legs subsided and his weight decreased about seven pounds. He had a little fever for three days early in September.

His physical examination was entirely normal except for slight arcus senilis in both eyes and a mediocre arterial pulsation in the right foot. The pulse was 84 and regular. The blood pressure was completely normal at 120 mm. systolic and 80 mm. diastolic. Fluoroscopy, that is x-ray examination, showed the heart normal in size and shape, with clear lungs. The electrocardiogram was essentially normal.

I made a diagnosis of a probably normal heart and bilateral leg edema due to phlebitis, the result of an injury. I did refer him to a blood vessel consultant, who concluded that he had had phlebitis (inflammation of a leg vein or veins) of the right leg, and that there was no need for any radical treatment.

With the rush of events of the Second World War and for years afterwards, I completely forgot about Admiral Oldendorf and failed to follow him up, which has been true of some of my cases, although I have often for special reasons made very careful follow-up studies of other individual patients or groups of patients. At a medical meeting in Brooklyn a few years ago I was engaged in conversation with a middle-aged doctor who reminded me that he had been one of the young naval doctors who years before had brought the Admiral to see me in Boston. He asked me if I knew what had happened to him. He knew, but I did not, and so he filled me in with the events of the previous twenty-odd years. The Admiral, he said, had won one of the biggest naval battles ever fought—the battle of Leyte Gulf—which sank a large part of the Japanese fleet in the Pacific. The Admiral then went on, my friend said, to take a leading part in the many naval battles which followed and which eventually permitted the landing of our armed forces in the Philippines and the driving out of the Japanese.

After hearing this news from the doctor in Brooklyn, I wrote to the Admiral, who had retired and was living on the Keys in Florida. He very cheerfully answered me that he was in excellent health, about to take a trip around the world with his wife, and that he would get in touch with me after he returned. This he did, and he sent me an admirable photograph of himself in uniform. He wrote me that he had had several important battle accidents during the rest of the war in the Pacific and had had to be in the hospital on several occasions. He had finally retired on September 1, 1948, and since his retirement he had had operations to clear away various difficulties, but never any indication of heart trouble. He had always taken regular exercise, playing golf whenever possible, and lately swimming in the ocean, because he could not find his golf balls any more on account of his eyesight.

Not all victims of phlebitis of the leg veins come off as well as did Admiral Oldendorf, but a good many do and may not need any radical treatment. He was fortunate in not having any pulmonary emboli, that is, blood clots going to the lungs, which is an important complication of phlebitis of the leg veins. His golf and swimming have helped to keep his legs clear of trouble and have been important reasons for his longevity. In February, 1969, the Admiral wrote to me about his more recent health, again good during the preceding year, after removal of cataracts from his eyes, and a tumor from his colon, complicated by hepatitis and phlebitis, all that now past history.

And so we learn that if we use our leg muscles properly, with the help of the valves in our veins we may certainly expect to benefit greatly in our health and to avoid, at least at an early age, some of the circulatory diseases so common today: leg vein thrombosis, embolism to the lungs, and possibly atherosclerosis too, leading to damage to heart and brain. I am grateful to Charles Thiery, my aged friend and patient, and to Admiral Jesse Oldendorf, both of whom taught me so much of value to pass on to others.

People, Patients, and Personalities

CHAPTER X 🙣

I have discussed in Chapter VIII the wide range of physical findings so far as the human is concerned, and now I would like to explore the range of the normal, or indeed of the abnormal, so far as I have encountered individual personalities. This, of course, leaves the physical aspects of my patients for the moment, except as they are manifestations of the effect of the psyche, and turns to the mental and spiritual sides of man (and woman), dependent on the function of the brain. Although it is true that many of the very interesting persons I have known as patients have been famous, many other fascinating personalities have been relatively impoverished and obscure, sometimes by choice.

I would like to refer to people in broad categories, lumping together under the heading of "the Arts and the Humanities" writers, artists, and musicians; under "Science" both the "pure" and the "applied" scientists; under "Explorers" both those of the earth and the astronauts; under "Professionals" lawyers, doctors, nurses, financiers, teachers, secretaries, clergymen, military men, politicians, accountants, architects, archaeologists, anthropologists, astronomers, philosophers, and psychologists; under "Business" merchants, and industrial workers of all sorts, many of whom had once worn the blue shirt; under "Laborer" the largest group of all, those who tend machines, or animals in the field; and finally, under "Housekeeper," most of the wives and women of the land, who often double their days with additional jobs. My patients have been in all these categories, a great kaleidoscope of people—some 15,000 in my private practice and as many more in hospitals and clinics.

Despite the differences in professions and life styles, there were some social and psychological factors common to all. The first of these factors is that of family, its relationships and problems. In order to treat the whole patient it is necessary for the physician to discover the answer to many questions. Is this family a patriarchy? Or a matriarchy? Or is there a wholesome sharing of responsibilities? It is often important for the doctor to have some idea of this, for it can play an important role in his diagnosis as well as in his treatment. For this reason it is helpful to see both husband and wife, if either one is the patient, either together or separately if it can be tactfully arranged. If the couple is senior, it is well to be in touch with one or two of the children; if the patient is junior, with one or both of the parents. The degree of happiness or unhappiness in the marriage can have a very important relationship not only to the spiritual health of the patient but also, through the effect of the psyche, to the physical health. Most physicians are well aware of the psychosomatic aspect of physiology and disease, but sometimes seem to pay less attention to the somatopsychic side, which I find equally vital. The body's influence on the mind can be just as important as the mind's influence on the body!

It is, I believe, important for the physician to inquire about the family relationship early in his care of a patient. If he does so and also acts discretely it may be quite unnecessary to prescribe psychiatric consultation. Nearly every patient I have ever seen has had his or her family problems, often unknown outside the family and often not even known to all members of the family itself. There may be an alcoholic husband, wife, father, mother, or child. There may be a member of the family in a hospital for the insane, in an institution for the feebleminded, or even in jail. There may be a delinquent child, a hippie, or a drug addict. There may be a divorce in the making, with fear of publicity or of its effect on the children. All this should be known to the family doctor, to the hospital or group clinic, and to the consultants.

Today there is little or no taboo about the discussion of sex and it is much easier for both doctor and patient to discuss than it was a generation ago. Some of my patients now consult me accompanied by their new partners, whom they may introduce as a brother or sister, employer or secretary, or simply and more frankly as paramour. I have found myself, as I have grown older and as attitudes have changed, asked sometimes to act as a marriage counsellor, in one case to a couple who had been married nearly fifty years.

Some writers condone or even recommend extramarital or premarital sexual relationships for some individuals, and inasmuch as we have not ascended in spiritual evolution much above the level of the farmyard, this is one way of accepting what is a rather common practice. But certainly experience has shown through the ages that monogamy works better than does polygamy, and is a much more practical way of life. The ideal marriage is doubtlessly far less common than is to be desired, and needs to be fostered by a striving for improvements in the selection of partners—fostered in part in the home but also in the schools by discussion of the elements and attitudes that go to make a good marriage that is creative and life-enhancing for both.

An interesting lesson that I have learned myself in the last decade is not to back any one part of the family against another—as we did at first in the program called "Hearts and Husbands," which I have described elsewhere in the book (see Chapter XIV). In that program, we urged the wives to help change the habits of their menfolk, habits which were leading to earlier coronary heart disease in their husbands and which were partly responsible for a six-plus-year difference in longevity between men and women in the United States today (sixty-eight years versus seventy-four). But as the program continued we found that in the eyes of other members of the family we seemed to be backing the wives too strongly and thereby creating resistance among the men; after three years we changed the title of the program to "Husbands, Wives, and their Children," and placed our foremost emphasis on prevention of disease among children.

Before leaving the subject of the family I would add a word about the present rebellious generation, which of course is not historically the first such generation. I suspect that about once in every century there has been something of the sort (like extremes of weather, hurricanes, and the like) and that except for occasional aspects of violence, it is by no means a wholly undesirable happening. Dean Sperry of Harvard once wrote: "Were it not for the perpetual succession of rebellious sons, we would still be gnawing bones in the caves of Mousterian man." I myself have advised the children of the present generation to rebel against their fathers' bad habits, but not against their fathers themselves. It is quite possible that the extreme permissiveness of the last generation will be followed by a considerable degree of discipline, we may hope optimal, of the next.

The numerous professions which I listed earlier have been represented in my practice by several thousand individuals, no two just alike and many of them fascinating personalities and pioneers in their fields. I would like now to turn to some observations about the members of these categories.

I will take first the Arts, which includes in particular writers, artists, sculptors, and musicians. I have found that writers, in particular, are prone to live too sedentary a life and also to be overnourished—unless their particular job, as in the case of a newspaperman, requires considerable physical activity or unless they develop a schedule of exercise that keeps them fit. Thus writers may be particularly prone to develop cardiovascular disease. And so may editors, whose jobs often require that they sit at a desk all day.

Artists have as a rule a more active schedule, since they must often travel about to paint scenes or people. I noted with interest that the portrait painter who "did" me twice (occasions about twenty years apart) was active physically as he painted, constantly walking around and about to view the canvas from all sides and angles. Musicians, too, must practice their music or take part in frequent concerts, requiring them to move about. Consequently, artists and musicians may be slightly less prone to heart disease than are writers, but I know of no adequate statistics on this.

Among my musical patients who have done very well despite a considerable amount of heart disease there are three about whom I would like to add a few words. The first was a composer whom I saw a good many years ago, named Henry Gilbert, who despite a very serious congenital deformity of the heart which we call the Tetralogy of Fallot (the cause of the intense cyanosis of the "blue baby" which resulted in the blue appearance of this man), became internationally known and honored as a pioneer of native American music. He lived before it had become possible to relieve or cure this condition by surgical therapy such as is possible today. When I saw him first, on March 8, 1927, he was fifty-eight years old and he told me that because of the seriousness of his condition his parents had been told that it would be a waste of money to educate him because he would not live to grow up. Therefore he learned at home as best he could and finally ran away and worked his way to study music in Europe. On his return to the States he concentrated on the folk music of the U.S.A., and I was told that one of his chief accomplishments was to make American jazz classical. The reason he came to me at his age was to find out if I considered his somewhat fragile state of health a bar or not to his acceptance of a series of invitations to take part in musical festivals in Europe during the following summer. I realized that this was the culmination of his career and that the modest risk was well worth while. He went abroad, had the time of his life, and survived not only the many concerts, but also the beer drinking and the multitude of banquets. On his return he became somewhat overconfident, exhausted himself conducting orchestras playing his music all over the U.S.A., and finally succumbed to cerebral thrombosis at the age of fifty-nine years and eight months, a new record, by many years, of longevity in a patient with pronounced cyanosis in a classical case of the Tetralogy of Fallot, proved by postmortem examination.

The second noted musician whom I was honored to see for a good many years as a patient and whom I greatly admired and loved was Charles Muench, conductor of the Boston Symphony Orchestra. Despite angina pectoris due to coronary heart disease, he carried on brilliantly with the help of nitroglycerine for a good many years, including several years after he returned to Europe following his retirement from the Boston Orchestra.

The most remarkable of all has been Pablo Casals, the world renowned cellist and conductor whose fascinating memoirs in the book called *Joys and Sorrows* have been edited by Albert Kahn and published recently (1970) by Simon and Schuster. On the evening of April 18, 1957, while taking part in a medical meeting in Texas, I was called by Governor Munoz Marin by telephone from San Juan, Puerto Rico, to come at once to see Pablo Casals, then eighty years old, who had been suddenly struck down by a serious heart attack that morning while rehearsing for the first of the notable annual musical festivals presented in his name at San Juan. I arrived by cross-country flight to Florida and thence to Puerto Rico at about

4:30 A.M. the next day, and found Casals very ill with acute myocardial infarction, but under the very able care of Dr. José Passalacqua and Professor Ramon Suarez, one of the leaders of contemporary cardiology, and of several devoted nurses, including a pupil, Matita Montañez, who later after his convalescence became his wife, in August of that same year. Not only has Casals continued in good health and spirits since that heart attack but he has maintained an extraordinarily active musical career as a teacher as well as a world renowned cellist and conductor. Recently, in August, 1970, my wife and I attended a concert at the Marlboro Music Festival in Vermont and watched him conduct with vigor Beethoven's Emperor Concerto, the fifth, which had been dedicated in 1810 to Napoleon, then emperor, but later rescinded. When I examined his heart the next morning at his temporary home in Marlboro I found it apparently in quite good condition. He spoke to us with emotion and vigor on the subject nearest his heart—world peace—and also of his distress about modern music. He and his wife Matita were about to fly to Israel where he would conduct and play his cello. He was ninety-four in December, 1970.

The so-called artistic temperament is well known to be exaggerated in some artists and writers as an excuse for over-indulgence in alcohol, tobacco, or other injurious habits. In fact many of my nonartistic patients have blamed their bad habits on an "artistic temperament," a confession which I have often found used as an excuse.

Just as the artistic temperament is not limited to artists, so the "absent-minded professor" as a designation can be applied to many and perhaps more of my nonscientific friends and patients than it can to those who are so involved in scientific research and teaching that they cannot afford to let their minds wander. On the other hand they often do have to concentrate on their work so intensively that like myself in medicine, they have, or at least take, little time for anything else. It has been sometimes said that the "pure" scientist, whether mathematician, physicist, or chemist, looks down on his colleague, the applied scientist, be he engineer or physician, but this I have found to be rare. Sometimes, in fact, the shoe is on the other foot and the applied scientist feels superior to the "pure" one. Most of such ideas are based on popular clichés; they are the exceptions and not the rule. Finally, I have found that leading scientists tend to be modest despite their accomplishments.

In my experience explorers are, in both the terrestrial and the celestial sense, a tribe apart. They tend to be individualistic, with great courage and enthusiasm, and at the same time a determined nonconformism which often gives them a reputation of being eccentric or difficult. This has been true in my dealing with several Arctic and Antarctic pioneers and one astronaut, but my experience with this profession is limited and should not be taken too seriously.

Among the outstanding physicians I have been privileged to treat was Sir Wilfred Grenfell, whose mission hospitals on Newfoundland and Labrador pioneered for the health of the disease-ravaged Eskimos and Indians of those lands, and still carry on.

Another noted physician who asked me to examine him when I visited him at his hospital in Africa was Albert Schweitzer of Lambaréné in Gabon. I found hm an impressive personality, whose very primitive hospital has been rehabilitated since his death by his daughter Madame Eckert, with plans for the building of an important modern medical center nearby. This could be a great contribution to the health of that part of Africa as well as a memorial to the philosophy of Dr. Schweitzer.

Other noted physicians (although less world-renowned) who asked for my medical advice or care have included several of my own teachers in this country and abroad. One was the late Richard Clark Cabot, professor both of medicine and of social ethics at Harvard University. A remarkable man, he pioneered in hospital social service, in hematology, in physical diagnosis, in clinical ministry, and in clinico-pathological correlation; his famous case records are still being published every week in what is probably the most famous local medical journal in the world, the *New England Journal of Medicine*. Richard Cabot played the violin in a string quartet and led a group of carolers every Christmas Eve on Beacon Hill. He left a trust in memory of his wife, Ella Lyman, which for the past thirty-one years has given a helping hand specifically to many creative young people at critical moments of their careers in the arts, sciences, ministry, and medicine, rather than to "causes" in general or to institutions as such.

A second teacher who became a patient was David L. Edsall, chief of medicine at the M.G.H. when I was interne and resident; he later became dean of the Harvard Medical School. He was a warm friend of the young house staff and the man who started me on my career in cardiology. He pioneered in modern medical education, and his authoritative biography has recently been written by my old friend and colleague Dr. Joseph C. Aub.

Third among these early teachers and incidentally also a coronary patient, was Sir Thomas Lewis, physiologist and pioneer in electrocardiography, who taught me how to burn the midnight oil in London and sent me back to Boston with a basis for my cardiological career. He himself in the 1920s suffered from his first coronary thrombosis, but he survived and worked hard until he died of his fourth attack twenty years later, still only middle-aged. He was one of the best teachers I ever had, a hard taskmaster with a brain as sharp as a razor.

Finally, I shall never forget Dr. Maude E. Abbott of Montreal, a most remarkable and lovable woman, pioneer in the field of congenital heart disease, directed to this specialty by the great Sir William Osler.

All in all, my medical patients, colleagues, and friends have given me much challenge in their care, much stimulation and help in my work, and much comfort in my own difficulties. Every so often I have been on the other side of the office door, so to speak, and have required their advice and care. In my childhood I suffered attacks of diphtheria, scarlet fever, and the usual childhood diseases; in my adult life I have experienced tonsillitis (and tonsillectomy), pneumonia, frequent respiratory virus infections, herpes zoster, and a broken leg (from playing softball in a back pasture).*

The nursing profession is also one which I deeply respect. For a few years when I was a young doctor I was assigned the job of taking care of the medical needs of the nurses at the M.G.H. and I still occasionally see some of these ladies. Several nurses have established notable careers in this country or abroad as heads of training schools, nurses like Sarah Parsons, Sally Johnson, and Ruth Sleeper of the M.G.H., or superintendents of hospitals, such as Sophia Eastman Bock, head of the Massachusetts Eye and Ear Infirmary, or Nina Johnson, who was a nursing missionary in China and who at this writing is still a patient of mine at an advanced age.

Deans and professors of law, practising attorneys in criminal and civil cases, judges and investigators, have also kept me busy in the analysis of the stress of their work and its relationship to their heart disease. I found in the course of time that the law embraces even more specialties than does medicine. I also have found that some patients in the legal profession were fortunately able to shift from work of great strain to a job with little stress, possibly more easily than a physician. I learned over the years how useful and interesting a knowledge of the law could be; however, I do not relish legal debate and have always avoided appearance in court except as it has been absolutely necessary.

One of my most interesting lawyer-patients was Gren-

* And also at Christmastime, 1970, a minor heart attack.

ville Clark, who was nationally known for his work in the field of world "good government." A former New York lawyer, during the years I knew him he made his home in Dublin, New Hampshire, where he became deeply interested in the cause of international law and world peace. With Professor Sohn of the Harvard Law School he published a book called *World Peace Through World Law*, which was primarily a recommended revision of the Charter of the United Nations. Another significant contribution of Grenville Clark was his participation in the very important first Dartmouth Conference of Russian educators and humanitarians with a similar number of Americans of the same professional standing. There have been four similar conferences since then—I had the privilege of serving as a member of the fourth one in Leningrad a few years ago.

The next categories of patients whom I remember with great warmth are those of educators and of the ministry. My respect and sympathy for teachers in the grammar schools and high schools of this country today is enormous, and I have greatly enjoyed my friendship with many of them. Theirs has been a difficult, often underpaid, and still more often thankless job. The same may be said today (as not always in the past) for the presidents, deans, and faculties of the hundreds of colleges and universities throughout the land; I am sure that they will survive the present turmoil on the campuses as their forebears have done in centuries gone by, but they have had a difficult time of late.

My patients among the clergy have represented many different religions and sects and have made me feel that I myself easily could have become a member of any of their faiths. Their sincerity and devotion to their parishes have been impressive despite the spiritual revolution going on around them; I have not found them hypocritical and whether of low or of high estate they have been warm friends of mine.

Their prayers have been comforting in these days when cursing and foul language have become so widespread.

When I began my practice I saw a good many laborers who really labored; they were poor but would abandon the free clinic for my office for a little while, at a modest fee. Quite naturally, then as now, many of them have needed essentially free study and treatment, and so they have formed only a small portion of my practice. But I still see some of my old friends among them, at little or no expense. However, many of these one-time poor laborers have prospered and now are among my well-to-do patients. It is cases like these which make one see that upward mobility is still a feature of American life.

I cannot take the space to write about *all* the categories, for almost every kind of business is represented by my patients, from a Wall Street banker to a Vermont farmer. They make clothes or shoes, or even hats. They work in or run factories of all kinds, or mills, or shops or drugstores or circuses. They are butchers or bakers or candlestick makers. They run hotel or restaurants or theaters, or boats or buses or plane lines. They are wreckers or builders or publishers or printers. They are jewelers, librarians, bartenders, housewives, barbers, or auto dealers. One man who is a patient of mine makes one small part of a tool by the millions. I have become familiar with many trades. Such memories I have of this host of friends! Many have died, but I have frequently kept in touch with their families, some of whom I have continued to see as new patients in the second and third generations. I can see, in my mind's eye, some of these old friends of thirty, forty, or even fifty years ago, friends whom I followed over the years to the emergency operating rooms of various hospitals, to the wards or hospital rooms and even to their death beds at home and then to their graves. This life, which I now relive, has certainly been a tremendous experience.

Finally among these categories of mine, I must mention the

famous politicians or political figures, to whose bedsides I have often been called in consultation, particularly in recent years. I cannot deny that this activity has certainly lent an element of excitement to my life!

The publicity which fell to my lot shortly after I had been consulted about President Eisenhower (which I will describe in a separate chapter) resulted in my being called to examine President Trujillo of Santo Domingo, who wished to be sure that his heart would stand the strain of the challenges to his dictatorship that surrounded him. The busy day that I spent in his presidential palace I shall never forget—it was a bit like spending time in a fortress under siege. Having assured him that his heart was sound, I was asked to examine his wife and other members of his family, and also several of his trusty lieutenants. Not very long afterwards Trujillo was assassinated.

There have been three other dictatorships in the western world with which I have been directly concerned. One experience had to do with the health of two members of the Argentine cabinet, the prime minister and the minister of health under Juan Peron. A few years later these same two ministers came to Boston for a check-up and were on their way, they said, around the world. Their departure from their country was shortly followed by that of Peron himself, and the trip around the world turned out to be, in a sense, permanent.

Another South American dictator with a precarious hold on his country suffered a very severe coronary heart attack, at which time I was asked to see him in consultation. He was seriously ill and obviously in no condition to stand the strain of a revolution. I advised his abdication for the sake of his survival and he thereupon retired to Spain, a beneficial event both for him and for the nation. A third dictator, in Central America, while still much too young, suffered an attack of coronary thrombosis. I was asked to see him to advise him as to how best to change his environment to avoid a further attack. How much he changed his risk factors, I never found out, but he died a few years later of another heart attack. Incidentally, his father is said to have been assassinated by a poisoned bullet.

Other political figures whom I have attended in the western world, including cabinet members, governors, and mayors, have been less dramatic although often of great interest and sometimes of great charm, as in the case of our own President Eisenhower. The "Veep," Alben Barkley, a patient who fascinated me greatly because of his political skill and wisdom, gave his full support to governmental aid to medical research, training, and education at a critical time in the early days of the new National Heart Institute and National Advisory Heart Council. He was suffering from myocardial fatigue, caused by a long spell of uncontrolled "atrial flutter," incident to his successful but over-vigorous campaign to re-elect President Truman in 1948. This was in the days of extreme secrecy about serious illness of important government officials, and I had to visit Mr. Barkley at the Naval Hospital in Bethesda more or less incognito. Later, of course, President Eisenhower quite wisely abandoned this tradition of concealing medical truth.

In Europe I have had a few interesting patients, including a prime minister who asked me, while he was recovering from a coronary heart attack, if I thought he might be able to stand the strain of one more revolution. Although I told him he could, he cautiously retired before the revolution occurred.

In the Near East there have been several notable patients, in particular Sami Sohl, prime minister of Lebanon, to whose sick bed I was called late at night on April 30, 1957, at the time of a critical illness. He recovered and was later re-elected in a colorful campaign. The local Beirut newspapers the next morning, May 1, 1957, carried two special headlines, the first of ominous significance, namely that the Sixth American Fleet had arrived, and, to balance it, a parallel headline that Dr. White had arrived to advise about a sick man: "war and peace," an interesting coincidence, made the most of by the U. S. State Department. Sami Sohl recovered and was later re-elected in a colorful campaign which began on May 12 with a political parade led by twelve camels, a parade in which I was unexpectedly involved, while believing that I was to conduct him from the hospital to complete his convalescence in his country home. Instead I found myself seated in the back seat of his car between Sami Sohl on my right and Charles Malik, Ambassador to the United Nations, on my left and with armed motor cycle police on both sides of the car. As we drove slowly along between huge throngs of his cheering friends I felt his pulse which seemed thready at first until some whiskey and the plaudits of the multitude revived him, and when we arrived at the center of the city he insisted on climbing two flights of stairs to his old attic room. When I examined him there, it was evident that this strenuous effort had given his psyche such a boost that no harm had come to him from the physical strain.

Another notable patient was the wife of the Prime Minister of Iraq, whom I saw with her English physician. I was conferring with them both when the King of Saudi Arabia, who was visiting Iraq on a state visit, entered the room with four tall sons. Our introductions were interrupted by one of the periodic Moslem calls to prayer, and were only resumed after the five Saudi Arabians had turned to face Mecca and to recite their praises of Allah. A few months later the prime minister of Iraq was assassinated. The two events, I should add, were unconnected.

A third friend in the Near East was Ben Gurion, the strong leader of Israel. I joined him one day on his regular four-and-a-half-mile walk, a few years after he had retired to his kibbutz in the Negev. He was a forceful personality, very pleasant to talk with and to walk with and extremely impatient with the government which had succeeded him. His wife seemed to plan his whole day and made me fit my plans to theirs, agreeably but in turn forcefully. I found him in good health, although at an advanced age, and I have no doubt that his daily walk contributed a great deal to his well-being.

My most numerous contacts with Asian political patients have been in Pakistan, India, and the Philippines. Since my Point Four Mission to Pakistan in 1951, I have had the pleasure of advising several other Pakistani heads of state, local and federal officials, and a number of ambassadors. I suppose that I have traveled more extensively in Pakistan than in any other country in Asia. My relationship with the Philippines has also been quite close, as over the years I have helped to train many of their graduate students and physicians; I have often been asked to give medical advice in that country to heads of state, senators, and other officials. The same has been true in India, about which I have more to say in later chapters.

There are three other smaller countries in Asia whose leaders have asked my professional advice, either during my visits or during theirs to the United States. These are Afghanistan, Nepal, and Kuwait. Years ago the mother of the King of Nepal was a patient at the New York Hospital, where I was asked to see her; later on, when my wife and I visited Nepal, I examined her again and became acquainted with the King. When the King recently had a coronary heart attack at the moment of shooting a tiger from a tree at his hunting lodge in the Himalaya Mountains, the United States State Department was requested to send a heart consultant. Dr. Willis Hurst of Atlanta, cardiologist to President Johnson, was unable to go and so I was asked for. Since I too could not go because of other important commitments, Tom Mattingly of Washington flew to Nepal. He told me later that he found the King being well cared for by Nepalese physicians in a hospital tent which had been set up at the foot of the very tree from which he shot the tiger.

Finally, in Australia and Japan and Taiwan I have been consulted by leading officials, who have still more convinced me that we are all fellow citizens of one world. This conviction has been further strengthened by several Russian and Chinese immigrants to this country, who have become my patients. The human body is truly international and the basic rules of health apply everywhere in the world.

Although there are extremes of courage and of cowardice, and of constant complaining and of stoicism under the stress of illness—and I believe that I have seen them all—it has been my experience that the average person, over a wide range, is a "good" patient and with adequate information from his doctor (and I would like to stress adequate and full information and discussion) , he is satisfactorily cooperative. Sometimes there is overmuch bravado, or assumed lack of interest in his illness, which attitudes the doctor must penetrate, just as there is excessive fear of symptoms and of the future, which demands at least sympathetic understanding and ample reassurance when justified. Less than one per cent of my patients (men and women alike, although the latter are somewhat preponderant) , make up about fifty per cent of my perpetual telephone callers. One naturally hesitates to tell them off, because once in a great while, sometimes after years of apprehension, a call is justified, and my reply may quiet the caller for months to come, though rarely much longer.

Most physicians lack the time and patience to devote to these hypochondriacs, who are looking for attention which they fail to receive from family or friends—a few finally outgrow such dependency on the medical profession, particularly if some brightness comes into their lives. It is a few such patients who can drive a doctor to distraction or, I imagine, even to drink. I suppose that we all have our share. But thank God for the other patients, who are much in the majority.

There is proverbial fear of anything wrong with the heart in contrast to other organs, except perhaps for the brain. This has been more or less natural throughout the ages, since the heart has always been recognized as the vital organ ever since man recognized that it pulsates and that to pierce it is likely to cause death. Superstition is still rife in much of the world but is rapidly melting under the glare of medical publicity. And it is not so very long ago that my father accomplished wonders with his sugar pills, which were often more effective than more official psychotherapy of the day— but of course the sugar pills were also psychotherapy. At any rate by that time, at the turn of the century, bleeding, vomiting, and purging were happily no longer popular in New England.

Another question that has been asked me concerns racial, climatic, and geographical differences. I have already mentioned the rugged health and great longevity of certain mountain people who have weathered the infections and accidents of youth, as in the Hunza Valley in the Himalayas, and certain districts of the republic of Georgia in the Caucasus. The fame of certain hill people, as in the Northwest Territory of Pakistan, the Sikhs of India, and the Evzones of Macedonia, as warriors, is well known, but I doubt if this can be ascribed wholly to their physical way of life, although vigorous physical activity and the avoidance of gross obesity are prominent features of them all. Heredity and local cultural traits are doubtless more important factors. But in every civilization and race and all through history there have been heroes and cowards, both physical and spiritual, in every land on earth.

Finally, I am sometimes asked about my fees for consultation. They vary, of course, depending upon the means of the patient, and have ranged from zero and five dollars on up. In the case of the truly wealthy, such as industrial magnates, kings, and dictators, I have also asked on occasion for additional hundreds or thousands, to be donated to heart research and other cardiological causes.

Retirement and the 1950s

CHAPTER XI

I found rather suddenly a new freedom, when in the late 1940s I retired from both the active directorship of the Cardiac Laboratory and Clinics at the M.G.H. and also from my undergraduate teaching position as clinical professor of medicine, in order to devote more time to the new interest and duties concerned with the United States Public Health Service, and to international medicine.

For over thirty years I had been a sort of prisoner in the hospital, spending most of the days and sometimes the nights, on duties concerned with the care of patients, on clinical research, and on the teaching of residents and internes. I now had a private office about a mile from the hospital at 264 Beacon Street, and during those first few months I walked the streets and paths along the Charles River Basin to and from the hospital with great enjoyment. However, I soon found that my captivity in the hospital was to be followed by a different kind of captivity, not in one place, but in a multitude of places outside the hospital.

My time continued to be fully occupied, but in a much more diffuse way. Private practice continued unabated with many new patients (although with an occasional struggle to reduce their number) and with the follow-up of old patients to whom I had become devoted and who wished to continue with me no matter what I might be doing otherwise. This situation has continued right up to date. I did see more of my family and my nights were less crowded with immediate obligations of practice and writing, but I have continued to take home with me from the office about three hours of work on letters, manuscripts, and journals to read, in order to keep up to date. This last is a heavy task for any doctor, especially in the recent two or three decades, because of the tremendous amount of published research and articles of clinical interest. However, I have always tried to divide my working time evenly, with one third for research, one third for teaching, reading, and writing, and one third for my patients.

Following an expedition to England, Scotland, Scandinavia and Germany en route to the First World Congress of Cardiology in 1950, my wife and young children and I continued as a family to have occasional travels, though not abroad again. Our chief vacation interest was in visits to Wyoming, where we took part in the activities of a working ranch and rode a good deal in the mountains and valleys there. We did not encounter any great difficulties, although we were sometimes on the trail of bears and other wild animals. We visited Yellowstone Park, the Grand Teton Mountains, and other parts of the Rockies. My particular hobby on such expeditions and on my medical travels has been that of three-dimensional photography with a Stereorealist camera, and I now have thousands of interesting stereoscopic photographs from all over the world.

Other family expeditions took us into New Hampshire, Vermont, and Maine and we have tramped, swum, and occasionally golfed and fished in various pleasant spots. In the winters for some years we skied in Canada on the Maple Leaf Trail in the Laurentian mountains, but since my wife and I took up this sport only in middle age we never became experts. But we have continued, even quite recently, to enjoy the skiing across country along the old abandoned roads in southern New Hampshire. One especially ritualistic annual event was to drive in October to southern New Hampshire and Vermont, especially to Newfane, and to climb hills such as Mts. Monadnock and Chocorua, to see the autumn foliage at its brightest. We never took to the sea, although we have enjoyed being guests of real sailors on short boat trips.

In the last few decades our more distant travels have usually been made by air. Actually, my first air travel was in 1922 from Brussels to London, in a very primitive plane; and in 1924, when we went to Europe on our honeymoon, we flew from London to Paris on a ride which was both rough and unpleasant. I did not resume flying until 1944 when Sam Levine, Duckett Jones, and I flew to Mexico City to attend the inauguration of Mexico's National Heart Institute. Following this renewal of flying in 1944 I have spent many, many hours and have covered hundreds of thousands of miles in the air, with only two or three narrow escapes. One of these was in 1948, when I was flying in an unpressurized plane from Prague to Rome. The plane was flying high over the Dolomite Mountains to escape thunderstorms when it was struck by lightning. We were all inhaling oxygen at the time. There was a sudden jolting of the plane, a roar, and a blaze of light lasting a fraction of a second. Then all was quiet and I felt that I had lapsed into eternity. Gradually we all recovered and in half an hour we landed safely in Rome. On another occasion when I was trying to catch a plane from Paris to London a good many years ago, I was much annoyed to arrive too late at the airport for my scheduled flight and was forced to take a later one. On reaching London I saw headlines in the newspaper—the plane I had missed had crashed and everyone aboard had been killed. When I reached my hotel and called up Dr. John Parkinson to tell him that I was sorry to be late for our meeting, he said: "Is it really you? Thank God! We thought you had gone down with the plane."

Now for my professional activities during the decade. There have been three chief interests aside from the continuation of my medical practice. These have been new since my retirement from the M.G.H. staff in 1949 and I shall take them up in order.

The first special interest was that of the Public Health Service appointment in the fall of 1948, as Executive Director of the National Advisory Heart Council, the advisory body to the National Heart Institute, both of which had been set up earlier that year by act of Congress. There were three aspects of this public health activity which together consumed about a third of my time throughout the 1950s. The first was that of the Heart Council meetings in Bethesda, Maryland, attended by six cardiologists and six prominent laymen, who met with us several times a year. There was also present at least one representative of the American Heart Association, a private body, and one cardiologist from each of the military services, Army, Navy, and Air Force, and several of the full-time staff of the National Heart Institute itself. Thus, in addition to the twelve of the Council, there would be a group of perhaps twenty to thirty other concerned persons. At these meetings we would discuss mostly policies and the development of the special interest of cardiovascular research, cardiovascular training, and cardiovascular teaching, both medical and lay. The twelve councillors were selected from across the country so that all regions were represented in the course of a few years. Three new councillors were elected each year to take the place of those who had finished their service.

My experience through the eight years in which I served the National Advisory Council was extraordinarily interesting, for one reason because it enabled me to become acquainted with leaders both in the cardiovascular field and among prominent nonmedical laymen. These friendships have endured. Many important decisions were made at each meeting, helping to direct and support the work of the Institute itself. During the 1950s, a large research hospital connected with the National Institute of Health was built. Each one of the National Institutes of Health—those of Cancer, Heart, Mental Health, Dentistry and others—had its place in this important clinical research facility at Bethesda. Meeting with us on each occasion would be the surgeon general of the Public Health Service, and we learned from him a great deal about the political aspects of the relationships of the Public Health Service to the Administration and to Congress. He kept us informed, for instance, on impending or possible changes in the attitude of Congress or of the White House toward our own efforts in behalf of public health. This information was always useful.

A second very important activity of ours, which was theoretically unofficial and which had to be done at times in which we were not obligated to the duties of the Institute itself, was that of attending hearings on heart and blood vessel diseases held by committees for appropriations for public health, both in the House and in the Senate. Among the chairmen of these committees who stand out in my memory were three individuals—John Fogarty of the House, with whom I had many years of fruitful experience and friendship, and Senators Chavez and Hill. John Fogarty and the two Senators had acquired through their experience at these hearings a great mass of information and knowledge about diseases of all kinds and of all systems. They had become so expert that they were able frequently to ask the right questions to stimulate the support of the House of Representatives and of the Senate in allocating needed funds for the development of our programs. Our testimony at the hearings was recorded in the Congressional Record, and much important information on the evolution of the governmental heart program can be found in these records, dating back to the first hearings in the spring of 1949.

We also became acquainted as lobbyists with many other individual congressmen and senators, including our own Massachusetts Leverett Saltonstall and John Kennedy; the former I had known when he was governor and I continued to call on Kennedy after he became president. They were both very helpful to our cause.

Gradually money became available through these hearings, about $3,000,000 in the first year and after that slowly increasing year by year until well over $100,000,000 was allocated out of public funds (tax money) by the House and Senate each year for the national cardiovascular program. To strengthen our testimony at the hearings it became our custom to bring recovered patients to the hearings, as concrete evidence of the benefit that previous funds had procured for the citizens of the United States. This practice was most effective. It happened not infrequently that prominent members of the government became especially interested in our work when they themselves developed heart disease (as many of them did) and became our patients. This happened in the case of Vice-president Alben Barkley, who suffered congestive heart failure secondary to uncontrolled atrial flutter, and whom I attended in great secrecy at the Naval Hospital in Bethesda (as I mentioned in Chapter X). After the Veep had convalesced and he and his wife had come to learn something about his own case in particular and heart problems in general, he took me to see President Truman, who in turn sent me to the Bureau of the Budget; it seemed at the time a good idea to try to have an adequate allocation of funds presented by the Bureau of the Budget as an administrative act under the president. Later, however, we decided it was far better to have the

Paul Dudley White and his wife, Ina Reid, in front of their antique cottage on Poor Farm Road in Harvard, Massachusetts, 1963.

Courtesy of Theodore F. Polumbaum

legislature increase the annual amount of our needed funds than to have it all fixed originally by the Budget Bureau. This was chiefly because we realized that we were gradually educating both bodies of the Congress, and through them, the public at large. This decision has been fully justified in the years that have passed since we made it.

Committee members of the House and the Senate were also not immune to heart attacks, and like Mr. Barkley they became more interested in our work after they themselves had suffered. This helped very much in the evolution of the tremendous heart program in this country during the last twenty years. For example, Mr. Fogarty of Rhode Island developed coronary thrombosis during his and my tenures of office and became a regular visitor to me in Boston for some years before his death. On one occasion during my years of attendance at his committee hearings in Congress I brought with me, as was my wont, an interesting and prominent patient of mine from a southern state, a businessman who had had a very successful surgical operation for valvular disease of the heart. After I had introduced him to the committee and described his case, proving thereby that previous funds for research which had been voted by Congress had been very useful, Mr. Fogarty asked my patient three questions, as follows:

Mr. Fogarty: "Were you forced to retire from your work because of complete invalidism before that operation?"

Mr. X: "Yes, Sir."

Mr. Fogarty: "And now you are back working full-time again?"

Mr. X: "Yes, Sir."

Mr. Fogarty: "And again paying taxes?"

Mr. X: "Yes, Sir."

That conversation was printed in the Congressional Record for all the other legislators and the public to read.

Finally, in connection with our activity with the Public

Health Service, we spent much time making project site visits all over the country in groups of two, three, or even more of the staff of the Institute combined with members of the National Advisory Heart Council. These project site visits to determine the justification for grants applied for by medical schools, hospitals, and public health programs in various states were very instructive to us and we became acquainted with important work developing in many of the centers in this country. The tremendous progress made in the United States in the study and control of cardiovascular disease can be directly related to these project site visits and decisions of the amounts and places of funding.

Some very interesting places visited were Negro medical schools and other areas where so-called "seed money" was needed in order to develop research and training. I remember, for example, a visit to the University Hospital at Jackson, Mississippi, where a marvelous transformation had taken place: within a relatively few years the institution had changed from a sleepy small medical unit to a thriving large center, fully equipped and staffed to carry out intensive research and extensive training, in addition to providing the best care possible for its patients.

During this decade I was also involved with American Heart Association activities, especially in supporting and stimulating interest in the annual heart drives and at the annual meetings of the affiliates during the month of February each year. In the spring of 1969 I myself visited fifteen different states to support the local heart associations in their fund raising, especially necessary since government support has had to be reduced because of inflation and the war in Viet Nam.

Suddenly in 1949 there had occurred the same sort of change in public attitudes that took place in governmental support of the cardiovascular program. Lay membership in the American Heart Association stimulated the annual drives and from almost no private money for research during the previous twenty-five years, the private support of research increased into surprising millions—although never so voluminously as the funds from the Public Health Service. It has been very important to have the private as well as the public arm of this support, since now and then we need to take a little risk in the backing of individuals or of programs that can be dramatically successful in the end but may seem too chancy to take a risk with tax money. Many of us were involved in both programs, public and private, moving constantly from one to the other.

Possibly even more important to me in the 1950s than the heart programs and my own practice, was my increasing and intense preoccupation with international cardiology. I have already written of the beginning of this in 1944 in Mexico City, and of the First World Congress of Cardiology in Paris in 1950. Between 1950 and 1954 there were efforts made to begin some international cardiological research through a special committee of the International Society. However, we had very little in the way of funds to develop any of this. In 1954 I went for my first epidemiological research training in the field to Naples in Italy, to work under Ancel Keys, with his team of international investigators from six or eight countries, in a comparison of the findings of four groups of the population. About seventy-five of the leading citizens in business and the professions who constituted the membership of the local Rotary Club, 150 steel workers, 150 city firemen, and 150 city clerks were studied physiologically, biochemically, and medically; the physical laborers in the steel mills were compared with the partially physically active firemen, the relatively inactive clerks, and the almost wholly inactive "patricians." The amount of coronary heart disease varied accordingly, being least in the physical laborers and most in the well-to-do, who had their own automobiles and other such luxuries and who were also overnourished. Professor Mattioli of Naples, who has been a very able cardiologist with large private practice, was at the time of our investigations there preparing a second edition of his book on coronary heart disease, based on 2,000 of his own well-to-do patients in Naples and environs. This was further evidence that the disease did exist in that area as it had in Boston years earlier, but was largely limited to the small minority of the inhabitants who were not seen in the hospitals, which were still limited to the care of the poor.

We also made a brief study of the population of Bologna, where there is a much higher level of rich diet, and we found more coronary heart disease than we had found in Naples. Incidentally, the only woman that I myself encountered in Naples with coronary heart disease was an American tourist. Taken sick there, she became a patient of mine, at first in Italy and then at home; she lived about fifteen years after that attack.

The next important event in connection with international cardiology occurred in 1957, three years after the Second World Congress of Cardiology in Washington. That was the beginning of the International Society of Cardiology Foundation, a mixture of laymen and doctors, incorporated in Chicago by Dr. Louis Katz and myself in 1957. (It is now called the International Cardiology Federation and is based in Geneva.) The purpose of this organization was wholly to support the International Society of Cardiologists by raising money for research, training, and education, and for Congresses and other meetings. This had a slow start but was expedited when we found a vigorous international businessman, Albert Baer, who at a Youth Hostels Board meeting volunteered his services to me, and who later became Chairman of the Lay Committee of our International Cardiology Foundation. Some of my medical travels since then have been with him, to stimulate the formation of programs like our own here in the United States that we started earlier in the fifties. We have been to many parts of the world to-gether—Latin America, Israel, Egypt, India, Japan, and European countries. We found that everyone was interested in our suggestions, but that Finland, India, Ireland, and Italy and now Japan and Mexico have been especially receptive.

Finally, before writing of the professional subjects which concerned my colleagues and myself during the 1950s, I would like to mention a few special foreign missions in which I was involved.

Late in 1950, a telephone call from the State Department asked if I would go to Pakistan at the request of Governor General Ghulam Mohammed, an old patient of mine, who had asked for me as part of Point IV aid.* Early in 1951 I carried out this mission, starting in Karachi, where I lived in the governor general's palace and worked with the staff of the medical school. I then went on to Lahore in the West Punjab and Peshawar in the Northwest Frontier, where I was a guest of the local governors. Finally I flew to Dacca, in East Pakistan, where I had another stimulating ten days as guest of the local Governor and his wife. In each of these places I was asked to spend the evenings busily examining the heads of state and their families, to complete my daily schedule of medical conferences.

During these travels I was particularly interested to note that each of the Governors had, as aide-de-camp, a former British general or colonel, left over from the days of British rule in India. Evidently their deep affection for the country in which they had served for so many years led them to stay on in a subordinate position when the British rule ended. Before we left Pakistan my wife and I were driven to the

---

* My wife reminds me that on an earlier visit of the governor general to the U.S.A., when he was Pakistan minister of finance, he had come one evening to our home for dinner, and before he left he lined the four of us up in the front hall and measured our feet. A few months later there arrived four pairs of beautifully and intricately embroidered shoes with gracefully turned-up toes, for us to wear on state occasions.

remarkable ruins of Mo-en-jo-daro, the ancient brick city on the Tigris River, contemporary of Ur of the Chaldees, and only partly excavated.

At the end of my stay in Pakistan, the governor general telephoned Rajkumari Amrit Kaur, then Minister of Health of India, and suggested that she might like to act as hostess to my wife and myself. Happily, she agreed. And so we spent ten days in the President's palace in New Delhi, where we were privileged to walk in the glorious gardens. We visited some of the countryside and saw also the beautiful Taj Mahal in Agra. We had conferences with the Indian doctors, and became better acquainted with a remarkably able and attractive lady doctor named Sivaramakrishna Padmavati. Soon afterward, she became the first member from India to attend one of the early meetings of the International Council of Cardiology; this was despite protests of some of her male colleagues, who referred to her as "only a woman." But in most of Asia women have been "liberated" since then.

On my way back from Pakistan and India, I paid my first visit to Israel and saw the medical school in Jerusalem, then housed in separate buildings, one of them a former harem; the important Hadassah Medical Center had yet to be constructed. I did this for the Hadassah ladies in Boston and made a report to them when I returned. Since then I have revisited Israel on several occasions and have watched the medical growth of that remarkable little country with much admiration.

My first mission to Latin America came when I went to Cuba in the 1940s, to give some lectures and to see some patients. I made several visits to Cuba after that, the final one in 1956, when the Fifth Inter-American Congress of Cardiology was held in Havana. At that time Batista was still the president, but he was soon displaced by Castro. Four years before this, the previous Congress had met in Buenos

Aires,* and I had taken the occasion at that time to travel widely throughout South America and to increase considerably my acquaintanceship with Latin American cardiology.

The Second World Congress of Cardiology, over which I presided, brought 1,000 participants to Washington in 1954, and was a wonderful experience for many of us because it brought together not only our old friends from all over the western world, but also doctors from many other areas— including two Russians, Professor Petrovsky, a thoracic surgeon and now minister of health, and Professor Tareev, a medical man and author of an important text book. They came unexpectedly and were our first contact with Russians after many years. It was only after we had been able to arrange for them to stay in the United States longer than the five days originally allotted and to be given permission to take the post-Congress tour, that they became less restrained and joined in our various activities. At the end of the Congress they invited a small group to the Russian Embassy and gave a delightful luncheon, which was followed by the film "Swan Lake." They joined the tour of about 100 doctors to Baltimore, New York, Philadelphia, and Boston, and we became well acquainted with them; from that time on, we have been able to talk to Russian doctors with reasonable frankness, and to our mutual benefit.

In 1956 I took part in four very important expeditions. The first was to Finland, where I addressed the president and Parliament in the great hall (aula) of the university and talked of our experience in the United States in the development of cooperative and coordinated medical and lay team work in the U.S. Public Health and American Heart Association programs in cardiovascular disease. From Helsinki, I led a group of five other doctors to Russia, the first U.S. doctors officially to go to Moscow after the death of

* The Sixth Inter-American Congress of Cardiology was in Brazil in 1960.

Stalin. There we had a most interesting contact with the Soviet cardiologists, headed by Professor Myasnikov. We met at his institute but we traveled elsewhere too, and saw again the two professors who had come to Washington in 1954 for the Second World Congress of Cardiology—Professors Petrovsky and Tareev. It was during this visit that I came to understand the monumental problems which the Soviet Union had faced and was trying to surmount.

Under the Czars there was a very limited number of well-trained physicians, although world-famous Russian medical scientists included Botkin, Machnikov, Pavlov, Korotkov, and Samoiloff. The handful of physicians and surgeons with close connections with Western Europe served a very small proportion of the population, namely the well-to-do, and vast numbers of peasants, serfs, and paupers in the cities had only the most primitive care, if any at all. There had long been a cult of healing, without scientific background, and this was passed on from father to son. Bleeding, cupping, the use of native plants to induce vomiting or purgation were the rule, as in medieval times. Also (as in China) acupuncture—a procedure of needling in "strategic" areas of the body—was practiced. Often patients were better off with no "therapy," trusting to nature for spontaneous cure. Periodically epidemics carried off tens of thousands of victims.

At the time of the Bolshevik Revolution, Russian medicine reached its lowest ebb because of the flight or deaths of many of the intelligentsia, including almost all the well-trained professors and practitioners of medicine. The doctors who did not leave the country were, like uncounted millions of other Russians at that time, victims of the great plague of exanthematic typhus or of starvation, and often the two were combined. Many towns and villages were destitute of survivors. It was a fearful period, of which we in the West heard little. I have mentioned it in Chapter III.

From this holocaust Soviet medicine very slowly emerged, but for years there were far too few well-trained physicians.

Public health was very wisely their first objective, and slowly but surely their high death rates of infants and their mothers from dysentery, child bed fever, and tuberculosis were reduced to levels comparable to those of Western Europe and North America. Advances in internal medicine and surgery and the specialties were much slower, due to lack of facilities, instrumentation, and intensive training. At the time of my first visit to Moscow and Leningrad in 1956 cardiology was only just beginning to emerge as a growing interest, although the country was still riddled by rheumatic fever and hypertension. Coronary heart disease was beginning to attract attention as a growing menace, as it had been already with us for almost a generation.

After the death of Stalin, Soviet physicians were finally allowed out of the country and more of us were allowed in, and the isolationism of Soviet medicine began to dissolve as we established warm and understanding friendships with a host of Soviet physicians and surgeons. In the last decade all the specialties in Soviet Russia have made great strides.

At the time of this first of my visits to the U.S.S.R. Dr. Maria Kovrigina, who was Minister of Health and had sent me the original invitation, was most cordial and arranged a ten-day program for us. Then, as well as before and since, there was a preponderance of women over men in medicine in the U.S.S.R. in the ratio of 3 to 1, but in leading positions the ratio seemed to be reversed. It was still a man's world. Apparently three factors were responsible: first, the high mortality among the men in both world wars; second, the low prestige of medicine after the Bolshevik revolution, engineering being much more in demand; and third, since women were obliged to work for the state, quite naturally they preferred the profession of medicine to hard labor in the streets. When we visited hospitals and research institutes we found women manning most of the laboratories, many of them in the role of technicians.

I have paid several visits to the U.S.S.R., besides the

ones in 1956 and 1966. The occasion for one was a cancer congress in 1960, after I had been made a member of the Soviet Academy of Medical Science, one of the first ten foreign members. These members were half from noncommunist countries (England, France, Italy, India, and the United States) and half from communist countries (China, Czechoslovakia, Hungary, Poland, and Roumania).

To return to 1956: my wife and I went to Japan to join Ancel Keys in a study of a population of miners, doctors, and American servicemen stationed at Fukuoka on the southern island of Kyushu. This was chiefly at the invitation of Noboru Kimura, an old friend, who had first traveled to Buenos Aires with me to attend the Congress there in 1952. This Japanese research again proved of much importance in the study of possible causes of coronary heart disease in younger people.

As we had done in Naples in 1954, so in Fukuoka we recorded data of several hundreds of young and middle-aged male subjects as to their height, weight, thickness of skin folds (for obesity), pulse, blood pressure, heart examination, electrocardiograms, blood chemical findings, hemoglobin, urine, and also their family histories, past illnesses, habits, physical activities, and symptoms. We then compared the three groups (miners, doctors, and American servicemen). We found the Japanese miners to be freer from risk factors, which are primarily a diet rich in animal fat, obesity, physical inactivity, heavy use of tobacco, and high level of serum cholesterol. (We found the American Air Force to be more involved than were the Japanese doctors in between.) An important part of the study was prospective, that is, follow-up examinations of the same individuals at intervals of five years. This plan has been followed in the so-called epidemiological (cause of disease) population studies all over the world. To date they all indicate that young males of the United States have the highest degrees of risk factors.

We followed that visit to Japan by the first studies in Hawaii of the Japanese population, which had originally come from Fukuoka. There we found among the same race much more coronary disease than we had found in Japan. They were already beginning to be contaminated by American ways of life; later it was shown that there was a still higher degree of trouble among the Japanese living on the West Coast of the United States. This is a characteristic contagion that comes to every immigrant to the United States, no matter where he or she is from.

During this Asian swing in 1956, my wife and I also went to the Philippines. In Manila, working with several of our Filipino graduate students in cardiology and with Dr. Kempson Maddox (now Sir Kempson), we organized the Asian Pacific Society of Cardiology. That was its first meeting, succeeded every four years after that by meetings in Australia, Japan, and Israel, respectively.

This whole Asian trip was partly due to another of those "links in the chains of chance," which so often appear in one's life. In the early mid-winter of 1956 I was attending a medical meeting at the Naval Hospital in Bethesda, Maryland, where I gave a talk. At the reception which followed I met Admiral Hogan, surgeon general of the Navy. When he heard that I might be planning to go to Japan later that spring to join Professor Keys in a research project, he turned to me and said, "Would you and your wife like to be guests on my plane when I go with my headnurse to inspect our naval medical installations in the Pacific?" He could arrange this, he said, if I would agree to give lectures and clinics at each of the naval medical centers which he would visit. I readily agreed and so we were guests of his from Hawaii to Japan, Taiwan, Hong Kong, the Philippines, Guam, Kwajalein, and back to Hawaii. We were greatly interested to find on the hot, windblown desert atoll of Kwajalein a remarkable cultivation of the plant life in nurseries, and collections of shells, fostered by the military personnel, who were inspired to do so by the wife of one of the officers.

One of the most useful and instructive of all my missions overseas was initiated in 1958 by an invitation from the students (and faculty) of the medical schools of the universities of South Africa at Cape Town and Johannesburg to spend a month as Visiting Professor. I decided to travel there down the east side of Africa and up the west. I flew to Cairo where I arrived at the renovated historic Shepheard's Hotel late on the 28th of February, 1959. The next three days I spent with members of the faculty of the University Medical School, in particular Professors Ibrahim, Sami, Sorour, and Badry, with Dr. Tarazi as my guide. I discovered that the U.S. Navy had an important medical research center near Cairo called NAMRU.

On the 4th of March a long starlit night flight brought me to Nairobi in Kenya, where I was an all day guest of Dr. A. D. Charters, who took me to the clinic of the King George VI Hospital, to the beautiful National Game Reserve where between tea time and dinner I saw my first lions, impalas, zebras, and giraffes in the wild, and finally to dine with the doctors and their wives. The next morning I flew to Kisumi on Lake Victoria in Uganda, whence I was driven to Kampala by Dr. John Davies, now pathologist in Albany, New York, and Dr. Alexander Galloway, dean of the Makerere Medical School, who was my genial host for the next four days. I had the pleasure of meeting the faculty at work, including Drs. Hutton, Williams, Shaper, Somers, Wellbourne, and Dean. While in Kampala, I saw something of the protein deficiency disease of young children called kwashiorkor and of the unusual kinds of heart disease described by Davies and others in Uganda, especially the extensive endomyocardial fibroelastosis of unknown cause in young people. In Kampala I visited Makerere Medical School and Mulago Hospital, which are devoted to the medical education of the native black people and are the best institutions of the sort that I saw in Africa.

Then I went on to South Africa where I was lecturer at Cape Town for three weeks and at Johannesburg for one week. It was at that time that I first met Dr. Christiaan Barnard, who was later to perform the first human heart transplant. The medical school at the University of Cape Town was on a par with any that I had seen anywhere in the world, and so I was not surprised when the first such operation was performed there.

While in Cape Town my wife and I had many outings, in addition to our sessions with the students and faculty. One of my outings was a climb up 3,550-foot Table Mountain, where I was initiated into membership in the club called "The Babooneers," which required a climb up the mountain and on the way, imitation of the baboon call. Also, there was a fascinating visit to the famous bird sanctuary islands off the coast of South Africa, where guano (droppings of seafowl, used extensively as fertilizer) is an important governmental export. We also visited one of the large vineyards north of Cape Town, noted for its fine wine.

In Johannesburg we were guests of the Susmans, Moses, an old friend and leading cardiologist, and his wife Helen, often the only member of the opposition in the South African Parliament, a vigorous proponent for the rights of the black population, and for their admission to the universities. They treated us to a visit to the wonderful wild animal preserve at the Kruger National Park, where the giraffes interested me most, both as the most remarkable animals there but especially because of the adjustment of their circulatory system by nature to meet the needs of their great height. In the intervening years their hearts and blood vessels have been studied and have shown a high blood pressure needed for blood to reach the brain, but also a safety vascular mechanism to protect the brain from the effect of the hypertension on lowering the head, and thick arterial walls in the legs to counteract the effect of gravity from the weight of the blood above.

On returning from South Africa we stopped at Leopoldville in the Congo, and there I met Professor Beheyt, Belgian cardiologist, who showed me much of his important work on 1,000 cardiac patients, with not a single case of coronary heart disease, but much hypertension and considerable rheumatic heart disease. Also we visited the famous and beautiful new university and medical school near Leopoldville called Lovanium. This was just before the revolution which drove the Belgians out of the country; after many troubles the Republic has finally settled down, and the university has now reopened its doors with a mixed faculty of native and foreign teachers. It was rather grim in Leopoldville when we were there, with obvious evidence of the impending rebellion, and we were quite fearful on some occasions, although we were not actually harmed. We were sorry for the governor general, who was obviously distraught, at a state dinner honoring a number of foreign guests, including ourselves.

From Leopoldville we went across the Congo River to the other republic of the Congo and visited the headquarters of the World Health Organization for Africa, at Brazzaville. There we inquired about the possibility of their adding certain cardiovascular subjects such as hypertension to their other health investigations. They begged our patience, since as they said, there were so many more urgent things to do— such as the identification of 1,000,000 lepers needing diagnosis and treatment. From Brazzaville we went to Gabon, to Libreville and thence to Lambaréné, a town across the river from Schweitzer's hospital on the Igooué River. At Schweitzer's hospital we were guests for a week and had many talks with this extraordinary man, more philosopher than doctor, who had spent the better part of his life working hard to treat the poor sick natives of that countryside but making little impression on the country's sad state of public health. He did, however, stimulate many others to take up the challenge. (See *American Journal of Cardiology,* 1962, X, 432.) His daughter, Madame Eckert, is one of the many people who has devotedly carried on and expanded her father's work.

During the decade of the 1950s I was involved in the publication of five new books and two new editions, the fourth of *Heart Disease* in 1951 and the third of *Electrocardiography in Practice* (with others) in 1952. The new books included *Coronary Heart Disease in Young Adults,* a pioneer classic, published by a group of us who had carried out important research on the subject. Another was *Clues in the Diagnosis and Treatment of Heart Disease,* with two editions in 1955 and 1956. This was translated into five other languages—Russian, French, Yugoslavian, Japanese, and Spanish. The next, in 1956, was *Cardiovascular Epidemiology* with Ancel Keys reporting a symposium of the Second World Congress of Cardiology in Washington in 1954. Then there were two small books on rehabilitation, one in 1957 called *Cardiovascular Rehabilitation* and a Symposium in 1958 called *Rehabilitation of the Cardiovascular Patient.* Both books were written by Howard Rusk, Philip Lee, Brian Williams, and myself.

I would add that although I had retired as chief of the Heart Unit at the M.G.H., during the 1950s I saw a good deal of the twenty-two cardiovascular residents and fellows and the forty-four graduate students (thirty-two of whom were foreign), who were involved for longer or shorter times in our researches and follow-up.

Subjects which especially interested us during the decade (in great contrast to the 1920s) included in the first place coronary heart disease. Next was the long (twenty-five years and more) follow-up of many of my patients, who had taught me much which I eventually assembled in book form.

I have always recommended a careful follow-up and recording of their rich experience to other physicians, whether specialists, internists, or family doctors.

Just as we had always been interested in the heart diseases of youth, so we* analyzed the autopsies of the aged—968 of them over sixty years of age. We found that heart attacks were often less severe in the aged but that kidney diseases tended to contribute importantly to the mortality of the very old. A noted patient was Charles Thiery, already referred to in Chapter IX ("Swollen Ankles"), who with familial longevity and good health habits, lived to the age of 107½ and finally succumbed to pneumonia. During this study, I recommended much walking at whatever pace seemed suitable, for my aged patients as well as for all other patients. Clarence De Mar, the famous marathoner, was still racing (although not too fast) in his sixties and eventually died of cancer at seventy. His heart, when examined post-mortem, was healthy and strong, and his coronaries, though sclerotic, were wide open.

It was during the decade of the 1950s that I realized and preached by voice and by pen that the prevention of heart disease should have the first priority over diagnosis and treatment, vital though those were. I had also become convinced that both hereditary and environmental factors played perhaps equally important roles, but needed much more study as to their relative importance. Both themes were over and over supported and emphasized by the epidemiological population studies in which I had become involved.

In describing the events of the 1950s I have omitted one of great importance to my own life: President Dwight D. Eisenhower's heart attack in 1955, my own role in his recovery, and the overwhelming publicity that unexpectedly came to me after I was called to his bedside as a civilian consultant. This episode deserves a chapter of its own.

* Dr. Leon S. Medalia and I.

Gunsbach, Alsace, France, 1959. Seated by the roadside in his native town, Dr. Albert Schweitzer discusses plans with Dr. White concerning an investigation of the jungle villages of Gabon, West Africa. It was from these villages that many patients journeyed by canoe to the Schweitzer Hospital. *Courtesy of Erica Anderson*

Dwight D. Eisenhower and Paul Dudley White at the dinner of the International Cardiology Foundation in New York City, October 29, 1963. *Courtesy of Wide World Photos*

President Eisenhower's
Heart Attack

CHAPTER XII 🙚 What I have written in this chapter is a very detailed account of my own participation in the care of a man notable in his time, but that is not the reason that prompted me to write as I have. The occasion was an opportunity for the medical profession to publicize widely the details of such an illness, because coronary heart disease was reaching epidemic proportions and demanding attention both because of its increasing frequency and its danger, and also because of the need of recognition that it is not always fatal or even permanently incapacitating. For at least twenty years before the President's heart attack we cardiologists had been seeing increasingly hundreds of patients with similar acute disability who had returned to work and had lived for years. For these reasons, and because many of my medical colleagues and lay friends have asked me to present the President's illness in all details as I witnessed it, I have done so. For some it may be dull reading, for others not, but this is the first time that I myself have published it from the very beginning. I talked to the country during those next few weeks as I had talked to families of many private patients.

The twenty-fourth of September, 1955, was indeed a very special day in my career. In the first place, I was put in contact with one of the most dedicated persons in government or military service anywhere in the world, a sincere, honorable, and courageous individual whose greatest desire was to promote world peace. Secondly, I was for weeks, with others, under the stress of the critical care of a man who filled the most important political position in the world of his day. Thirdly, because of these events I, again with others, assumed the obligation to present an objective non-political assessment of his fitness to accept the heavy burdens of the presidential office for a second term. And finally, I myself was suddenly thrown into the spotlight glare of intense publicity for the next year or two, a situation to which I accommodated myself slowly and with difficulty, emerging from the relatively quiet life of a practicing physician and teacher of medicine.

To begin at the beginning, my wife and I were just leaving our home in Belmont, Massachusetts, in the early evening of the twenty-fourth of September to dine with former neighbors of ours in Chestnut Hill, when we turned on the car radio and learned of the President's heart attack. It had occurred early that morning at the home of his mother-in-law in Denver, Colorado; from there he had been taken by his family physician, Major General Howard Leroy Snyder, to the Fitzsimmons Army Hospital. As we left the house in our car my wife turned to me and said that it was a good thing that we had left our host's telephone number with the graduate student who was living with us, but I answered that it was quite unlikely that I would be summoned.

On arrival at the home of our host, an ophthalmological colleague, we joined the other guests at cocktails and met the special guest of the evening, Professor N. M. Gregg of Australia, who had discovered (and reported in 1941) the connection between German measles in the mother during the first three months of pregnancy and various congenital defects, including those of the eyes and of the heart, in the new-born baby.

No sooner were we seated than I was called to the telephone and found a *Boston Globe* reporter, an old friend of mine, on the line. She asked me if I had heard the news and if I were going to Denver. To the first question I answered. "Yes" and to the second "Not that I know." She then said, "If you should be invited to go, please let me know and I'll be there to support you." (I did and she was.) I returned to the party but in a few minutes I was again called to the phone, and this time a *New York Times* reporter repeated the questions that the *Globe* lady had asked and my answers were the same. Once more I returned to the company but once again I was summoned. This time the Surgeon General's office in Washington was on the line and the new question was "Will you go to Denver? If so, we will get in touch with you later about details of travel." My reply, cognizant as I was of both the responsibility and the honor, was "Yes."

After a brief dinner we returned home, where I was alerted to be ready early the next morning to be flown by the U. S. Air Force to Denver. I was told that the President's condition was stable and that my old friend Colonel Thomas Mattingly, chief army cardiologist stationed at the Walter Reed Hospital in Washington, had already gone to Denver and would meet me at Lowry Field, the military airport there.

Early the next morning, September 25, I was taken by army car from Belmont to the Logan Airport in East Boston, where I boarded a huge Air Force jet—the only passenger. The flight was uneventful except that on landing we blew out a tire and came to a stop at the edge of the airfield in a pall of black smoke. A ladder was brought out to the plane and I climbed down to meet the doctors and Sherman Adams, special assistant to the president and a man who was to prove consistently helpful to me both in Denver and afterward in Washington.

On entering Fitzsimmons Army Hospital we were greeted by the staff and went at once to the nurses' station just outside the President's bedroom. We looked over the temperature record, the notes of the doctors and nurses, the laboratory test data, and the electrocardiograms. It was obvious that very careful records were being kept, in apple pie order, with as little fuss as possible. It was now the middle of the afternoon. We made only a short visit to the President, so as not to tire him. He was in a large and comfortable oxygen tent, drowsy under sedation and free from any pain, shortness of breath, or other symptoms. It was the first time that we had ever met, and he smiled when I greeted him. I felt his pulse, took his blood pressure, and listened to his heart and lungs. All seemed normal. This took about twelve minutes. I told him that he was doing well and that I would examine him more fully the next morning. This was now thirty-six hours after a perfectly typical coronary heart attack (thrombosis) with damaged (necrotic) heart muscle (infarction, later to become a scar) about the size of a large olive, in the anterior wall of the left ventricle (heart chamber).

The next event, which quickly followed my examination of the president, was a short medical consultation between Colonel Mattingly and me on the one hand and General Snyder and the hospital staff on the other. We were all in close agreement as to diagnosis and treatment, and happily we remained in accord throughout the President's seven weeks in Denver.

Immediately after the medical consultation Tom Mattingly, Colonel George M. Powell (the director of the hospital), and I met with Vice-President Nixon, Sherman Adams, James Hagerty (press secretary to the President), and a few other key personnel to discuss first the President's illness in some detail and the prognosis (the future); second, what should be done concerning the President's job during his illness; and third, what to tell the country at the official news conference—the first of these having been scheduled for 10 A.M. the next morning.

Up until this time, it had been the custom to maintain a high degree of secrecy concerning the illnesses of high government officials. Thus the nature of the incapacitating illness of President Woodrow Wilson was kept from the public; not until after his death did it become generally known that President Franklin D. Roosevelt had suffered a cardiac and cerebral illness for several years and was in bad health at the time of the fateful Yalta Conference. As recently as November, 1950, I myself had been forced to practice great secrecy in my visits to the bedside of Vice-president Alben Barkley. Now all this was about to be changed.

Jim Hagerty told us that he had been so concerned over the question of publicity that he had felt obliged to open the oxygen tent in the hospital and wake the President, who was sleeping from the effects of medication. He asked the President how much publicity he would recommend in letting the public know about his condition. The President opened his eyes, thought for a moment, and then said three words, and went to sleep again. Those three words were: "Tell them everything." This wise order was greatly appreciated and fully followed by the physicians and others involved and was the key to all our news gatherings. A breath of fresh air had blown through the old policy!

Following this conference I met Mrs. Eisenhower and their son John, and was able to give them some reassurance based on the fact that the President's general condition was satisfactory and without complications some forty hours after the onset of his heart attack. After dinner with the hospital staff, Tom Mattingly and I visited the President again briefly at 9:45 P.M., took a pleasant walk on the hospital grounds, and retired for the night in one of the bedrooms provided for visitors to the hospital. After going to bed, we discussed at length details of the President's illness and its treatment and also plans for our press conference the next morning. It had been a busy day.

The next morning at 8:30, Drs. Mattingly, Pollock, Snyder, and I visited the President again and I made a more complete examination and more critical review of the evolution of his illness as best shown in his electrocardiograms. The nurse reported that he had slept from 10 P.M. till midnight, had awakened to be carried by two strong and expert Negro corpsmen to the toilet for a very helpful bowel movement, after which, with the aid of a hypnotic, he had slept soundly till 6 A.M. He had enjoyed his breakfast of prunes, oatmeal, and milk just before our arrival. We found him in quite good condition, now fifty-four hours after the onset of his attack, except for frequent premature beats, both atrial and ventricular as shown by electrocardiogram, for which quinidine sulphate every few hours proved to be helpful. He was already receiving anticoagulant therapy, begun on his entrance to the hospital by Colonel Pollock, one of the pioneers in the use of coumadin. His pulse (heart) rate was a little fast at 90 per minute, and his blood pressure was 115 millimeters mercury systolic and 65 diastolic. The heart sounds were mediocre but there were no murmurs, gallop, or pericardial friction, although the superimposed pericarditis did become manifest by ear and by electrocardiogram later that evening and the next day. The rectal temperature was still normal at 99.6° but that night and the next day it reached a maximum of 100.4° and then subsided. At the same time there was a slight elevation of the white blood cell (leukocyte) count to 9,800 and a rise of the blood sedimentation rate to 29.

All these tests were consistent with the diagnosis of damage of the heart muscle (infarction) but of only moderate degree, and their rapid subsidence was favorable evidence of the probability of a good recovery (that is a good prognosis or future) unless some unexpected and unlikely complication should supervene in the next ten days. These tests, the good so-called vital signs, blood pressure and lack of evidence of heart failure, the physiologically normal bowel movement, and his clear mental state except when somewhat subdued by medication, were justification for our reasonably favorable forecast later that morning at our first press conference. I note, however, that on my record cards of that day I wrote: "Still seriously and acutely ill but no complications so far. I don't like the heart sounds or rather fast pulse, and many premature beats, but there are favorable points otherwise. The next few days are critical."

At ten o'clock that morning we assembled in the large press room at Lowry Airbase. There were about 150 White House and other noted and mostly senior reporters present from all over the country. Five of us sat at a kind of head table. I, having been asked to be the spokesman, sat in the middle, with General Snyder on my right and James Hagerty on my left. To Hagerty's left was Tom Mattingly and to Snyder's right was Colonel Pollock. We began with my fifteen minute statement concerning President Eisenhower's condition and a description of the disease itself. This was later broadcast throughout the country and I suppose did more than any previous efforts to inform the public about the disease that had become the great American epidemic. In fact, thousands of patients who were having fresh attacks of this nature during the next few weeks and months and even years, had listened to this first of our Denver conferences and to those that followed and were already helpfully informed.

After my initial statement there followed fifteen minutes of questions, most of which I answered, except for those of a political nature, which I turned over to Jim Hagerty.

I must add one more item about this press conference. During my statement about the President's illness, I had mentioned the good news that we had received on our visit to him that morning, of a successful bowel movement. As far as I knew, nothing of this nature had ever before been announced at a press conference, but knowing that a good many thousands of physicians would be listening to my statement, I emphasized this normal physiological event so early in his illness as a favorable prognostic sign, because I wanted my medical colleagues throughout the world to be fully posted. After the conference one of the British reporters said to me: "Dr. White you certainly are very frank. Just suppose that our Queen were ill!" Later, I did receive in my copious fan mail two or three letters, the writers of which said that although they were pleased to hear of the President's good progress, they wished I had not mentioned his bowels. But as I told a reporter at the time: "I insisted that this item be put in because I knew the country would be well pleased, especially the doctors."

Before I left Denver that afternoon, I wrote a number of recommendations on the President's hospital record. For the sake of any medical readers of this book, I now reproduce them: "Continue careful nursing and quiet atmosphere. Chest up at 30° angle much of the day [a position much easier for the heart than sitting straight up or lying flat]. Continue to lift and carry to toilet for bowel movements, and to move legs. Oxygen tent to be omitted at intervals today. Medicines symptomatically except for anticoagulant routinely. Light Diet. Dr. Mattingly to remain another two days and Dr. Pollock to report by phone to P.D.W. twice daily for a few days. P.D.W. to return to Denver and to see the president in two weeks with Dr. Mattingly and later at his farm at Gettysburg."

That same day there was some debate about the altitude of Denver, which is about 5,000 feet. Some people felt that it, plus a busy day of fishing and golf, had been responsible for the President's heart attack and that it would be wise to move him at once to sea level. However, we learned that Dr. Samuel Gilbert Blount of Denver had taken care of heart patients both at sea level and in Denver and had found that there was no difference on either count between the two barometric pressures; he advised us not to move the president and we were glad not to, because of the extra strain, both physical and emotional, that would ensue were we to move him in the first critical days of his illness. Incidentally, when some persons blamed the President's golf for his heart attack, my answer was that quite likely if he hadn't played golf so much he might well have had his heart attack years earlier. I felt that his golf itself had been largely protective of his health and that the heart attack was about due anyway.

Some doctors and laymen, that day and later too, thought that I should remain in Denver constantly for a few weeks. I believed and acted differently for two reasons: first, because I wanted the country to know that I had implicit confidence in the army cardiologists, Colonels Mattingly and Pollock, and that there were also excellent civilian consultants there in Denver; and second, because I was optimistic myself about the recovery of the President and I wanted the country to share my optimism, though, of course, with our fingers crossed.

And so on the afternoon of the twenty-sixth, I returned east in the President's private airplane, the *Columbine*, with the Vice-President and Sherman Adams. That evening at 11 P.M. I received from Colonel Pollock a telephone report of his late findings concerning the president's condition and for the following week I discussed his state of health twice a day with either Colonel Pollock or Colonel Mattingly before we issued our daily news bulletins.

At home I faced a steady barrage of reporters, who not only invaded my office by phone and in person but who also haunted my home in Belmont, day and night. They appeared at breakfast time—we gave them coffee—and at all other times, quizzing my wife and watching and photographing every move I made, even to recording the weekly event of my son Sandy's and my bringing our emptied trash barrels down the drive to the house.

One of the interesting but often bothersome results of my attending President Eisenhower has been the *effect* of all this publicity, which has been both helpful and troublesome. Among the helpful results have been my greater influence in both medical and lay circles in promoting good medical causes of all kinds. The public prestige that came my way increased my usefulness as a speaker at meetings, both medical and lay, and I know that frequently my name has helped in fund raising or even in the passage of useful legislation. Also, my contacts abroad have been enhanced. Happily, some of the affection that most people throughout the world held for Ike was passed down to me. I was indeed fortunate in having been one of his physicians.

On the other hand, my mail and telephone lines both at the office and at home were for many months swamped with letters and calls from reporters and writers galore. The great majority of these letters and calls were pleasant and often of interest; but I felt obligated to answer more than half of them, and this was time-consuming. Some of these correspondents, whom I have never seen, still send me Christmas cards every year. Many of them have been cardiacs themselves and now and then their doctors write me.

Another troublesome but infrequent result of my publicity has been the unauthorized use of my name and even photograph in advertisements in newspapers or journals. This sort of thing requires the bother of writing to the advertiser and requesting him to desist, and it continues right up to date.

One other result of my publicity has been recognition of me on the streets, in the shops and hotels, and in the airports in many cities in this country and sometimes abroad. I try to avoid awareness of this, except when spoken to, and I try not to take advantage of it by being ushered into planes ahead of others. Once in a while it has been troublesome to be recognized by my neighbor on a plane just as I am settling down to work (as I usually do in the air). However, a friendly explanation suffices, and we converse when the luncheon or dinner trays are served.

All in all, the publicity, I think, has been more helpful and pleasant than the reverse.

After a few days of this glare of publicity, my family and I fled to Vermont at what happened to be, in any case, the time of our usual annual pilgrimage to Newfane in early October, when the foliage is at its best. At subsequent press conferences back in Denver, I was able to give the reporters a good description of the beauty of a New England autumn. The Newfane Inn, incidentally, had installed a direct private line to Denver so that I was not out of touch.

Another of the reasons for my return to the East was that I felt the need for consulting the most expert advice obtainable about the President's electrocardiograms. Although I had had, myself, much experience concerning the changes resulting from ischemia (lack of blood supply) and scarring (infarction) of the heart muscle, I believed that my medical colleagues and the public at large would appreciate the sharing of my responsibility with one of the world's foremost authorities, Professor Eugene Lepeschkin of the University of Vermont at Burlington. So I arranged to have him drive down to Newfane with his wife, and after dinner we spread over the beds all of the President's electrocardiograms that had been taken to date, and studied them carefully. I was happy to observe that Professor Lepeschkin and our Denver team were in agreement. The next day, upon my return to Denver, I reported this consultation at my second press conference. Dr. Lepeschkin was immediately besieged for further comments as to prognosis, an onslaught which his equanimity managed to survive.

Slowly, but steadily, the President convalesced. When I examined him with Drs. Pollock, Snyder, and Mattingly, on October 8 (a fortnight after his attack), I found him in good spirits and looking and feeling perfectly well. His heart rate was regular at 72, his blood pressure was 132 systolic and 80 diastolic, and his heart sounds were much improved, without murmurs. His serum cholesterol was a low normal at 174 mg.%; it had been normal in 1950 when he was President of Columbia University. The electrocardiogram was typical of a healing anterior heart muscle scar (myocardial infarct of moderate size) with no R waves in chest Leads to $V_1 V_4$ inclusive.

We decided to keep him at rest for another week, but to allow him—because of his restlessness about the state of the nation and of the world—to begin to see his cabinet members. I suggested that he begin with the Postmaster General as the one least likely to bring up a difficult problem, but he demanded to see John Foster Dulles, Secretary of State, first of all. That conference was held three days later, on October 11, and lasted for twenty-five minutes; it was so successful and refreshing to the President that further visits were arranged in sequence with his brother Milton on the thirteenth, Mr. George M. Humphrey, Secretary of the Treasury on the fifteenth, Secretary of Defense Charles E. Wilson on the seventeenth, and so on.

All continued to go well, and I made three more visits to Denver of about twenty-four to thirty-six hours each. These were on October 22, when the President was sitting up in a chair a few hours each day and having daily conferences about his presidential duties, on November 7, when he was walking about and beginning to take the stairs, and on the tenth, the day after he had been visited by the President of Guatemala.

On November 11, we all returned to Washington together on the *Columbine*. Although we would have allowed him to travel back two or three weeks earlier to complete his convalescence at Gettysburg, he did not want to ride a wheel chair to the plane and be carried up the steps. And so he was able to walk into the plane under his own power and to get off in Washington to greet the people there with a show of good health. We all agreed that this was a good thing to do and when we assembled in the White House that evening for dinner we watched the taped moving picture of these events with great pleasure and satisfaction.

There are a few other stories connected with those seven weeks which are of special interest. One of them concerns our press interviews, which were usually exactly one half hour in duration. We quickly discovered that if we could distract the reporters for five to ten minutes at the beginning of these conferences we would have fewer difficult questions to answer, particularly at the end of the half-hour when the questions tended to take on a political tone. I myself had quite innocently created consternation among Republicans by remarking at the beginning of the President's illness that I personally would not want such a hard job a second time, and later among Democrats by saying that I had voted for Mr. Eisenhower in 1952 and would do so again if he decided to run. One reporter, referring to my political ignorance combined with my unexpected honesty, compared me to a character out of the pages of James Thurber. Whether or not this is an apt comparison I do not know, but I do know that I learned to confine my statements and answers to nonpolitical events.

One of these events, which served as a helpful distraction, occurred on one of my October visits to Denver. On a previous visit I had noted that the President wore a bright bathrobe, on the collar of which were embroidered five gold stars in a circle; when I mentioned this to my secretary, Helen Donovan, she suggested that I ask one of our jeweler patients to make a large gold star pin. This I did, and on a day of bright October sunshine, when the President was seated in a wheelchair on the hospital roof outside his suite, I pinned the new star in the center of the circle of the other five, and made him a six-star general as a special award for good behavior. This pleased everyone, including the press in the conference that followed, and no awkward political questions were asked. The President in a letter to me from Denver dated October 28, 1955, wrote: "I suspect you know by now of the great hit the 'sixth star' has made with the doctors and nurses and members of the press corps. Of course I am highly complimented, and trying hard to live up to the distinction conferred upon me."

Another event that took place at one of our very last press conferences, in Gettysburg, was the bestowal on Jim Hagerty of the honorary degree of D.J.D. (Doctor of Journalistic Dietetics), engraved on a beautiful parchment; this was done because week after week Mr. Hagerty had reported the President's menu for each meal, in order to add flavor to the often dull reports. In this connection, I remember particularly the pleasure with which the President often enjoyed Canadian bacon at breakfast, and the careful way in which he scraped the inside of a soft-boiled eggshell.

And finally, to complete the events of 1955, is the story of my vain effort to persuade the President not to run for re-election in 1956—a story which was extremely confidential at the time and for many years afterwards.

After that last press conference at Gettysburg on December 17, the doctors, White House people, and reporters all left, but the President asked me to stay behind to discuss his future. It was winter now, but the day was pleasant and we sat, that early afternoon, on the veranda of the farm house, enjoying a light picnic luncheon; later we were engrossed for an hour or more in a philosophical discussion about the decisions the President must soon make. I contended that since I knew from previous conversations that his major aim in life was to promote world peace, he should not run for re-election. His heart would stand the strain, I told him, but I felt that the inevitable political maneuvering might endanger his peace-making role. (I had learned a lot about politics by this time.)

He answered that as an ex-president he might have little influence, but I replied that he didn't realize the high respect, prestige, and affection in which he was held the world over. He still thought that he would have more influence as president, but he also said that my proposal interested him greatly and he would consider it seriously.

During the next two months we occasionally corresponded about my proposal, and I believe that much of the delay of his decision to run for re-election was the result of his seeking advice from colleagues and friends. Finally he wrote me at the end of February, 1956, that he had decided he could promote world peace better as president than as ex-president. (And I might note that the Republican party needed him badly in order to win the election; I was heavily outnumbered.) Political difficulties did hamper him as a peace-maker near the end of his presidency, but whether or not he might have been more successful as a nonpolitical free citizen of the world we shall never know. I have always felt that it would have been worth the trial.

On the fourteenth of February, 1956, the staff of the Walter Reed Hospital, including in particular Dr. Mattingly, Dr. Pollock (who had come from Denver), Dr. Snyder, and myself, issued a statement from the White House—where we had assembled after examining the President—to the effect that we considered President Eisenhower physically fit for resumption of his office for a second term "if he so wished and the country approved." We added, however, that "the choice was his and not ours." We prophesied that the chances were that he should be able to carry on an active life for some years to come, which might be "in the neighborhood of five to ten." He lived for a little more than thirteen years after that, till March 28, 1969.

There was one more dramatic event concerning the President's health in 1956, in which I was involved. On June 8, I was called to the Walter Reed Hospital in Washington to meet in consultation my old friends General Snyder and Tom Mattingly, and eight surgeons, the senior four of whom were General Heaton, chief of the hospital, Dr. Ravdin, surgical consultant from Philadelphia, Dr. Blades of Washington, and Dr. Lyons. The junior surgeons were from the Walter Reed staff.

I made the following notes on my medical record card number 37 of President Eisenhower's file in my office:

This morning, June 8, 1956, after a long period of excellent health and a White House party the evening before, the President was awakened by low abdominal cramps and vomiting which continued from 12:45 A.M. until he was moved for study and treatment to the Walter Reed Hospital at 1:30. More comfortable since, but x-rays showed an obstructed small bowel based apparently on an old area of chronic ileitis. No fever. White blood count 15,000. Pulse and blood pressure o.k. Electrocardiograms at 6:30 A.M. and 2:30 P.M. showed normal rhythm at a rate of 90 to 100 and slighter higher ST segments and evidence of the old scar produced by the coronary attack nine months earlier.

At 8:45 P.M., June 8th, P.D.W. visited the President and found him comfortable and cheerful though moderately distended. The vital signs were good. At 9:30 the surgeons were still uncertain about the exact diagnosis except for at least partial obstruction, so that they continued to postpone an exploratory laparotomy. Dr. Mattingly and I kept circling the eight surgeons who were in a close huddle, urging them for the sake of his heart to make up their minds. At midnight new x-rays showed no more obstruction. Finally a rising pulse forced the issue and at 3 A.M., June 9th, the abdomen was opened by Drs. Heaton and Ravdin, working together, and a 50 centimeter long area of chronic ileitis was exposed. The small bowel was attached to the transverse colon and the operation was completed at 4:55 A.M. Dr. Mattingly and I monitored his heart throughout the operation (which was done under general anesthesia) and all went well. When I visited the President at 8 A.M. he was sleeping. He looked well, his color was good, his pulse was regular at 84 and his blood pressure measured 130 systolic and 80 diastolic.

When I called on him a day or two later he was convalescing very well.

On January 31, 1957, at the beginning of his second term as president, President Eisenhower was visited by General Snyder, Dr. Mattingly, and me, and found to be in excellent health. The only abnormality on examination was the electrocardiographic evidence of the well-healed and symptomless myocardial infarct (heart muscle scar), then sixteen months old. After the examination we doctors were taken by the President to the golf cage, which he had set up in the basement of the White House. We watched him drive, approach, and putt in full vigor for forty-five minutes without symptoms. He was evidently expert at the game. He handed us the clubs to try, but, compared to him, we were rank amateurs. He offered to play with us some day to improve our form, but the actual game never took place.

On November 26, 1957, two weeks after a complete checkup at Walter Reed Hospital, which showed apparently an excellent state of health of both the President's cardiovascular system and his gastrointestinal tract, General Snyder phoned me to say that the President had had a slight stroke the day before, involving particularly his speech. He recovered in a very few days and was able to carry out an important political assignment in Europe shortly afterward. On inquiry, I found that the anticoagulant therapy had been continued constantly on an average dosage of 35 milligrams of Coumadin weekly. I find in a note on his record as of June 30, 1961, that General Snyder wrote me that this program of anticoagulation was still being maintained with good control and that Ike was keeping his weight down to 175 pounds or less on a low animal fat diet. The electrocardiogram was unchanged.

I visited the General briefly five years later at his winter home at Palm Desert, California, where my former student, Dr. Seeley Mudd, vice-president of the University of California, arranged a very pleasant reunion dinner on February 27, 1962. I examined General Eisenhower briefly, and found him in excellent health. When I arrived at the Golf Club that day I watched the players all riding by in golf carts. Soon Ike himself drove up and was embarrassed momentarily when I chided him for riding instead of walking. He explained that out there the players were not permitted to walk, because of the great demand for speedy playing due to an oversupply of players. When later I played a round myself with Dr. Mudd I tried to persuade the management to let me run between shots, which would have been faster than travel by cart, but even that was not permitted.

My next note, on card number 41 of the General's medical record, tells of my visit on November 13, 1965, to the Fort Gordon Army Hospital in Augusta, Georgia, where he was under the care of Tom Mattingly and another former student of mine, Dr. Harry Harper of Augusta; he had suffered a second but mild heart attack.

On November 9 he had been awakened at 1:15 A.M. by moderately severe substernal pain lasting half an hour. Nitroglycerine was ineffective. He was given demerol and taken to the hospital where he had, after another twenty-four hours, more severe substernal pain lasting, until controlled by demerol, an hour or more, accompanied by sweating and temporary hypertension. The next day he had slight fever, a considerable increase of transaminase (a muscle enzyme), slight leukocytosis, and the characteristic change of a small inferior-lateral myocardial infarct. When I examined him he looked and felt well. The findings on physical examination were entirely normal. My comment was that Ike was apparently convalescing satisfactorily from his second coronary heart attack (thrombosis) with a minor infarct in a different region of his left ventricle from that of his first one ten years before. He was receiving admirable treatment.

President Eisenhower's Heart Attack

Two years later, in 1967, General Eisenhower had his third attack of coronary thrombosis, a mild one, to be followed in the spring a year later by his fourth attack, which hospitalized him for much of the last year of his life.

Most of the President's illnesses in the years that followed his second inaugural were related either to his intestinal troubles or to his arterial disease, the atherosclerosis that was responsible for his heart attacks and his stroke. But in the main, his health was good and he was able to lead a fully active life consistent with his age until he was struck down by his fourth coronary thrombosis in California in May, 1968, after which he lived for the most part an invalid existence until his death.

Recurrence of ileitis and peritoneal adhesions associated therewith, caused repeated attacks of intestinal obstruction which plagued him sorely during the last year of his life, when he was a chronic patient at the Walter Reed Hospital after the fourth heart attack. Despite his cardiac invalidism, it was finally necessary to operate again to give him relief from the distress of the serious attacks of intestinal obstruction, but he died a few days later.

Most episodes of cardiac nature which occurred during that last year in the Walter Reed Hospital consisted of various paroxysms of arrhythmia, including atrial flutter, atrial fibrillation, and also several instances of cardiac standstill due to ventricular fibrillation, all of importance and at times critical, requiring resuscitation, but not to be ascribed to constantly recurrent attacks of thrombosis, except for a typical fifth acute occlusion in June, 1968.

When I called on him at the hospital in February, 1969, a month before he died, he was clear mentally and quite cheerful except for the terrible nuisance of his bowel condition. It was evident that an operation was necessary, despite the serious risk involved. The odds were, however, too great. His death was a merciful release from the intolerable suffering, which was too much for even such a heroic spirit as was that of General Eisenhower.

Both during his second term as President and for years afterward, both Ike and Mamie were very helpful in promoting interest far and wide in the prevention and relief of heart disease. By word and by deed they took part in the annual February Heart Drives of the American Heart Association. Ike served as honorary chairman, and I remember the Valentine Day ceremony in the White House when Mamie and a young girl who had had a successful heart operation in the earlier years of cardiac surgery lit the candles on the huge birthday cake. On October 29, 1963, Ike presented me with a gold stethoscope at a special banquet of the International Cardiology Foundation in New York—an act which of course provided our campaign of preventive cardiology with much helpful publicity.

Other writers, much more interested and knowledgeable than I concerning the military, political, and literary exploits of Dwight D. Eisenhower, have presented and will continue to present aspects of his life which I knew only by hearsay, or in print, or in snatches of conversation with him. But I did become familiar with an artistic side of his life which stood him in good stead as a means of pleasant relaxation and which he used helpfully during various periods of convalescence from illnesses. I greatly enjoyed receiving from the President on several successive Christmases, pictures of scenes that he had painted in various parts of the world; these remain delightful souvenirs of our friendship.

I shall treasure always the memory of the spirit of this great American and world citizen. With patience and hard work throughout the world, his goal for universal peace can come to pass but science (irenology—See Preface) must play a major role; emotion is not enough.

The Long Follow-up

CHAPTER XIII 🙿   The long follow-up of any subject can be of great help in the
analysis of the importance of in-
dividual problems. I have found it to hold true, particularly
with reference to health and disease in my own field of cardiology. When I began my practice in 1920, I had of course
no patients that I had followed for more than a few years in
the clinic and in the Out-patient Department at the Massachusetts General Hospital. I decided early that I would make
the long follow-up one of the features of my medical career,
and so I had printed for me large sheets which were at first
loose-leafed in a binder but which were later bound in a
special volume after the collection of the first 5,000 cases.
The second volume contained another 5,000 cases; and I am
just finishing the third volume now.

These sheets contained two horizontal lines for each patient, divided by vertical columns with the serial number,
the name, the age, the sex, the diagnosis arranged according
to etiology (both cardiac and noncardiac), the structural
change and the functional condition of the circulation, and
a special column at the end of the lines devoted to some unusual reason why this patient might be particularly important to be followed up. Now, after all these fifty years, I find
these volumes of great value; they hardly require a computer,

because of the organization of this original tabulation, which has proved so useful. This type of follow-up can apply to any particular field in medicine or surgery, or any science as a matter of fact, or any other activity of life, but as the years have gone by and the organization of my material has become so helpful I have emphasized more and more the importance of this relatively simple technique in the practice of medicine and in the collection of information otherwise. One of the difficulties, however, is that the practitioner of medicine, the family doctor, and the specialist too, is "too busy," or does not write legibly, or does not arrange to have the description of his cases typed, but especially in that he has had no realization of the usefulness of his material. As a result, he has almost nothing of definite value to look back to after many years of practice. The doctors who might be more orderly in their collection of data are the medical professors, but either they do not have the opportunity to see many private patients to follow through many decades, or they do not specialize, or they move to other posts, often in other cities.

My own increasing interest in the subject culminated first in an editorial in the 1950s and eventually in a book, published early in 1967, which has been considered of great usefulness clinically by a widely scattered group of physicians. It is a kind of book different from the usual textbook and is called *Hearts: Their Long Follow-Up.* In it there are recorded the cases of eighty-odd private patients of mine, followed for at least twenty years and some of them for much longer. They are grouped according to their etiological diagnoses, first the variations of normal, then congenital heart disease —beginning during the first years of life—then rheumatic heart disease and other infections in early life, and going on to the cor pulmonale (pulmonary heart disease), hypertension, coronary heart disease, arrhythmias, pericarditis, and a few other such subjects.

The very first page of the introduction of this new book

presents the immediate reason for the stimulus to write the book. I shall quote and also summarize from some of these first few pages.

"On October 29th, 1964, a healthy appearing man, E.G., aged sixty-four years, appeared at my office early one morning with his wife, saying that they had come down from northern Vermont to do some Christmas shopping in Boston, and while here he thought it would be good to have a checkup after a long interval. I asked him how long it had been since I had previously examined him, and he said he thought that it was forty years. This interested me greatly. I had no time to examine him that morning, but I had him come back a week later. I found him in perfect health. I had not remembered him, since he had not been a private patient of mine, but he said that he had been a surgical patient in the M.G.H. when I was a young visiting physician in charge of the new cardiac department comprising laboratory, clinics, and consulting service. He told me he had been seen by me on one of the surgical wards of the M.G.H. and had been very ill, that I had been called in consultation to examine him and to give advice at that time, and that I did see him two or three times. I looked up the hospital records and found that he had indeed had a miraculous recovery; my handwriting was still clearly legible on that record of forty years earlier.

"It was this particular checkup after an interval of forty years that made me call my former secretary, Helen Donovan, and tell her that we must write a book on the subject of the long follow-up, illustrated by our own cases. Much of the medical writing of today is based statistically on scores, hundreds, even thousands of cases, but in such studies we often miss the individuality of the patients who are included in such mass statistics. It is these individual single cases that often teach us the most.

"E.G. is a striking example. I have added a further note that these are real people, not just cases. To be sure they are exceptional in that they have survived a long time, sometimes after some very serious disease, but they balance in many respects those who die early and in this way we get an average picture of the condition we are studying. In E.G.'s case it was infection.

"When he was twenty-four years old he was a law school student. He entered Ward D of the M.G.H. on January 5, 1924, with a story of five days of pain on swallowing associated with aching of the left lower jaw. A dentist had extracted three abscessed roots and curetted the mandible. Swelling, tenderness, and pain in the left jaw followed rapidly with cellulitis in the neck. On admission to the hospital his temperature was 102.8 degrees F. with a leukocyte (white blood cell) count of 28,000 (normal is 6,000 to 10,000). He was operated upon at once by one of our ablest surgeons who incised and drained an abscess of the jaw, which was shown by x-ray to include osteomyelitis. During the course of this illness his temperature rose to 105.5, and he had several chills. On January 13, eight days after his hospital admission, he complained of pain in the front of his chest, and on that day his pulse slowed markedly, at first to the forties, later into the thirties; on one occasion it was only 26. A pericardial friction rub was heard and there was some enlargement of the heart shadow by x-ray. He was put on the danger list. An electrocardiogram taken on January 13, 1924, showed a very high degree of partial atrioventricular electrical block up to 4:1 and 5:1, with an atrial rate of 108 and a ventricular rate varying from 26 to 37.

"By good fortune and with excellent nursing care, E.G. slowly recovered. The heart block lasted for a week, and he was discharged well except for weakness on February 23, 1924, six weeks after his admission.

"When he came to the office to be re-examined nearly forty-one years later, he was very well and fully active, practicing law in northern Vermont. Incidentally, he had received an honorary degree from the University of Vermont the previous June (1964). Examination showed no abnormalities. He looked well. His pulse was regular at a rate of 66. His blood pressure was 140 systolic and 90 diastolic. The heart sounds were good and there were no murmurs. There was an old scar from the drainage incision over the left lower jaw of a generation earlier. Fluoroscopy showed a full-sized heart shadow within normal limits by measurement. The electro-cardiogram in the autumn of 1964 showed normal rhythm at a rate of 65, and was wholly normal."

I added the comment about this case that "one of the important lessons we have learned these many years has been the ability frequently encountered, of patients to recover from serious degrees of heart disease, no matter what the cause, as soon as the acute process or strain has subsided, either spontaneously or through medical or surgical measures. The most striking, more or less spontaneous, recoveries, with a return often to excellent health, can occur in the cases of active rheumatic myocarditis, generally in childhood, through the subsidence of the process, and in older patients with high degrees of coronary insufficiency due to atherosclerosis of the coronary arteries or actual coronary thrombosis via the development of an adequate collateral circulation. The possibility of such natural recoveries to complete health later in life was not appreciated in the early days of this specialty of mine, but now such are well recognized by experienced observers.

"In addition, of course, we now have medical and surgical therapy to treat conditions such as many of the congenital defects of the heart and blood vessels, acquired valvular deformities, and hypertension. The possible reversibility, in many instances, of every kind of heart disease is now an established fact and of vital importance in prognosis, appreciated by the medical profession, by the underwriters of life and disability insurance and—not to forget him—by the patient most of all. It is fascinating to know that one can grow healthier as one gets older and not necessarily the reverse. One of the chief reasons for writing this book was to emphasize the importance of this evolution of our knowledge of both natural and man-made miracles, but at the same time we recognize that we are still faced with many failures and many tragedies. We expect that as time goes on we shall have more miracles and fewer tragedies. All in all, however, I have learned that it is wiser to err on the optimistic side in prognosis rather than on the over-pessimistic. It is important also to recognize that around the corner there may be some therapy that can completely change the prognosis, whether by medical treatment or by surgical operation."

In many patients the reversibility of cardiovascular disease back to normal health is only partial, but even slight to moderate degrees of recovery are welcomed not only by the patients themselves but also by their families, their doctors, and their nurses. Such rehabilitation has been greatly advanced and scientifically developed by one of the great pioneers of our day who has stimulated others to follow him, Dr. Howard Rusk of New York University.

Autopsies are still needed as well as cardiac catheter data, angiograms, biopsies, and surgical exploration. However, it is wise to avoid excessive investigation as well as excessive therapy. Both are tiring and expensive for the patient and once in a while they are downright dangerous.

In another chapter of this book I have written on the range of the normal. Most of the findings we talk about in general are averages with very wide ranges above and below the average. I have spoken in that chapter on heart rate, blood pressure, electrocardiographic findings, and on other so-called parameters, or measurements. I mentioned murmurs which may be innocent or physiologic, that is, functional and not due to any organic disease of the heart. In young children such murmurs are very common, and may sometimes be confused with important murmurs. Sometimes months or years of observation are necessary to distinguish between them. Also, it is true that in certain cases of rheumatic heart disease or with other infections the heart may be dilated due to involvement of the muscle itself; murmurs may then occur, which, when the disease and the dilatation subside, may disappear. In the case of some of these murmurs it may not always be possible to distinguish between important or pathologic murmurs and unimportant or physiologic ones. I would like to add here observations about an interesting murmur that has been frequently confused with the murmurs of heart disease, namely, the venous hum in the neck in a patient with a normal heart in early childhood. On page 17 of my book on the long follow-up I had the following to say.

"J. S. H., aged 4, son of a physician, was examined by me on March 18, 1944, because a loud basal heart murmur (that is, at the base-upper end of the heart) had been heard during routine examination a month earlier. But he was perfectly well and fully active.

"Physical examination showed him to be a healthy appearing boy weighing 36½ pounds with normal heart sounds and a fairly loud (what we call a grade 2 to 3 out of a possible 5 to 6) continuous humming murmur over the right jugular vein at the base of the heart and also down the right side of the breastbone, loudest at the aortic area just below the collar bone and obliterated by pressure over the right jugular vein. The murmur also disappeared when the boy lay down in the supine position, that is, on his back. The pulse was regular at a rate of 100. There was no cyanosis, that is blueness, or clubbing of his fingertips.

"X-ray examination and electrocardiogram were perfectly normal."

We stated to this parent and to the patient that this was a perfectly normal murmur due to an active circulation in an active boy, made by blood running down the jugular vein from the head and upper part of the body into the heart, causing a subdued roar. We would expect it to disappear as the child grew older, since we do not often see it in adult life. My associate, Dr. Edward Bland, examined this lad two years later, and there was no evidence of any disease. He still showed the loud venous hum above the right clavicle, with a thrill. The murmur was dispelled as before by pressure on the jugular vein. We saw the boy again on July 21, 1966 and at this time, twenty-two years later, he was twenty-six years old. He was perfectly well, working hard, but was not very active physically. Physical examination showed no abnormalities. He now weighed 173 pounds. There was a very faint diastolic hum on inspiration just below the right clavicle, abolished by pressure over the right jugular vein, a faint residual of his old venous hum. We were able to reassure him again, but we did advise him to stop smoking, to take more exercise, and to lose some weight.

Now I shall speak of some of the types of heart disease that we have followed in special cases. To illustrate further this chapter about the long follow-up, I shall discuss several of my long-lived patients representing different but common types of heart disease—congenital, rheumatic, hypertensive, and coronary—and who were at the other extreme of longevity from those patients who die quickly from one of these acute or subacute causes. There are many such at both ends of the spectrum. I shall begin with congenital heart patients. An important such patient with cyanosis (a "blue baby" type) has already been presented in Chapters IV and X, the famous musician, Henry Gilbert. I shall now present two noncyanotic patients.

L.S., aged three, was seen in the Children's Cardiac Clinic of the Children's Hospital by Dr. John Hubbard in 1934. She was born normally at full term. There was no cyanosis noted at birth or during the postnatal period. The family history revealed no important hereditary diseases. Physical examination showed signs suggesting congenital malformation of the heart with a precordial thrill and a loud murmur. The carotid pulsations were marked and pistol shot sounds could be heard over the brachial and femoral arteries. The blood pressure was 104 mm. systolic and 0 mm. diastolic. There was definite cardiac enlargement. The diagnosis was congenital malformation of the heart, with a large patent ductus arteriosus.

During the next four years, she continued to be observed at the Children's Hospital and her case was discussed with me. At no time had cyanosis been observed. Dyspnea developed after moderate exercise, and her physical activities had been limited accordingly. Her mother noted a "buzzing noise" in her daughter's chest.

On August 17, 1938, she was seen by Dr. Gross, and the physical findings, as reported by him and Dr. Hubbard in the *Journal of the American Medical Association*, 1939, *112*, 729, were as follows:

> At the time of admission the patient was slender and undernourished. The pulsations of the carotid arteries were abnormally forceful. The radial pulse was of the Corrigan type, and a capillary pulsation was readily seen. The veins over the chest were somewhat prominent. There was a precordial bulge. The heart was definitely enlarged by percussion, the enlargement being for the most part to the left. Over the entire precordium there was a prominent coarse thrill which was most intense in the third interspace to the left of the sternum. This thrill was continuous but was accentuated during systole. There was a rough 'machinery' murmur heard with maximal intensity over the pulmonic area to the left of the sternum in the second and particularly in the third interspace. It was continuous throughout the cardiac cycle but like the thrill was greatly accentuated during systole. It was transmitted to the left along the third interspace and into the axilla with only slightly

diminished intensity. The systolic element was heard faintly over the vessels of the neck and could be heard clearly in the right axilla and over the mid-thoracic region posteriorly. Blood pressure readings were respectively right arm 115/40, left arm 110/50, right leg 150/55, left leg 140/40 mm. of mercury. There was no clubbing of the fingers and no evidence of peripheral edema. The liver edge was palpable at the costal margin. The examination in other respects was negative.

A 7-foot x-ray film of the chest showed the transverse diameter of the heart to be 11.7 cm. compared to an internal diameter of the chest of 20 cm. There appeared to be definite enlargement of the left ventricle. There was questionable prominence of the pulmonary artery. A mottled increased density around the lung hili was interpreted as representing circulatory congestion. Fluoroscopic examination showed a 'hilar dance.' An electrocardiogram was normal showing no deviation of the axis.

On August 26, 1938, an operation was done by Dr. Gross, who carried out ligation alone since the ductus was too short to tie double and divide. Postoperatively, the patient did well, and the following day she was allowed to sit in a chair. By the third day she was walking about the ward; she was discharged on the thirteenth day. When the dressings were removed the thrill had completely disappeared. There was a faint systolic murmur in the left third interspace, which was not transmitted over the precordium, and no murmur could be heard in the axilla, in the neck, or over the back. The average of the daily pressures prior to operation had been 114 mm. systolic and 38 mm. diastolic, as contrasted with the postoperative daily average of 108 mm. systolic and 80 mm. diastolic.

When seen by us for a follow-up examination on January 24, 1966, she was thirty-five years old and was in excellent health, fully active, with no symptoms of any kind. In the interval she had married and had had two sons. Her weight was 133 pounds and her height was 5'5". Her habits were excellent. She was accustomed to quite a bit of exercise. A tonsillectomy was done in 1952.

Physical examination showed no abnormalities whatsoever. The heart was normal in size, and without murmurs. The rhythm was regular at a rate of 72. The blood pressure was 100 mm. systolic and 65 mm. diastolic. There was no evidence of congestive failure or of clubbing or cyanosis of the fingers. The pulse was felt in both ankles. Fluoroscopic examination showed a heart of normal size with clear lung fields and very slight prominence of the pulmonary arc. The lung hilus shadows were normal. By orthodiagram the transverse diameter of the heart measured 10.6 cm. and the internal diameter of the thorax 25.3 cm. The electrocardiogram showed normal rhythm at a rate of 75 to 80 and was perfectly normal in all 12 leads.

Happily, this patient has remained in perfect health since the complete cure of a widely patent ductus arteriosus by a surgical operation done thirty-two years ago, the first successful case in medical history. It is of further interest that the ductus was too short to divide and was closed by ligation alone. During the first seven years of her life before the operation, she had a very abnormal circulatory defect responsible for the water-hammer pulse, dyspnea, and limitation of her activities. She herself and her mother were aware of the noise in her chest. Fortunately, all of this was corrected by a relatively simple operative procedure.

A second case I would like to present now, a very interesting one of a congenital defect different from that of the first. It was that of a woman who has never had any operative treatment, partly because we discovered her before there was any such treatment, and partly because she has done so well since then that she has constantly refused surgical repair. I saw her first early in 1944, when she was forty years of age and came in for a checkup prior to operation for a large fibroid tumor of the uterus. There was no history of heart disease, although a systolic thrill (a sensation by palpation) over her heart had been noted since birth. Her family longevity was excellent. There were four brothers and three sisters, all well and without heart disease. The thrill accompanied a very loud murmur indicating the presence of pulmonary stenosis, that is, marked narrowing of the pulmonary valve which she had had since birth. It is now correctable by surgery, and we advise that any child with this condition should have the valve opened and repaired, the repair carried out with a good risk in almost all cases. This patient I am describing was examined annually, and did very well. On December 18, 1950, she reported that she had gotten along well. The findings on examination were the same as when I first saw her in 1944. There was a note on her record in 1954, when she was found to have the same signs, and she was referred to Dr. Robert Gross, who advised cardiac catheterization, but the family refused to allow it or to consider cardiac surgery. She continued to be examined annually. When I saw her in September, 1966, she was very apprehensive because of the mistaken x-ray diagnosis of a chest tumor which should be resected, it was said. This tumor was simply an aneurysmal dilatation of the pulmonary artery which was associated with the pulmonary stenosis and which she had had for years. I was able to reassure her and she has continued to be well right up to the present. She is now in her sixty-sixth year. There is no reason why she should not pass the usual three score and ten without operation. Of course, if we had noted this condition when she was a young girl or if surgery had been available at that age, this condition would have been corrected decades ago.

I would like now to discuss two rheumatic heart cases, one with natural longevity and the other helped very much by surgical operation. Marcial Lichauco of Manila, aged eighteen, a Harvard sophomore, was first seen by me on January 10, 1921, when I was beginning my practice. He had had tonsillitis and rheumatic fever at the age of eight, and another acute rheumatic attack in December of 1920 at seventeen, for which he had been hospitalized for ten days in the college infirmary at Harvard. He had had no symptoms except for palpitation after exercise. On examination the heart was a little enlarged. There was a murmur characteristic of aortic regurgitation, that is, a leaking through the aortic valve resulting from the rheumatic fever. Otherwise he was quite well. During his college course and during his law school education I saw him annually, and there was little or no change in his condition of chronic rheumatic heart disease with aortic regurgitation. He went back to the Philippines to carry out his legal career; he was one of those who helped to establish the documents for the independence of the Philippines. In time he became a noted lawyer, and on the occasion of the Japanese invasion he held a prominent place in the Philippine legal profession. However, with this prestige he had become too busy to take care of his health, and he had put on weight, and had taken little or no exercise. It was about then that the Japanese invasion occurred, and I personally believe it was that which saved his life. With his automobile taken away from him, he was forced to walk, he was more or less malnourished, and in the course of a few years he had become very thin, but not otherwise sick physically. When he came back to the States at the end of the war I found him in quite good condition. He had recovered some of the twenty-five pounds that he had lost; he was quite active and continued so. I saw him at intervals when he came back for college and law school reunions, and noted that he slowly developed some aortic stenosis superimposed on the regurgitation, that is, narrowing of the valve, which compensated somewhat for the leak, and this has helped him.

There are a few more points about this remarkable man.

In the first place he became in the early 1960s Philippine Ambassador to the United Kingdom in London. In my book on the long follow-up, there is a picture of him and his wife, with seven of their eight children. Late in life, despite his crippled heart, he went big game hunting in Africa. In 1966, I examined him at his home in Manila, and although he had developed Parkinson's Disease, his heart was doing well, though it was still enlarged and he still showed aortic stenosis and regurgitation. It is nearly half a century since I first saw him as a Harvard sophomore, when he was eighteen years old. In May, 1970, I examined him again, and found his heart holding its own and his Parkinsonism helped by L-Dopa.

One of my most remarkable patients is Sara Gordon whom I first saw when she was at the age of sixty, in May, 1953. She had a considerable degree of rheumatic mitral stenosis and invalidism therefrom. She had an enormous heart, and there was very little we could do for her. However, after considerable reflection, we decided that it would be common sense to offer her surgical treatment of the mitral stenosis by the simple procedure of breaking the valve with a fingertip or by a knife inserted with the finger. (This was before open heart surgery was being carried out.) With the helpful cooperation of Dr. Dwight Harken, and with the family—including a brother who was a physician—in agreement, she was restored to good health by Dr. Harken's operation and to an active life, which she has carried on ever since.

She has had a most amazing career. I am sure that, in this case, not only was the disease less important than the patient, but the treatment, too. Sixteen years after my first examination, I talked with her. She was then in her mid-seventies, having survived much illness, including fracture of her hip with recovery therefrom. She has always had a buoyant spirit, and has been an inspiration for many others with heart disease and other diseases as well. I wrote in my book:

This lady is one of the most remarkable persons we have ever met, both as a human being and as a patient. By her indomitable spirit, her optimism, her superior intelligence, and her courage she has overcome all of her many serious ailments and has not only set an extraordinary example to healthy people half her age, but has contributed greatly both spiritually and materially to our campaign against heart disease, both nationally and internationally.

Next, let me talk of hypertensive heart disease, which we can now treat much better with drugs than we used to be able to do. But this particular case is an example of what we accomplished by Smithwick's sympathectomy almost thirty years ago. The patient, a thirty-one-year-old surgeon, entered our hospital in the late summer of 1942 for consideration of serious hypertension and treatment of his failing heart. He had had high blood pressure for several years, and on admission we found it to measure 165 mm. systolic, and 136 mm. diastolic, a very high level. He had become breathless. His heart showed enlargement with gallop rhythm and accentuation of the pulmonary second sound. There was alternation of the pulse. He was in a serious state of heart failure from high blood pressure. His electrocardiogram was abnormal.

Surgical resection of the lower sympathetic spinal nerves, the so-called Smithwick thoracolumbar sympathectomy, was carried out, first on the right side on October 1, 1942, and then on the left side on October 13, 1942. Within two to three weeks the blood pressure and electrocardiogram became normal; the blood pressure dropped to 104 mm. systolic and 75 mm. diastolic.

One year later he felt perfectly well and was operating surgically four hours a day; the blood pressure was normal (120 mm. systolic and 80 mm. diastolic). Three years post-operatively he was still in excellent health and working hard, with normal blood presure. His only complaint was that he perspired excessively in the upper part of his body in hot weather.

On June 21, 1965, at the age of fifty-four, and twenty-three years after his sympathectomy, he wrote to us as follows. "I should come back to Boston for a checkup, but never seem to have the time. My blood pressure stays about 118/80 repeatedly. I have had no symptoms and/or signs of trouble that I know of, except that I did develop gout five years ago. This, apparently, has been successfully treated and I have had no attacks since 1961. I guess that this means that I have survived long enough to get the diseases of civilization. My oldest daughter is to be married Saturday. The other three children—all post partum, as far as surgery is concerned—are coming along. I keep busy in private practice and as a Professor of Surgery."

This patient illustrates the benefit of this type of surgery at that time, when medicines were of no avail. I am sure he would have succumbed to heart failure in a short time if he had not had this particular treatment, which was not often done at the time. When I saw him two years ago, he was still well and fully active. Now happily medicines are at last available to control high blood pressure and therefore surgical sympathectomy, a difficult and painful double operation, is no longer needed.

Now I come to the last case in this chapter, demonstrating excellent longevity in coronary heart disease. I have had many such patients who have survived thirty to thirty-five years, but none quite as long as this patient did—thirty-eight years.

Mr. H.H., aged fifty-two, an insurance broker, while emotionally upset in his work and after a hurried, hearty luncheon followed by golf (quite incidental, I think, and not a cause), developed in the late afternoon of May 11, 1927, severe precordial pain which persisted all night. The next day he saw his family doctor, who found his heart beat irregular. The pain gradually subsided under the administration of morphine. He had a little fever and his white cell count went up. His blood pressure came down moderately.

As consultant I saw him on the third day of his illness. He was in fairly good condition considering the severity of the attack. After a few weeks of more or less complete rest and another month of convalescence he returned to work, and remained quite well with respect to his heart. At the age of ninety, he died of pneumonia in May, 1965, thirty-eight years after his acute coronary thrombosis. Autopsy showed the scar in the front wall of his heart, which in all those years had not bothered him at all. He had been very active, playing golf and continuing to work until he retired at the age of seventy, twenty years before he died and eighteen years after his heart attack. At the age of eighty-one he had a little stroke, with dragging of his left leg afterward. In 1959, at the age of eighty-four, he had a fall downstairs and was badly, but not permanently, shaken up. He had pneumonia in 1960 and recovered well, although the next attack, in 1965, finished him off. A tough old gentleman, indeed!

This case illustrates several important points, including the extreme longevity, which is possible following a moderately severe attack of coronary thrombosis, given the absence of a very large scar, congestive failure, or coronary insufficiency (angina pectoris) following the healing of the infarct. In these matters he was fortunate, and he also benefited importantly by a favorable family longevity. Incidentally, he had no anticoagulant therapy, and for many years he carried on an active business and played a good deal of golf following his attack. This exercise, especially, kept him well.

I have hoped in this chapter to demonstrate my belief that man is more important than his disease, that these patients were really more important than their various kinds of heart disease. It was the combination of individual physical and spiritual stamina and heredity, as much as the treatment of their diseases, which helped them to survive. The combination included family longevity, hardihood of constitution, and an optimistic and determined mental outlook. Without a doubt, their psyches greatly helped their somas.

Physical Fitness:
Hearts and Husbands

CHAPTER XIV 🙋 This chapter was originally entitled only "Hearts and Husbands," but since its theme was primarily that of physical fitness, with particular emphasis on the prevention of presenile atherosclerosis with its frequently devastating sequelae, I have added "Physical Fitness" to the title. I would like to preface the text, as originally prepared, by two observations.

As most of my lay friends and medical colleagues know, I have always been, and still am, a strong advocate of physical fitness. But I have two reservations. Preoccupation or concentration full time on physical fitness should not exist at the expense of sacrificing mental and spiritual values and contributions and the happiness of a full life. One must, or should on occasion, honestly compromise between the constant effort to be physically fit and the normal urge to get something done in behalf of the welfare of others, either as individuals or for humanity as a whole, or indeed for one's own welfare. Thus, I am myself justifiably, I believe, too busy in my writing, in my research, or in my care of my patients, to look, on a good many occasions, after my own health, which I do try as best I can to control and I admit that sometimes I am too lazy. Thus, physical fitness need not, in fact should not, consume all our time, except perhaps for the relatively rare person whose job it is to teach it.

My second observation is that, actually, physical fitness includes the health of the brain. Thus those who are impatient with the idea of pursuing physical fitness should realize that for the optimum health of their mental and spiritual functions, they need a good circulation of well oxygenated blood, free of toxic substances, to and through the brain.

One of the most curious, interesting, and dramatic episodes of my life, and one of the most important in the evolution of my slowly developing program in preventive cardiology, occurred on the sixth of November, 1964, in Portland, Oregon. So far as I was concerned my part in this episode was quite incidental; Mrs. Ira Keller and Dr. Wayne Rogers, both of them leading figures in the Oregon Heart Association, deserve full credit for its astounding success.

For several decades it had become evident that coronary heart disease was much more common in young and middle-aged males than in females of the same age. As I have already mentioned, several of us had found that of 100 persons with coronary heart disease under the age of forty years, 97 were men and only three were women. Furthermore, it was known that in the United States in recent years women outlived men by six years or a little more, with an expected longevity of seventy-four years, compared to sixty-eight for men. This difference in length of life had been increasing for a generation or two and was being ascribed to increasing bad health habits affecting the males earlier in life, and the protection of the women by the female sex hormone (estrogen).

The Oregonians were greatly disturbed by this situation and wanted to do something practical about it *now*, without waiting for many years for a definitive research to be 100 per cent complete; they believed that the correction of health habits could begin to help the male to catch up in longevity with his wife and they therefore called their 1964 program

"Hearts and Husbands." They inserted invitations to their program in all kinds of routine mail, such as gas bills, going to women all over the state, and scheduled the meeting for noon in the Portland Coliseum to allow time for the women to come by bus, private car, train, or plane, and to return home in time to prepare the family dinner.

A short time before the meeting was to start, I was conferring backstage with some of the Heart Association officials; I shall never forget their excitement when they learned that every one of the Coliseum's 10,000 seats was occupied and that several hundred more women had been admitted as standees. The arriving ladies had, I later discovered, created one of the biggest traffic jams Portland had ever experienced.

In addition to the program of speakers and a question-and-answer period there were many interesting exhibits around the hall, including a large whale's heart, for my benefit. One of the exhibits was my own monitored electrocardiogram (from electrodes on my chest and a sending device) transmitted to a large monitor on the stage—so that all the audience could watch my heart beat.

I was asked to introduce the program, and my opening remarks (as recorded) were as follows.

"Wives and sisters, mothers and daughters, I have come to seek your aid in saving and prolonging the lives of your husbands and brothers, your sons and fathers, doomed to die before their time, leaving you to spend the last six years or more of your lives as widows, not only to grieve but to begin to succumb before your time, also, to the same afflictions which kill and cripple *us*. We must face this fact and do something about it, for if we act in our time I am sure that we can change not only our own lives, but even history as well.

"We are suffering from three great epidemics in this country today, which we should be able to control, at least in part within the next generation, if we really want to do so. Pessimism is not the answer. We have done a superb job in the last generation, ever since I was a boy, in the control of other great epidemics of the past, in particular tuberculosis, a high infant mortality, diphtheria, rheumatic fever, and syphilis. There is no reason why we cannot succeed in time in the control of the present threats to our lives, our health, and our happiness.

"I shall limit my remarks today to the three epidemics that kill us, for I shall have no time to discuss other epidemics that only cripple us, such as arthritis, and afflictions of the mind and of the very soul, about which much needs to be done. I shall concentrate on only one of the three current epidemics that kill, since that is the most common and in my own field. The other two epidemics, which rank second and third respectively as causes of death in this country today, are cancer and accidents, many of the latter being preventable at home, at work, or on the highway. You may be surprised that I call them epidemics, but that is what they are, for, as derived from the Greek *epi,* which means 'upon,' and *demos,* which means 'people,' an epidemic is something that has fallen upon the people. We think of it as bad, but equally well we should have an epidemic of good health for all of us all our lives."

After further discussion of atherosclerosis, the disease of the arteries which is responsible for coronary heart disease and death therefrom, I ended my address by asking and answering the question as to what the thousands of women in my audience might do to help prolong the lives of their menfolk. I said that risk factors both of heredity and of the environment needed consideration. Little could be said about the obscure, but certainly important, factor of heredity, about which much remains to be discovered. We are at present, I said, quite ignorant about the relative importance of heredity and environment in the background of causes of the atherosclerosis—

are they equally important, or do they vary greatly in different individuals?

Since it is obvious that we have at present no control of our heredity, we must concentrate on environmental risk factors, of which three are widely recognized: (1) obesity and rich diet, (2) physical inactivity, and (3) tobacco. Other possible factors, like stress, except as it may precipitate death in an already sick man, need further study as to their basic responsibility for the disease itself.

What can the women do? Two things, I said: first to set the example themselves by avoiding obesity, by being physically active, and by not smoking; and second to reduce the volume and richness of the diet of their menfolk, induce them to exercise with them, and to get the family to protest against their smoking.

Following my address, there was an emotional account of her husband's heart attack by a noted commentator. Then after the intermission came a lively question-and-answer period, with Dr. Rogers and two other cardiologists joining me in the quiz session. For weeks afterward the Portland team was busy answering many more questions which came in by mail.

This initial "Hearts and Husbands" program in 1964 was so successful that a very similar meeting, in which I again participated, was held in San Francisco the next fall and again many thousands of women came from central and northern California. A year later, in 1966, on the way home from the Fifth World Congress of Cardiology in India, my wife and I stopped off in Manila. There, Dr. Francis Chamberlain of San Francisco and I took part in the third "Hearts and Husbands" program, which was attended by about a thousand men and women—preponderantly the latter—including Ismelda Marcos, the wife of the president of the Philippines.

Then, out of the blue, there came a fascinating challenge

from a lady who was writing to the *Reader's Digest;* she sent me word that unless I could send her an adequate answer she was about to send in an "Open Letter to Dr. Paul Dudley White," accusing me of breaking up families. My answer must have satisfied her, for I heard no more of the matter, somewhat to my sorrow, for I would have welcomed publication of both her question and my answer.

The crux of her accusation was that I and other doctors were joining the wives against their husbands. She gave the following example: John comes home from work in the evening and asks his wife "What's for dinner?" She replies, "Soup and fish and vegetables." "And what's for dessert?" he asks. She says there is no dessert. "Why not?" he demands, for like most men he enjoys rich desserts. "Because Dr. White says 'No,' " she answers. Whereupon John slams out of the house to get his dessert somewhere else.

The more I thought about the editor's complaint the more I began to see that it might be valid. And so I changed the title of these meetings on preventive cardiology to "Husbands, Wives, and their Children," and placed the emphasis on the children, in whom atherosclerotic arterial disease often begins. It is easier, after all, to teach a child good habits than it is to reform a grown man.

In 1967 the more inclusive program was initiated, and several meetings of the sort have been held all over the country since then. The most interesting one of all was in the Mormon Tabernacle at Salt Lake City on September 13, 1967, on which occasion there was an overflow audience of 10,000 people, 9,000 of whom packed the Tabernacle. A delightful part of the occasion was a performance by the famous Tabernacle Choir, which sang at the beginning and the end of the two hour program. The members of the choir also took part in the question-and-answer period. They asked me if I thought that singing was good for the heart, and I allowed that it doubtless was, although not enough in itself—the other health rules also had to be obeyed. I then asked them a question, which I had been put up to earlier by the elders, who feared that some of their flock were smoking. My question was: "Can you sing better with or without tobacco?" Since they were not permitted to smoke, there was naturally no reply, but there were many smiles and much laughter.

Young Candidates for Early Coronary Heart Disease: Risk Factors

CHAPTER XV ⟡ Much more important than our meetings on "Hearts and Husbands" as outlined in the last chapter is the subject of the present chapter, namely a program to prevent, delay, or minimize the great hazard of serious atherosclerosis (the great epidemic of the twentieth century) in the middle-aged American, especially the male, of today. This preventive program should be applied to the young even in their teen ages and early twenties if they are identifiable in their youth as many of them are twenty, thirty, or forty years before they become victims of the disease. Therefore, while working hard to treat and to rehabilitate the senior citizens we should pay at least equal attention to their children and grandchildren (especially their sons and grandsons) before they get sick.

Since it is possible to identify the candidate for early coronary heart disease while he is still in his early youth, even a teenager, preventive environmental health measures can be started many years before his coronary heart disease would ordinarily become manifest, at perhaps fifty years of age.

How is it possible to identify these candidates? This is best told by an examination of the various risk factors involved.

Let me start with the environmental risk factors, which still need some research and refinement and almost certainly vary greatly in relative importance from individual to individual. I shall discuss them more or less in the order of general agreement as to their importance:

A. *Environmental Risk Factors*

1. Overnutrition: This I consider the most important type of malnutrition prevalent in the United States, in contrast to undernutrition or starvation, which, although existing in the impoverished areas of the country, is far less common. I as well as many others of my vintage have watched this type evolve right under our noses, with other evidences of the misuse of our prosperity. There have always been obese and overnourished people, even in antiquity, but relatively far fewer than in the United States today, when the great majority are prosperous enough to have indeed added more fat to their bodily frame and to the lining of their arteries than is good for them. In my own experience in medical practice the majority of my coronary heart patients have put on considerable weight by middle age, when their disease becomes manifest, twenty pounds or often much more over their weight in their very early twenties. Certainly this weight is not due to added muscle. Whether the harm that obesity does is worse (that is, compounded) by eating an excessive amount of fatty food than by eating an excessive amount of vegetable food of the same caloric value, no one knows. The American diet is overrich in all three food constituents, protein, fat, and carbohydrate. It is, however, believed by many that saturated, mostly animal, fat in the form of dairy products, eggs, and fatty meats, is more conducive to earlier atherosclerotic disease than the same amount in calories of unsaturated, mostly vegetable, fat.

We do know that undernourished or starving people have little or no atherosclerosis, at least in youth and middle age. There must be a middle of the road in reducing! I should add, however, that there has been an unnecessary proliferation of dietary books and dietary fads; it is far better to remember that *calories do count* and that good advice may be had from doctors and from the American or local Heart Associations. (See Appendix 2 for further comments on diet.)

2. Physical Inactivity, or Lethargy: This seems to be an environmental risk factor almost as important as an overrich diet, or probably, in some individuals, more important. We have found in our studies that if one labors physically very hard all day he can be lighter in weight and have less coronary heart disease. Dr. Fred Stare, of Boston, Professor Joliffe, of Dublin, Ireland, and their colleagues, including myself, found in a study of 500 pairs of Irish brothers that the brothers who worked hard with their arms and legs and backs on poor farms in Ireland had less coronary heart disease than their brothers who had lived in the United States for at least ten years and who had adopted our inactive physical life. Although the brothers in Ireland devoured more calories, including dairy products, than their brothers in this country, they were lighter in weight, and their electrocardiograms and blood pressures were more normal.

There must be a happy mean of muscular activity between the hard work of someone who labors physically ten hours or more a day, and that of a typical United States citizen who has hardly any exercise at all as he drives or is driven to work every morning, rides to his office floor in an elevator, sits at his desk all day, often has too much lunch brought in to him, rides home again in the late afternoon, sits and naps in front of the television set, is interrupted by several cocktails and an overhearty dinner, and finally goes to bed late after raiding the refrigerator. When I was a young doctor, nearly sixty years ago, I dealt with many laborers, the like of whom we see no more, and there was very little coronary heart disease among them, in contrast to our relatively prosperous blue collar workers today, who labor little and have more "coronaries."

What can take the place of the beneficent effect of the hard physical labor of yesteryear? In the last fifty years, our machines have become our masters, and the result is a great increase of coronary heart attacks, with strokes and sudden death in profusion in middle age, long before we are old. My own belief is that no one under eighty years of age should be so afflicted, certainly not under seventy, and yet they are common in the sixties, in the fifties, and now growing more common in men even in their forties and their thirties; recently I have examined two young men with coronary heart disease, both in their twenties—they were typical candidates.

Part of the answer lies in physical labor or exercise, such as gardening or farming, or work on trees, or substitutes like sports or gymnastics; the type of exercise doesn't matter much; what matters is that it should be vigorous from childhood on, and performed for at least an hour a day and a conservative minimum of seven days a week. If the individual is young, or has never ceased to exercise, it can be strenuous; if the individual is over fifty and unaccustomed to labor it should be less strenuous and begun under the supervision of a doctor.

It doesn't much matter what exercise you take, provided it involves the leg muscles in particular and suits you in age, strength, aptitude, and experience. There are, as in the case of diets, too many books on exercise of every kind. There are as many fads on exercise as there are on diet. For the healthy young or middle-aged man accustomed to run or swim or play squash or tennis, or golf without a cart, or to ski or skate, there is no reason why he should not continue to carry on for many years, cutting down somewhat the vigor of the sport as he gets older and checking with his physician annually in case diabetes, high blood pressure, or some other abnormality should insidiously appear, so that it may be treated early in its course.

The simplest exercise of all and the easiest for most individuals is walking, and that can be done without equipment except good shoes, in almost any terrain and weather and into very old age. The next simplest is bicycling, which I myself have enjoyed for many years and continue to enjoy, at home and abroad, as in England, France, the Netherlands—only recently I bicycled ten miles on the Atlantic City boardwalk, and found the experience most beneficial, especially as an example to my fellow octogenarians. One of my continuing campaigns is to try to persuade various cities and towns to put in special paths for the pedestrians and cyclists when they build new roads. I am pleased that this campaign is beginning to have an effect.

I believe that brisk walking or slow running on the toes is probably better than jogging, in which one comes down on the heels or on the flat of the foot; I understand that the orthopedists are seeing some joggers with symptoms of strain on hips or spine already become osteoporotic (a term referring to weakening of the bone) with age and disuse. I have also known of a few deaths of runners and joggers who suddenly began these more vigorous exercises after years of indolence; similar deaths have quite naturally occurred among snow shovelers.

If one joins a group exercising regularly in a gymnasium or running or jogging, he should be checked first by a physician and always report any new symptom which develops. In fact, the ideal is that one member of the group be a physician, who would be able to observe and help his lay colleagues, but I would add a word of caution, since one group reported to me that it was their doctor who dropped dead.

Calisthenics, which literally means "beautiful strength," can be a part of the exercise program, but it is important to remember that the largest muscles in the body are those of the legs, and that they should constitute the main object of the exercising for several reasons. Among these are the fact that the leg veins have valves (as have the arm veins too) and that, as already mentioned, these valves prevent the blood from falling with gravity to the bottom of the legs; also, when leg muscles contract they squeeze the veins and actually pump the blood up to the heart. It is important for the health of the heart, therefore, to see that the legs are well exercised. When this is done, a sense of psychological relaxation often ensues. In fact, physical labor is one of the best antidotes, perhaps *the* best, for emotional stress or mental fatigue. Also leg exercise helps to keep the leg veins themselves from developing clots (from thrombosis).

3. Tobacco: Here a complete taboo is advisable for everyone, since massive statistics have shown that cancer of the lungs is much more common in smokers than in non-smokers. So, too, is emphysema of the lungs, which is due to the breaking of the myriad of delicate little alveoli (air sacs), by the strain of coughing, to form large blebs with so much reduction of surface area of the total inner lining that the exposure to the outside atmosphere of the blood flowing through the lungs is inadequate for the exchange of gases, for the oxygen to enter the blood and the carbon dioxide to leave it. We know, also, that the inhalation of carbon monoxide in the tobacco smoke, more even than in the polluted air of our cities, displaces the essential oxygen in the hemoglobin in the blood. A switch to pipes or cigars is often thought to be safe, but this gives a sense of false security, since bladder cancer is more common in such smokers and results from the fact that the nicotine from tobacco juice is inevitably swallowed and is excreted through the kidneys. Tobacco is a poison, almost as addictive as morphine, although not so devastating.

4. Other Environmental Factors: Many of these— like emotional stress, for instance—are now being studied to determine whether they are basic causes of a heart attack or whether they only precipitate the eventual attack after the

body has slowly but steadily established the atherosclerotic disease. This atherosclerotic process can take twenty or thirty years to develop without any knowledge on the part of the subject. In fact, most of the American males that I see as patients in middle age with what we call coronary heart disease, have felt well or even unusually well until their heart attack suddenly hit them, or until their first symptom of angina pectoris slowed them as they walked fast or climbed up a hill or faced a cold wind, or got unduly excited.

Stress, physical or emotional—for example, shoveling snow in a blizzard or being excited nervously or emotionally (from anger, grief, joy, pleasure, or any other emotion)— does not, as far as I know, cause death or a heart attack in a physically healthy person. But if the coronary (heart) circulation is already compromised by a sufficient degree of atherosclerosis (an accumulation in the arteries of a deposit of fibrous tissue, blood clot and fat deposit, obstructing the flow of blood to the heart muscle), angina pectoris (heavy pain under the breastbone) may occur, or even rapid death. If in the same way there is an increase of blood pressure, when it is already high, there can be a hemorrhage in the brain (apoplexy) from physical or emotional stress. Or if the cerebral circulation through the carotid, vertebral, or basilar arteries is already compromised, ischemia of various parts of the brain can result in temporary aphasia (affection of speech), or weakness or paralysis or loss of sensation of a hand or some other part of the body. This has been sometimes called a "little stroke."

I was recently asked whether a man who is forty-five, overweight, unaccustomed to exercise, and a longtime smoker, could possibly reclaim his body by following the course I have recommended. My answer was that although some men by the age of forty-five have done themselves irreparable harm, the majority are salvable if they stop smoking, reduce their weight slowly and sensibly, and begin to exercise gradually by walking more each day, by golf or swimming, or by tennis later on if they feel up to it. This rehabilitation should be under medical supervision.

I have also been asked whether such a man should reduce the quantity and character of his sexual activities. My answer to that is, not necessarily, unless he has angina pectoris easily induced. I must add, however, that deaths during coitus do occur.

On this same subject I may say that, contrary to popular belief, sexual relations are not forbidden even *after* a heart attack. Like resumption of physical exercise, social activities, and one's occupation, whether sedentary or involving physical, mental, or emotional activity or stress, so sexual intercourse is a normal physiological function that can be beneficially resumed in the course of weeks or months in almost all patients after heart attacks, or, with the help of nitroglycerine, even while somewhat limited by coronary insufficiency, or even after the clearing of congestive heart failure.

Before leaving the subject of the environmental risk factors, we should note that life begins nine months before birth and what the mother does or is subjected to, may have a potent effect for good or bad on the foetus. We know that a few things, like German Measles in the first three months of pregnancy, can deform the baby and that the sedative thalidomide taken at the time of the development of the limbs can deform them. But there must be many other environmental factors like other viruses or other drugs or the overuse of tobacco or alcohol by the mother, or trauma, that may have important influences on the foetus; much more work must be done before we can define all the risks during those first nine months of life.

B. *Heredity*

Now I shall end this chapter by discussing one of the most important considerations of all, that is, the identification in his teenage years or twenties of the candidate for early coronary heart disease, which becomes manifest in his thirties, forties, or fifties—a subject lost in mass statistics of populations and of lipid tests. No two persons are exactly alike and in every population there are candidates for earlier atherosclerosis and others who are almost immune. Although there is still much to learn or to confirm, there are some factors of which we are already aware:

1. Sex: The male sex is preponderantly affected in youth and middle age and lives a shorter life than his consort, as already noted. It is the female hormone that protects against early atherosclerosis of serious degree up to the time of the menopause, but we don't know why. A male who is castrated early in life is late in developing any atherosclerosis, while a female who is deprived of her ovaries early in life loses her immunity and can develop coronary heart disease early.

2. Age: It is true that atherosclerosis usually increases with age, but in many patients the correction of overeating and other bad habits may initiate an indeterminately long period of good health, with recovery from some of the more serious manifestations of the atherosclerosis.

3. Mesomorphy: Body build, evident even in childhood, is also of importance. The youngster stocky in build, with relatively big bones and strong muscles for his age, doubtless needs protection against overnutrition and obesity in contrast to the ectomorph (person of skinny build) , as I was, and am.

4. Diabetes: This disease is often inherited, and its presence, unless found and controlled early, makes one about four times more likely to have important degrees of atherosclerosis. In fact, even a family history of diabetes is a threat and a "prediabetic" state should be investigated in every member of a diabetic family.

5. Hypercholesterolemia: Too much cholesterol in the blood, a condition which must be confirmed by repeated tests, makes one a candidate and may be a family trait discoverable even in the teenage years. By usual testing, a cholesterol fig-

ure constantly at 250 to 300 milligrams per cent, is slightly to moderately elevated above normal. When over 300, it is importantly high and demands effort at reduction by diet, exercise, omission of tobacco, and (as a last resort) the use of medicine. (See Appendix 2 for more about cholesterol.)

6. Hypertension: High blood pressure has been rare in my young cases of coronary heart disease, but when it does come in middle age or older it is certainly an aggravating factor.

7. Excessive Stress and Excessive Reaction Thereto.

8. Family History: Finally, a history of presenile coronary heart diseases or strokes in both branches of the family is important and should be ruled in or out by careful history-taking, which sometimes is difficult. This investigation should also include brothers and sisters.

We are in a serious health crisis in this country today because of the prevalence of this disease of the arteries. Although we can undoubtedly improve the situation by advising and effecting a general change in our ways of life, we can attack the problem first and best by helping early in life the more obvious candidates for the disease. We need to start now to help to save the next generation. I am optimistic that we will do so.

But we also still need much more research on all the risk factors mentioned above, with our minds open for the possibility of as yet unrecognized factors. One of these is that of trace minerals or chemicals in small concentration that have not yet been identified or are already under study. Another possible factor is that in some individuals the arterial wall may be delicate and unable to stand the wear and tear of the simple hydrodynamic pressure of the vigorous blood flow with the early development of scarring in streaks or at certain vulnerable areas of the intima (inner lining) as pointed out by Meyer Texon.

The Decade of the 1960s

CHAPTER XVI 🙚   As I look back in this final chapter on the last ten years, in time the decade of the 1960s, and in age my own seventies, I am profoundly grateful. I have been permitted by circumstances not only to follow up in practice many of my private patients but also to continue three other main and special interests which had begun in the previous decade, the first to help in the support of public health with the triple partnership of physician, layman, and government, the second to help in the evolution of preventive cardiology, and the third to help to promote international medicine through cardiology, one of its most important fields, and thereby to improve the international relationships of both physicians and their patients, a process basic to world peace. Judah Folkman, in an address to the graduating class of 1970, published in a recent (August 1970) issue of the *Harvard Medical Alumni Bulletin*, paraphrased Francis Weld Peabody's famous precept "The secret of the care of the patient is to care for the patient" by substituting "people" for "patient," thereby broadening the context. I would go a step further to the ultimate for all physicians, and laymen too, on earth, namely to be concerned with the health and happiness of *all peoples*, all nations, all races.

At the beginning, in 1920, I started with private patients,

their clinical research, and local teaching; happily thirty years later, in 1950, I was led into the two larger fields, but I regard the two careers, the earlier one and the later one, as equally important and complementary, and each a continuing learning process.

I fully recognize that the fortune of good health allowed me to maintain a very active program throughout the 1960s. Since a good many people have asked me if I have ever been sick at all, I shall for such enquirers list my relatively few maladies. My illnesses have been mostly minor to date, except for scarlet fever and diphtheria in childhood. I have had two disagreeable "colds" every year, a broken leg during a medical softball game in our pasture thirty years ago, pneumonia in Washington in 1950, an annoying intestinal irritability ever since an attack of herpes zoster (shingles) in 1963, a very little and decreasing angina pectoris on effort during the last few years (which began just before the age of eighty-one), and more recently, a severe sprain of my right ankle from a silly skiing accident. I have a wise medical adviser who examines me annually; my only medicine is a vitamin mixture for my undernutrition, attested by a loss of twenty pounds in the last twenty years, so that my frame today resembles that of the late Mahatma Gandhi.

Let me discuss a few of the details of my chief interests of the 1960s, to which I referred in the first paragraph of this chapter.

First, my patients and those whom I have seen as a consultant: there were perforce and by intention fewer new patients in the 1950s and the 1960s than in the earlier three decades, because there were so many old ones to follow up. I actually listed and tabulated 10,000 private patients from 1920 to 1950, and 5,000 more between 1950 and 1970. When I began to see patients, at first only in the hospital from 1911 until I started private practice in 1920, they were almost all poor, since the Massachusetts General Hospital was a so-called "charity hospital" like all the large hospitals in the rest of the country. Quite naturally, when I began private practice, these earlier patients were unable to pay more than a very modest fee—ten dollars for the first visit and five for later visits, which then seemed adequate to me. I can recall that thirty years earlier my father in his family practice had charged two dollars for a house visit and one for an office visit. This difference between 1890 and 1920 and again between 1920 and more recent years has been, in considerable degree, the result of the decrease in the value of the dollar, but it also reflects the fact that in the budding practice of any doctor the wealthier patients do not come until the physician has established himself in his community by experience and ability. Many of my patients during my first year of practice were young and poor and often were recent immigrants; almost all of them, by dint of hard work, have prospered, and a few have become wealthy. Many have made donations to my research fund and to the national and community heart drives every year, contributions for which we are all most grateful.

Another special reason for my gratitude to these patients of mine through the years has been their willingness to serve as examples in my teaching clinics for medical students, both undergraduate and graduate, and also at the larger inter-hospital and even national and international congresses and at the committee hearings of the House of Representatives and the Senate in Washington.

Finally, one of the special advantages and joys of a long practice in one community is the involvement with the patient's family through the years. I have had as patients a good many of two generations of the same family, and, not infrequently, of three generations. It is in part this experience that has convinced me that certain heart diseases *do* run in families, and of the need for family doctors.

In my teaching, I suppose that I have been most effective in passing on what I have learned directly from my patients, especially in my clinical researches. The excitement of the research has often been contagious and has attracted able students as volunteers. The research teams of today, made up of workers from multiple disciplines, are generally more effective in the long run, but the division of the investigation into fragments tends at times to dull the interest, and can make it more pedestrian to the individual member of the team. Despite this criticism, however, I have greatly enjoyed and profited by being a member of some of the international teams carrying on epidemiological cardiovascular investigations in various parts of the world. I have been lucky to belong to both groups, first, to the doctors involved with individual patients in practice and in clinical research, and second, to those involved in statistical studies of large groups in public health through population investigations. In this way, while recognizing the significance of the forest, I have not lost sight of the individual trees. I believe this to be significant, for to me every patient is an individual and usually the individual is more important than his disease.

I turn now to my major interest in the 1960s: prevention of heart disease. Earlier chapters in this book made it clear, I hope, that until the mid-thirties heart disease was not a major epidemic and that it only became so in the 1940s and especially so in the 1950s. The result of this increasing challenge has been that during the last ten years I have spent more and more of my time in the struggle to save our men, through prevention of the disease, while they are still young, than in trying to cure it, when it may be too late.

To recapitulate, this epidemic disease is not one of an infection, or of a poison, or even of the heart or brain, which are secondarily affected, but of the arteries (the tubular branching vessels which carry the blood from the heart throughout the body). It is called atherosclerosis, a kind of "rusting" of the inner wall of the artery, which delays the flow of blood and frequently results in a complete blocking of the artery by a blood clot (thrombosis), with death of the tissue (called infarct) of heart or brain or other tissue, and the formation of a scar if the victim survives.

This frightful disease has developed insidiously and steadily right under our very noses throughout the middle of this century and now causes half of all the mortality in the United States, much of it under the age of sixty. It demands attention at once, despite the rather casual references made to it. Many people, even doctors, call us alarmists, as they used to do about epidemics of the plague, or of typhoid fever, or of diphtheria, saying that we should not interfere with the pleasure of an individual in his tobacco, his overeating, and his physical laziness. But in the last few years I have personally seen and helped to take care of too many young men in their thirties, and even in their twenties, to be able to be complacent about this epidemic.

I am certain, from what we have done with other diseases in the past, that we can control this one, despite its complexities. We know enough to begin, and we must start with the children, to prevent the disease while doing all we can to save and to rehabilitate those who acquire it in middle and older age. The most important thing that we have learned about it is that the arteries begin to be affected often in the teenager, some thirty years before symptoms begin, and that the first symptom can be sudden death. I suppose that almost half of my waking hours these days are concerned, in thought, reading, writing, speaking, or in actual practice, with this dreadful disease—and yet of its very existence I was hardly aware at the beginning of my professional career.

As a final theme of my life, I would like to emphasize once more the desire which was part of my boyhood dreams—

inherited in large part from my parents—that I might have some small part in the work of establishing a true brotherhood of man on this contentious earth. I feel fortunate in having been exposed to such a brotherhood in my youth; I had many Irish Catholic and Jewish playmates who were neighbors, and in college, medical school, and hospital I had many acquaintances and friends among Negro Americans and recent immigrants from Ireland, Italy, and central and eastern Europe; I very nearly went to China as a medical missionary early in my career. My grand tour of Europe in 1913 and my year of study in London, with its opportunity to become acquainted with Welshmen and Scots as well as English, greatly broadened my international base, so that all of the many travels that have followed in the past half century were a natural consequence.

I shall mention only a few of these travels during the 1960s. To include more could be boring but a full list of medical travels during that decade can be found in the appendix.

Useful for the purpose of appraising the progress in the field of cardiology throughout the world and in becoming acquainted with the young new pioneers from every country, were two World Congresses—the fourth in Mexico City in 1962 and the fifth in New Delhi in 1966. The one in Mexico City was a reunion of many of us who had attended the inauguration of the pioneer National Institute of Cardiology of Mexico (the real beginning of international cardiology) in 1944. Later, in the fall of 1969, there were still a good many of us survivors who took part in the twenty-fifth anniversary of the Institute in Mexico City.

On June 6, 1966, my eightieth birthday was quietly feted by a small gathering of intimate friends at the new villa of Ancel Keys on the southwest coast of Italy at Pioppi, some thirty miles south of the renowned Greek temples at Paestum; somewhat later, during the World Congress in New Delhi, the birthday was belatedly but happily celebrated by a host of international friends.

To go back briefly to the first year of the decade, my wife and I took part in 1961 in one of the most interesting and successful campaigns of our lives. As the result of an initial visit to Australia in 1958 we helped to persuade the Australian doctors to organize a public drive for funds for cardiovascular research, training, and education, along the lines of the very successful annual drives of the American Heart Association. To give impetus to the initial Australian campaign, my wife and I, during the last ten days of April, 1961, made one-night stands all over Australia by television, radio, luncheons, dinners, and receptions, campaigning in the cities of Sydney, Brisbane, Melbourne, Hobart, Perth, Adelaide, and finally Canberra, where, on the night of April 28, Prime Minister Menzies and I launched this first heart drive via the newly established national television network. The goal was for 1.5 million pounds, but when through the month of May that goal was surpassed by a million pounds, everyone was jubilant.

On the thirtieth of April, my wife and I flew 2,000 miles, from Sydney to Darwin, and then the 2,100 miles on to Singapore, where we conferred with our Malaysian and Chinese cardiological friends and attended the first dinner of the new Singapore Society of Cardiology. (Incidentally, the next Asian-Pacific Congress of Cardiology will be held in Singapore in 1972.) It was a week of cardiological beginnings, for during the next few days we visited our medical friends in Bangkok, Calcutta, Kathmandu (Nepal), and in New Delhi, where, early in May, 1961, the Indian Heart Foundation began its existence under the able leadership of Dr. Sivaramakrishna Padmavati, and with the approval of Prime Minister Jawaharlal Nehru, with whom we discussed the project. This was the only time that we met this great man, so beloved by his countrymen, but we rather regretted the need to meet him at this particular time, since we found him obviously exhausted from overwork.

On the eleventh of May my wife and I flew from New Delhi over the Himalayas to Tashkent in the U.S.S.R. and thence to Moscow, where we joined an American team of cardiologists and were guests of the Myasnikovs at their apartment in the city. Their walls were covered from floor to ceiling by the works of great Russian painters, especially Levitan. We went for the weekend to their country dacha, and enjoyed the hospitality of many other Russian friends also. We have always felt an affinity with the citizens of the U.S.S.R. on the streets, in their homes, and at public and private conferences (and of course through their literature), but they seemed to be almost as distant from their political leaders as had been the common people under the czars.

My wife then left for home and I went on to Leningrad with my American cardiological colleagues to continue our conferences with local doctors there, then back to Moscow to complete our discussions. Then I went off to conferences in Greece and in Paris, and finally flew home at the end of the month.

I have described this particular world tour as a typical example of the many medical missions which took me abroad so frequently during the 1960s. There are a few other travels of special importance.

One of these was a trip which took place in the fall of that same year, 1961. This began with a conference on international research in Brussels, where in 1958 the Third World Congress of Cardiology had been held; continued with my attendance at the Fourth World Congress of Angiology (a congress concerning the study of blood vessels), chaired by Professor Bohumil Prusik of Charles University in Prague, Czechoslovakia; and thence with a visit to the Caucasian Republic of the U.S.S.R., where Dr. Keys and I carried out a brief study of that area's world-famous centenarians. I myself examined wrinkled but alert and physically active men authentically aged 105, 118, and 126; the oldest of these three was somewhat deaf. Our conclusions were that they had inherited their longevity, and that it wasn't just the result (as sometimes claimed) of the noted wine of the country, or their outdoor life, or the consumption of butter-milk—we had hoped to carry out a complete research on this particular population with our Georgian medical friends, but their invitation was not approved in Moscow.

After that I took off for Kabul, the capital city of Afghan-istan. This mission, as I have already mentioned briefly, I undertook at the request of Tom Dooley, who, a few months before he had died, had asked me to help in the establish-ment of the American medical and nursing team at the highly respected and historic Avicenna Hospital in Kabul. As a guest of Ambassador Byroade and his wife, I visited that hospital several times, and I also lectured at the Univer-sity Hospital and at the Shara Hospital, famous for its school for midwives. I was delighted to find that Medico (later a branch of Care) was taking on the responsibility for the American medical, surgical, and nursing staff at the Avi-cenna Hospital—a contribution to the health of the Afghans which was much appreciated by their health ministry.

From Kabul I returned home slowly via Teheran, Beirut, and Athens, stopping off at the beautiful island of Corfu where I observed an epidemiological cardiovascular investiga-tion of the population then in progress there under the wing of Professors Ancel Keys of the U.S.A., and Christos Aravanis of Athens. Professor Djordjevic of Belgrade was also an observer. Finally I flew to Dublin where I conferred with my Irish medical friends about the organization of the Irish Heart Foundation, which a few years later developed.

Early the next year, 1962, I returned briefly to Pakistan and the Khyber Pass to make sure that our medical supplies to the Avicenna Hospital were getting through despite a de-

Paul Dudley White addressing 10,500 women of Oregon in Portland's Memorial Coliseum at the 1964 Hearts and Husbands Conference. Throughout
the address a monitor in the foreground recorded Dr. White's electrocardiogram from electrodes on his chest.

Dr. White with several Russian friends at the First Annual Congress of the Soviet Society of Cardiology. From left to right: Dr. Evgeny Chazov, vice-minister of health; Paul Dudley White; Professor Pavel Lukomsky, first president of the Soviet Society of Cardiology; and Dr. Igor Shkhvatsabaia, director of the Myasnikov Institute of Cardiology. A bust of Professor Alexander Myasnikov appears in the background.

lay caused by an intertribal war which had closed the pass. I lectured in the picturesque city of Peshawar, situated near the eastern end of the pass. There I met again Dr. Edward Toomey, a young doctor whom I had known in the States and who was now serving his military duty at the U.S. Airbase from which the famous U2 plane took off to precipitate the international crisis so very difficult for President Eisenhower. Dr. Toomey obtained leave for a week and I introduced him to Field Marshal Ayub Khan, then president of Pakistan, who made it possible for him to visit the Hunza Valley, high in the Karakorum Range of the Himalayas, to study for me the health of twenty-five of the oldest men—approximately 100 years old. I had harbored the thought and desire to do this for some years but because of other commitments was unable to go myself.

Hunza is a very remote valley, and until recently the only way to reach it was to travel by foot or by horseback. A few years ago a jeep track was finally carved through the massive rock passes; before that time the inhabitants had been unaware of the existence of the wheel, and thought nothing of walking thirty miles in a day. They have been famous for their health, eating a great deal of fruit, and boasting that a man in really good shape can eat 3,000 apricots at one sitting. By and large they live to a much older age than do other inhabitants of the Asian subcontinent.

Dr. Toomey, who was, I believe, the first Western physician to obtain such data concerning the Hunzas, found that among twenty-five aged men whom he examined, the blood pressures, the electrocardiograms, and the serum cholesterol levels were all completely normal, a finding very different from similar studies in the United States, and one which is probably to be ascribed to the ancestral longevity, the hard way of life, with great dependency upon their legs, and to the largely vegetarian diet of these men.

It was in July of that year, 1962, that I took advantage of

the International Cancer Congress in Moscow to ask Professor Blokhin, president of the Soviet Academy of Medical Sciences, to call together the ten foreign members of the Academy to meet with the Soviet members in order to get acquainted. Almost all were present at the subsequent meeting, including the president of the Chinese Academy, with whom I conferred several times. He invited me for a month's visit to four cities in mainland China, but as we began to make plans for my visit during the next year, difficulties within China and the militant program of the young Chinese Red Guards made it necessary to postpone any such visit. Through various intermediaries the Chinese authorities have been kept informed of my continued desire to confer with the Chinese physicians interested in cardiology. The United States will now grant permission for travel to China, but the would-be traveler must first be invited by the Chinese. So far, no official and valid invitation has been issued to me, or to any other U.S. doctors so far as I know, but I am still hopeful.

In 1963 there were two events in my life that were especially enjoyable. The first was an errand in Izmir, the old Smyrna, for our secretary of commerce: to cut the ribbon of the United States medical exhibit at the annual Turkish fair. Consul General Byrne and his wife not only took me in as their guest but made it possible for me to visit the ancient ruins—in the south at Ephesus (the sacred city of Diana) and those in the north at Pergamum. It was during that fortnight that I was exposed first to chicken pox in Istanbul and then to severe smallpox at Schweitzer's Hospital and at the Government Hospital across the Ogooué River in Africa; apparently as a result of the exposure to chicken pox soon after my arrival home I broke out with the shingles (herpes zoster), which I thought at first might be smallpox.

The other special event in 1963 was the dinner of the International Cardiology Foundation in New York City, on

October 29, honoring General Dwight D. Eisenhower, on which occasion he presented me with a gold stethoscope. This was the first award of the sort, except for a private presentation to me by my associate, Howard Sprague, some years earlier in the Ether Dome of the Massachusetts General Hospital. Two years later, as president of the International Cardiology Foundation, I had the honor of presenting at an international dinner in Geneva, gold stethoscopes to three pioneer cardiologists of world renown, Professors Camille Lian of France, Sir John Parkinson of England, and Alexander Myasnikov of Russia, and incidentally a gold electrical vector of the heart to Professor Pierre Duchosal of Geneva.

I would like to record two events of 1964. The first was the visit which my wife and I made to Iceland to help celebrate the inauguration of their new cardiology foundation, to see the strange moonlike landscape, and to fly over the fiery new volcanic island. I believe that their literacy level is the highest in the world. The population is more or less static and is a marvelous field for the study of heredity. We had a hard time keeping husbands and wives straight because the women do not take their husbands' names but are always "daughters of ——." We found them a charming people. It is a historic land and we saw the medieval site of the world's first representative parliament and not far away the icy pool used for the dunking of unfaithful wives.

From Iceland, we went on to attend the celebration of the six-hundredth anniversary of the Jagellonian University, with the bestowal of honorary degrees, in Krakow, Poland —a country whose unfortunate, brave and long-suffering people have endured centuries of hardship imposed by their geographical position in Central Europe. These hardships continue to the present day.

The second event of 1964 was that of the Fourth Dartmouth Conference, held in Leningrad. A team of sixteen American educators, writers, economists, and scientists met with a similar team of Russians for a week, to discuss freely but confidentially, mutual national problems. One of the Russian team was the Mayoress of Leningrad, who acted as the hostess for us all. She led us one evening to the enormous graveyard where hundreds of thousands of the victims of the World War II Great Siege of Leningrad are buried— a beautiful memorial, full of roses. Each of the American conferees was given a rose at the entrance to the cemetery. We gave them all to the very able and articulate educational leader of our group, a beautiful black woman, who bearing her armful of roses laid them at the feet of the heroic figure of Leningrad surveying her myriads of dead.

The discussions that took place that week were transmitted in secret to the Kremlin and the White House and we can only hope that they may have improved Soviet-American relations. Two of us were physicians, Professor Blokhin of the U.S.S.R. and myself. With our prime interest in preventive measures in the political field we suggested that teams of physicians, half of them Russians and half Americans, working and living together to bring medical and surgical aid and health measures to needy populations in any part of the world, would show that these two nations can actually work together in a positive way. Our suggestion, alas, was never adopted. An amity close to this, however, exists in Antarctica.

One of the high points of my foreign travels in 1965 was my visit to Ben Gurion and his wife in their kibbutz in the Negev and his invitation for me to join him on his daily four and a half mile walk, after luncheon and his siesta. I found him to be as I had expected, a vigorous critic of the Israeli government, with which he was then in opposition. We talked at length about the ancient and modern history of Israel. I asked him about Sodom and Gomorrah, the supposed site of which I was about to visit at the southern end of the Dead Sea. We talked about the fine job that Dr. Toor (who took me there) had done in rescuing the laborers in the chemical works at the Dead Sea, far below sea level, by persuading the government to build a new town for them higher up just above sea level, where they could live and be able to breathe fresh air, at least at night and on weekends. Incidentally, I had been asked by Ben Gurion's younger physicians to persuade him to stop standing on his head during the Yoga exercises which he had adopted. I suggested that at his age (in the upper 70s) this was probably unwise.

In 1966 there was one outstanding event in addition to the Fifth World Congress of Cardiology in India. My wife and I spent Christmas week in Moscow, attending and taking part in the first annual congress of the new Soviet Society of Cardiology. This was a most stimulating and pleasant experience, meeting as we did hundreds of young cardiologists from all over Russia, including the Asian territories, and even students and physicians from Outer Mongolia and Cuba. My wife and I were the only visitors from the West. I shall never forget, the last evening, looking around the large horseshoe-shaped banquet table and seeing the very different kinds of faces—Mongol, Georgian, "Russian," Armenian, making us aware again of the richness and variety of races that make up the U.S.S.R. We had Christmas dinner on a Sunday at the dacha of the Petrovsky family. He was then, and still is, the minister of health of Soviet Russia, and was one of the first two physicians of the U.S.S.R. allowed to come to the U.S.A. in 1954 after the death of Stalin (the other was Professor Tareev). We were treated to a fascinating troika (three horse) sleigh ride over the snowy countryside before dinner. When I signed the register at the ranch where the horses were kept, I noted that my signature immediately followed that of Castro of Havana who had been there a week earlier.

There were three events of particular interest in 1969. First, we held two Irish-American programs on Preventive

Cardiology in the first week of June. On June 3, Professors Jessup and Mulcahy came from Dublin and addressed us at the Science Museum in Boston; four days later Dr. Frederick Stare, Dr. Mandel Cohen, and I reciprocated by going to Dublin. I would suggest that this type of international exchange can be a desirable program to promote in the future. It was supported by our respective heart foundations.

In September, 1969, we staged a most interesting conference in Geneva, bringing together one cardiologist and one leading layman interested in health from each of many countries, to discuss their cooperative endeavors both nationally and internationally. It was evident that such international cooperation can be very helpful indeed on a wide scale, even more so than higher level cooperation between any two countries. This experience takes time to spread abroad because of the common tradition of nationalism, which, though important in its place, should never exclude the need for international cooperation, particularly in the field of medical science and health.

The third particular activity in 1969 which involved travel was national rather than international. With a beginning of a decrease of government support for medical research and training (due to the war in Viet Nam and travels to the moon), I was asked to extend my exhortations to the American public to increase their contributions to the annual drive of the American Heart Association and to its many affiliates. In 1969 alone, I traveled to at least twenty-five states throughout the country to do this.

Three events overseas in 1970 bring us up to date. In April I greatly enjoyed heading a panel on the W-P-W Syndrome (see Chapter IV) at the Hamlet Hotel in Elsinore, Denmark, during an International Symposium on Cardiac Arrhythmia; and in May my wife and I were guests of the Japanese in Tokyo, where I took part in the inauguration of the new Japan Heart Foundation, in which industrial leaders joined the doctors as very vital allies in their struggle to control the serious menace of heart disease in that country, with the blessing of the government. The third event will be the Sixth World Congress of Cardiology in London in September.

Although preventive medicine in cardiology, epidemiological cardiovascular research, and international cooperation in the field have been my own chief interests, it is a pleasure to record other important developments in cardiology in the decade of the 1960s, carried out by laboratory investigators, clinical contributors, and cardiovascular surgeons who have been helped so much by their engineering colleagues.

There have been many refinements of diagnostic techniques, such as cardiac catheterization and x-ray delineation of arteries, called "angiography," all over the body, aorta, coronary, cerebral, renal, iliac, and femoral, and of the veins, especially the pulmonary and venae cavae (the great veins, superior and inferior) and those of the legs. The serum electrolytes and enzymes, glucose, cholesterol, uric acid, and other chemical substances can be expeditiously tested and at less expense than before—one of the few economies nowadays.

There has been more and more cardiological specialization, as for example in the newer surgical techniques of open heart surgery and assist devices attached to the aorta for a few days to rest the heart by taking on some of its pumping. Most recent of all have been the heart transplants and the continuing work on the completely artificial heart, which has been the object of intense research by a few individuals for more than a decade. Neither of these radical procedures has as yet succeeded; they both are still in the experimental stage. It is probable, however, that both will eventually succeed and play a minor, but useful, role in the late treatment or even the prevention of heart failure in severely damaged hearts, as in the case of certain complicated congenital defects or in the hopeless chronic failure of a grossly damaged heart, when the rest of the body is healthy enough to warrant this radical treatment. The technique of the transplant has been a brilliant technical advance shared by many surgeons, but the so-called rejection problem must still be solved, as well as the problem of obtaining an adequate supply of heart-healthy donors. There has been overmuch anxiety about the ethics of the surgeons involved, their enthusiasm being misinterpreted as unethical; many of these surgeons I know and trust; they are ethical and honest, though adventurous pioneers extending the boundaries of our knowledge, health, and longevity. It may be a long time before the philosophical aspects of the procedure, as in other areas of medicine, like euthanasia, find a satisfactory, humane solution.

Meanwhile I happily credit the surgeons with two other most up-to-date spectacular advances in the treatment of serious coronary heart disease. The first is that of the use of a saphenous vein from the leg to connect the aorta directly to the coronary arteries to bypass the points of block to bring fresh blood in larger quantity to the heart muscle. The second is that of the excision (cutting out) of the myocardial (heart muscle) scar which is either so large that it seriously interferes with the pumping action of the left ventricle or so irritable in its freshly damaged state that it is a threat to life by grossly disturbing the heart rhythm. This procedure is called infarctectomy.

This brings us now to the 1970s, 1980s, and 1990s. I am willing to join the guessing game about the future. It is probable that either by some spectacular biochemical breakthrough or, more likely, by the painstaking education of the very young candidates for the dreadful epidemic of atherosclerosis, a dramatic decrease of this kind of heart disease in youth and middle age may be achieved before the year 2000. Other advances will include more understanding of the causes (with at least some control) of genetic defects of the circulation and of those acquired during fetal life.

As I look back over the past I am grateful that my life has been so full of interesting experiences and people, and that I have been allowed to be of some service, as I hope to continue to be for whatever years remain.

People sometimes ask me, if I were a young man now, just beginning a career and looking for an unexplored field —as cardiology was when I began my work—what field would I choose? I usually startle them by answering that I would pick the study of the brain, which includes both so-called neurology and psychiatry. Yet why not? The brain is an organ, in many ways like other organs, and science is only beginning to know how it functions. The workings of the mind and of the *soul* are about as little understood today as the workings of the heart were sixty years ago. Yes, if I could begin again, I would study the brain.

As for the future of my own specialty, I am optimistic. However, the next few years, even decades, will demand concentrated and hard work by physicians and laymen alike in aiding the cardiologist in his difficult task of educating and caring for the public, as well as in promoting his research.

I shall close with four verses written by Oliver Wendell Holmes over 100 years ago, but as applicable today as they were in 1860:

What makes the Healing Art divine?
The bitter drug we buy and sell,
The brands that scorch, the blades that shine,
The scars we leave, the "cures" we tell?

Are these thy glories, holiest art,
The trophies that adorn thee best,
Or but thy triumph's meanest part,
Where mortal weakness stands confessed?

In vain our pitying tears are shed,
In vain we rear the sheltering pile
Where art weeds out from bed to bed
The plagues we planted by the mile!

And lo! the starry folds reveal
The blazoned truth we hold so dear:
To guard is better than to heal,
The shield is nobler than the spear!

Appendix 1

Paul Dudley White's international cardiological travels, 1961–1970

Date and Place	Center and Program

January 1961

PAPAGO INDIAN RESERVATION
SOUTHERN ARIZONA

San Xavier. Inspection of U.S. Public Health Service, several village centers and new hospital.

April

AUSTRALIA

Canberra. Assisted in first fund-raising campaign of Australian Heart Foundation following meetings in all provincial capitals.

May

SINGAPORE

Singapore. Lecture at Faculty of Medicine.

THAILAND

Bangkok. Visited doctors and hospital.

NEPAL

Kathmandu. Lectures at Nepal Medical Association.

INDIA

Calcutta and New Delhi. Lectures and meetings to promote All India Heart Foundation.

U.S.S.R.

Moscow and Leningrad. Second Exchange Mission between U.S.A. and Soviet Cardiologists.

GREECE

Thessaloniki. Lectured at University Hospital and attended 75th anniversary of Anatolia College.

September

BELGIUM

Brussels. Conference with insurance officials and Professors Keys and Lequime.

CZECHOSLOVAKIA	Prague. Fourth World Congress of Angiology.
U.S.S.R.	Tlibisi, Georgia. Study of centenarians with Ancel Keys.
AFGHANISTAN	Kabul. Lectures at Avicenna and university hospitals for Tom Dooley and Medico.
GREECE	Corfu. International Epidemiological Conference and population research.
IRELAND	Dublin. Conference re Irish Brothers study.

February 1962

INDIA	Bombay. Symposium on Atherosclerosis. Asian-Pacific Society of Cardiology Research Committee. All India Heart Foundation meeting.

Kanpur and Lucknow. Lectures at medical schools. |
| PAKISTAN | Lahore, Rawalpindi, Islamabad, Peshawar, Khyber Pass, Karachi. Visit to clinics, minister of health and President Ayub Khan. |
| ISRAEL | Tel Aviv and Jaffa. Hospitals. Nazareth, Jerusalem (new Hadassah Medical Center). Lectures. Fiftieth anniversary of Israeli Medical Society. |

March

CANADA	Toronto. Health Forum, Geriatric Panel.

May

ENGLAND	London. Royal College of Physicians, induction as Fellow.

July

U.S.S.R.	Moscow. Attended Cancer Congress and especially meeting of

Appendix 1

Soviet Academy of Medical Sciences to meet Chinese academicians.

October

MEXICO

Mexico City. Fourth World Congress of Cardiology.

November

PUERTO RICO

San Juan University. First Inter-American Conference on Forensic Science. Mock trial of suit by "Professor Jones (with heart attack) vs. Centervale College."

August 1963

TURKEY

Izmir. Opened U.S.A. Medical Exhibit at Annual International Turkish Fair, and lectures.

NIGERIA

Lagos. Interviews.

GABON

Libreville, with James Robinson of Crossroads Africa. Visit to Ministry of Health.
Lambaréné. Second visit to Dr. Schweitzer's Hospital; conferred with Mme. Eckert. Visit to Government Hospital—much smallpox.

September

YUGOSLAVIA

Makarska. Epidemiologic investigation of local population of fishermen and farmers.
Meeting of the Research Committee of the International Society of Cardiology.

U.S.S.R.

Moscow. Annual U.S.A.–U.S.S.R. Conference on Cardiology. Demonstration of Coronary Care Ambulances. Visit to Ministry of Health.
Kiev. Visits to Institutes of Gerontology and Cardiology.

HUNGARY

Budapest. Participated in International Congress of Cardiology at Academy of Sciences.

October

CZECHOSLOVAKIA

Prague. Cardiological conference at Ministry of Health.

November

GUATEMALA

Guatemala City. Participation in the Fourth Central American Congress of Cardiology.

May 1964

ICELAND

Reykjavik. Inauguration of new Icelandic Society of Cardiology. University and public lectures.

POLAND

Krakow. Attendance and honorary degree at 600th anniversary of Jagellonian University. Conferences re cardiology.

JAPAN

Kyoto. Third Asian-Pacific Congress of Cardiology.
Kagashima. Lecture to Medical Society.
Kurume. Cardiovascular conferences.
Tokyo. Plans for Japan Heart Foundation. Lectures at University Medical School
Sapporo (Hokkaido). Meeting with local internists.

June

CANADA

Ottawa. Parliamentary Committee on Health and Aging.
Montreal. Seventh Inter-American Congress of Cardiology.

July

U.S.S.R.

Leningrad. Fourth Dartmouth Conference, U.S.A. and U.S.S.R.

August

CZECHOSLOVAKIA

Prague. Fourth European Congress of Cardiology.

FINLAND

Helsinki. Conference on Muscular Metabolism.

Appendix 1

October

CHILE   Santiago. Meeting by the Interna-
                     tional Cardiology Foundation with
                     doctors and laymen re plans for
                     Chilean Heart Foundation.

PERU   Lima. Meeting of Peruvian Society
                     of Cardiology.

December

FRANCE   Paris. Addressed French Society of
                     Cardiology.

April 1965

ITALY   Venice. Research Committee of the
                     International Society of Cardio-
                     logy.

ISRAEL   Tel Aviv. Inauguration of Israeli
                     Heart Foundation.
                     Beer-Sheba. Visit to Negev Hos-
                     pital and Ben-Gurion.

SWITZERLAND   Geneva. Important meetings of the
                     International Cardiology Founda-
                     tion with Gold Stethoscope din-
                     ner: Parkinson, Myasnikov, Lian.

EGYPT, U.A.R.   Cairo. Meeting of International
                     Cardiology Foundation to plan
                     Egyptian Heart Foundation.

December

PANAMA   Panama. Fifth Congress of Central
                     America and Panama cardiologists.

May 1966

IRELAND   Dublin. Inauguration of Irish
                     Heart Foundation.

CZECHOSLOVAKIA   Prague. Meeting of new Czecho-
                     slovak Heart Foundation.
                     Sliac. Symposium on Coronary
                     Heart Disease by Czechoslovak
                     Heart Foundation.

GREECE   Athens. University Symposium on
                     Atherosclerosis.

June

SWITZERLAND

Geneva. Conference of International Cardiology Foundation and International Society of Cardiology.

ITALY

Minnelea (Pioppi). PDW's 8oth birthday with epidemiologists in Southern Italy (province of Salerno).

October

ISRAEL

Tel Aviv. Symposium on physical activity and aging.
Jerusalem. Israeli Heart Association meetings.

PAKISTAN

Karachi. Cardiac Department, Postgraduate Medical Center. Meeting of Pakistan Society of Cardiology.
Lahore. Lecture at King Edward Medical School.
Rawalpindi and Islamabad. Tour of hospitals.

October–November

INDIA

New Delhi. Fifth World Congress of Cardiology.

November

CEYLON

Colombo. Lecture at University Medical School. Plans for Ceylon Heart Foundation.

THAILAND

Bangkok. Met doctors to plan National Heart Foundation.

PHILIPPINES

Manila. Guerero Lecture at Santo Tomas University. "Hearts and Husbands" program for public. University of the Philippines Lecture "The Cardiac in Industry."

December

U.S.S.R.

Moscow. First meeting of the Soviet Society of Cardiology, Professor Lukomsky, President. Conference with Professor Petrovsky, Minister of Health.

January 1967

MEXICO

Scammon's Lagoon. Study of the gray whale.

April–May

SPAIN

Seville. Conference with cardiologists.
Madrid. Meeting of Spanish Society of Cardiology.

May

SWITZERLAND

Geneva. Inauguration of the new headquarters of the International Society of Cardiology and International Cardiology Foundation.
Meetings of the Executive Committees.

August

CANADA

Montreal. Lecture at Cardiological Institute.

October

SPAIN

Madrid. Inauguration of Spanish Heart Foundation. First Servetus Lecture at University.

ITALY

Milano. Planning Italian Heart Foundation.

CZECHOSLOVAKIA

Prague. Addressed Purkinje Medical Society. Visit to Minister of Health.

FRANCE

Paris. Conference re French Cardiology Foundation.

November

PUERTO RICO

San Juan. Annual meeting of Puerto Rican Medical Society.

April 1968

PERU

Lima. Eighth Inter-American Congress of Cardiology. Peruvian National Heart Foundation meeting.

June

ENGLAND

London. Royal College of Physicians dinner meeting.

September

ISRAEL

Jerusalem. Fourth Asian-Pacific Congress of Cardiology.

ITALY

Milano. Inauguration of Italian Heart Foundation.

GREECE

Athens. Fifth European Congress of Cardiology.

YUGOSLAVIA

Makarska. Meeting of Epidemiological Council of the International Society of Cardiology, and population follow-up.

April 1969

FRANCE

Paris. Conference re French Heart Foundation.

SWITZERLAND

Geneva. Conference with staff of International Society of Cardiology and International Cardiology Foundation.

ITALY

Milano. Program of Italian Heart Foundation.

June

IRELAND

Dublin. Irish Heart Foundation program on Preventive Cardiology.

July

PHILIPPINES

Manila. Meeting of Philippine National Heart Foundation.

September

SWITZERLAND

Geneva. Meeting of National Heart Foundations with the new International Cardiology Federation.

October

MEXICO

Mexico City. Twenty-fifth anniversary of the National Heart Institute of Mexico.

Appendix 1

April 1970

DENMARK
Elsinore. Participation in Symposium on Cardiac Arrhythmias and Wolf-Parkinson-White Syndrome.

May

JAPAN
Tokyo. Inauguration of Japan Heart Foundation.
Nagasaki. Lecture at University Medical School.
Kurume. Participation in Syposium on Rheumatic Heart Disease.

September

IRELAND
Dublin. Visited Irish Heart Foundation headquarters.
Blessington. Symposium on Cardiovascular Epidemiology. International student group.

ENGLAND
London. Sixth World Congress of Cardiology. Inauguration of International Cardiology Federation. Retired from presidency of International Cardiology Foundation.

October

CANADA
Ottawa. Annual combined meeting of the Canadian Cardiovascular Society and the Canadian Heart Foundation. Honorary membership.

January 1971

MEXICO
Mexico City. Inauguration of the Mexican Heart Foundation.

March

JAMAICA
Kingston. Inauguration of the Jamaica Heart Foundation. Address on *S.S. Hope.*

Appendix 2

ARRHYTHMIAS

At the turn of the century (about 1900) Sir James Mackenzie had been reassuring the medical profession and the public at large about the simple arrhythmias of premature beats, both atrial and ventricular, and of short paroxysms of atrial paroxysmal tachycardia, the seriousness of which had been grossly exaggerated and feared. This was at a time when myocardial ischemia and infarction due to coronary heart disease were far less common than now, seventy years later. However, today, with the justified attention to an increase of all arrhythmias precipitated by heart attacks, there has again arisen an unwarranted fear of the very common simpler arrhythmias in vast numbers of people with normal hearts. I spend a good deal of time reassuring and treating these otherwise normal people alarmed by the unjustified exaggeration about all arrhythmias.

DIET

A. Individuality of diet without strict rules is probably best for healthy persons, as in the case of exercise. Such individuality is dependent on one's digestive capacity and toxic reaction to certain foods, on one's nutritional state (over, under, or optimal), and on one's individual taste. There is still some truth in the old adage that "One man's meat is another man's poison."

B. One can live on a carbohydrate, so-called *vegetarian,* diet without fat, or on a *fat* diet without carbohydrate, provided there is adequate protein and the vitamins and calories are properly adjusted. Or the diet may be largely limited to *protein,* but man is essentially an omnivorous animal and probably does best on a mixture of food elements, provided the calories are adequate and not excessive.

C. The so-called *natural food diet* is doubtlessly healthful from the standpoint of nutrition, provided there is adequate protein and the vitamins and calories are properly adjusted, but it is probably not necessary to exclude all cooking. This regimen can certainly help some individuals in need of such a fat-free diet, but one of the great difficulties with these "natural" foods is that the change from one's current diet can be difficult and is probably not necessary for most people. One can live to be a very healthy centenarian on an average mixture of elements of cooked and uncooked food, as in the case of Charles Thiery, already presented in this book, who told me that he had ingested during his long life a good deal of ice cream, butter, pastry, and cream, and died at 107½ of pneumonia. The total calories are probably more important than the kind of food.

D. The amount of cholesterol in the blood is much more important than that in the food and they are usually not directly related. The total food and saturated fat calories are much more important.

E. Food calories should naturally be reduced in invalids and semi-invalids.

F. I would refer the reader to the following books for more details concerning diet:

Blakeslee, Alton and Stamler, Jeremiah: *Your Heart Has Nine Lives.* Pocket Books, Inc., 1966.

Keys, Ancel and Margaret: *Eat Well and Stay Well.* Doubleday and Company, 2nd edition, 1963.

Mayer, Jean: *Overweight—Causes, Cost and Control.* Prentice Hall, 1969.

Stare, Frederick J.: *Eating for Good Health.* Doubleday and Company, 1964.

MURMURS

Actually many murmurs, probably the majority of slight murmurs, especially in growing children, are normal and physiological, due to the normal hydrodynamic effect of a vigorous circulation, in particular with exercise or in different body positions. In every instance, however, a careful appraisal is called for.

SCIENCE WRITERS

I want to emphasize the great appreciation and gratitude of the medical profession, and of myself in particular, to the growing body of able and restrained medical science writers who have greatly eased our job of public education concerning both health and disease.

Index

Acute cor pulmonale, 77, 78, 122, 123
Adams-Stokes syndrome, 64
Afghanistan, 238
Africa, 170
Age, 228
Air travel, 155, 156
Alaska, 93
Alcohol, 7
American Heart Association, 19, 45, 114, 160, 161, 244
AMA, 44
American Red Cross, 30, 36
Amyl nitrite, 68
Anacapri, 55
Ancestors, 3
Angina pectoris, 64, 68, 108, 140
Angiocardiography, 66
Angiology, 237
Animal research, 16, 88
Ankle injury, 132
Antibiotics, 121
Aortic stenosis, 84
Argentina, 147, 164
Armistice Day, 1918, 33
Army officers, 109
Arrest as spy, 25
Arrhythmias, 20, 45, 54, 87
Arterial wall, 229
Artificial heart, 245
Artistic temperament, 141
Artists, 139
Asian–Pacific cardiology, 111, 169
Assist devices for the heart and circulation, 245
Athens, 36, 118, 238
Atherosclerosis, 2, 9, 233–234
Athos, Mt., 118
Auscultation, 65
Australia, 236
Autopsies, 62, 63, 174
Avicenna Hospital in Kabul, 238

Bangkok, 236
Baptist Church, 7
Baptist Hospital, Boston, 5
Barber surgeons, 68

Base Hospital #6 AEF, France at Talence near Bordeaux, 26–30
Base Hospital 22 BEF, 23
Beacon Street, Number 264, 114, 153
Beluga whale, 93
Beth Israel Hospital, 12
Bicycling, 6, 224
Bleeding, 66
Blood chemistry, 245
Blood pressure, 105, 107
Blood vessel surgery, 125
"Blue babies," 52, 125, 139
Body build, 228
Bohemia, 115
Boston City Hospital, 12
Boston Transcript, 3
Boston University Hospital, 12, 120
Brain, 247
Brazil, 165
Brazzaville, 172
Broken leg, 72
Brotherhood of man, 235
Brussels, 237
Brussels, Third World Congress of Cardiology in, 237
Bucharest, 36
Buenos Aires, 164
Bulgaria, 36
Bunker Hill, 3, 4
Businessmen and women, 146

Cairo, 170
Calcutta, 236
California gold rush, 4
Calisthenics, 224
Camp Becket, 8
Canberra, 236
Cape Town, 170, 171
Capri, 55
Cardiac catheterization, 65–66
Cardiology, 19, 38, 39, 58; history of, 59–70, 120
Cardiospasm, 86
"Cardiovascular epidemiology," 173
Cardiovascular military rejectees, 110
"Cardiovascular rehabilitation," 173

Index